Lost Animals,
Disappearing Worlds

Lost Animals, Disappearing Worlds

Stories of Extinction

Barbara Allen

REAKTION BOOKS

For my late husband, David, who
died during the writing of this book:

> *'You were my world.*
> *I spin, out of orbit, but*
> *your love lassos me.'*

Published by Reaktion Books Ltd
Unit 32, Waterside
44–48 Wharf Road
London N1 7UX, UK
www.reaktionbooks.co.uk

First published 2025
Copyright © Barbara Allen 2025

Printed and bound in India by Replika Press Pvt. Ltd

A catalogue record for this book is available from the British Library

ISBN 978 1 83639 045 9

Contents

— PART ONE —

Introduction 7

1. Extinction 9

2. Memorializing Grief 25

— PART TWO —

THE PORTRAITS

The Aurochs 35

The Dodo 40

The Rodrigues Solitaire 49

Steller's Sea Cow 54

The Great Auk 59

The Spectacled Cormorant (or Pallas's Cormorant) 66

The Falkland Islands Wolf 72

The Quagga 77

The Tarpan 84

The Rocky Mountain Locust 89

The Japanese Wolf (or Honshu Wolf) 100

The Passenger Pigeon 105

The Carolina Parakeet 115

The Syrian Wild Ass 122

The Heath Hen 125

The Thylacine 131

The Xerces Blue Butterfly 140

The Arabian Ostrich 144

The Ivory-Billed Woodpecker 150

The St Helena Earwig 159

The Eskimo Curlew 166

The Tecopa Pupfish 174

The Southern Gastric-Brooding Frog and the Northern Gastric-Brooding Frog/Eungella Gastric-Brooding Frog 178

The Dusky Seaside Sparrow 183

The Golden Toad 189

The Pyrenean Ibex 194

The Baiji (Yangtze River) Dolphin 199

The Pinta Island Tortoise 205

The Bramble Cay Melomys 210

The O'ahu Tree Snail 214

References 221

Bibliography 237

Acknowledgements 239

Photo Acknowledgements 241

Index 243

— PART ONE —

Introduction

IN THIS BOOK, I TRY to give voice to 31 extinct species and, via the individual species story of each, tell something of the broader story of extinction, through the circumstances of the species, be it on an island, in the ocean, roaming the mainland or skirting the skies.

This idea had its genesis in a moment of gazing at a trilobite fossil on my desk. I purchased it on a significant birthday several years ago; I had wanted something that was much older than I. Gently supporting the fossil, I wonder about its history. Its scientific, or biological, history can easily be read. Its name (meaning 'three lobes') is given; it was a part of an extinct marine arachnomorph arthropod. Trilobites were a casualty of the mass extinction (which killed at least 90 per cent of species) that took place at the end of the Permian period, about 250 million years ago. Before this happened, trilobites had been what would be considered 'successful' and diverse: trilobite fossils have been found in many parts of the world. They lived on this earth for more than 300 million years, burrowing in sediment or crawling on the sea floor.

There have been written descriptions of trilobite fossils perhaps as early as the third century BCE, and they were accorded magical properties by the Ute Indian Tribe. Trilobite fossils were worn by the Utes as amulets, believed to protect the wearer from the dangers of bullets and diseases. The trilobite's closest living relative is thought to be the horseshoe crab.

I carefully place it back on the shelf. I wonder about it, this particular one, not its species as a whole. Where had it lived? What was its habitat like?

I move on to my other fossil, that of a cross-section of a mammoth's tooth. Mammoths' teeth really meant life or death. Woolly mammoths had four functional molar teeth at a time, two in the lower jaw, two in the upper. What is remarkable is that a mammoth had six sets of molars throughout its lifetime, which were replaced five times. Its final set, its sixth, would emerge when the mammoth was about thirty years old. When that set of molars wore out, that signalled the end of the mammoth. No longer able to chew, it would starve to death. I don't think that was the cause of death of the mammoth whose tooth I held, but I am not sure.

Trilobites. Mammoths. Interesting creatures, but neither is explored in this book. Choosing the creatures to feature was both a conscious choice (ones that had lived in recent times) and an unconscious one (why did I choose Steller's sea cow and not the sea mink? The great auk and not the moa?). Living in Australia, why did I include the thylacine? Why not the lesser bilby? Or the toolache wallaby?

I do not know. What I do know though is that no book, with one exception, can contain stories about every extinct species; the only volume that can, and does, cradle those sad tales close to its heart, its core, is Earth. May we endeavour to add as few names and pages as possible to this book of extinction.

I wrote this book accompanied by many tears. I could not stay dry-eyed reading about the slaughter of the great auk, the seemingly endless shootings of the passenger pigeon, the destruction of habitat. A warning though: it is too easy to judge, to stay angry, appalled, but let us face forward, mindful of the past, but looking ahead, working to save the many endangered species, so fewer are added to the extinction list. May this book serve as a perpetual memorial.

1. *Extinction*

EXTINCTION: THE PERMANENT LOSS or depletion of a species. Among the dictionary definitions, lodged after 'no living representative; having died out', we crash head-on into 'complete destruction; annihilation'.[1] This definition is not sugarcoated, nor has it been gentled for our sensitive nature. It tells it as it is, highlighting trauma, tragedy and pain.

We live, knowing species will die out, and are dying out. Hundreds of them will become extinct before we know of them. If 'discovered' by humans, and given scientific names before they die out, then their extinction is more likely to be viewed as a human tragedy, our loss, rather than one for the now-extinct creature and species.

Species. We speak of and hear about 'species', but that word houses a collective. Every species is made up of individuals. When we label everything as a group, including human beings, we miss the individual, the uniqueness of that creature or human. How do our brains fathom such numbers?[2]

We live in an era of extinction. We live knowing about extinct species. Search engines, biologists and conservation groups keep us up to date about endangered ones who live precarious, tenuous lives. It is strange to be reminded of how controversial the notion of 'extinction' was. In 1796 French naturalist Georges Cuvier, speaking about the mammoth and the mastodon, coined the concept of 'extinction' by speaking of them living in a 'world previous to ours'.[3] He shocked his audience, the religious establishment and indeed the scientific world. Theologians were affronted by this idea that challenged a divine plan for all of creation. Why could or would God create beings that would later die out? Did

God make a mistake? Many believed in the Great Chain of Being, which encompassed beings from the tiniest form of life, to the 'higher ones' of human and angel. To propose the theory of extinction implied that some of these vital links were missing. Cuvier tended to push for the idea of cataclysmic extinction, a large, intervening event that wiped out species, whereas Charles Darwin proposed that extinction was a more gradual process, not a result of Cuvier's theory of great 'catastrophes'.

Nowadays, we know that extinction consists of both forms, large and catastrophic (though I would class all extinction as catastrophic) and smaller, due to adaptation or evolutionary changes (such as birds on islands adapting to new surroundings by evolving smaller wings over many years).

The eras and dates of mass extinction events are still open to debate. If we take one acceptable measurement of time (the last 500 million years), which comprises the Palaeozoic ('ancient life'), the Mesozoic ('middle life') and the Cenozoic ('new life') eras, then there have probably been six mass extinction events during this vast period of history. The first extinction event, which took place approximately 445 million years ago, was the Ordovician-Silurian extinction, when most of life on Earth inhabited its seas. It is estimated that 85 per cent of all Ordovician species died out during this period. The next was the Late Devonian extinction, approximately 370 million years ago, when an estimated 75 per cent of species, most being marine invertebrates, became extinct. The third extinction was the Permian-Triassic, around 252 million years ago, with an estimated loss of 96 per cent of all marine species, and 70 per cent of land-dwelling species, including the largest known mass extinction of insects. This extinction event is also known as the 'Great Dying'. It is thought to have been triggered by volcanic activity and an over-abundance of noxious gases, such as sulphur dioxide and carbon dioxide, which elevated the global temperature and altered the pH balance of the ocean. All of these mass extinctions happened during the Palaeozoic era.[4]

The Mesozoic era followed, with the Triassic-Jurassic extinction, and then the Cretaceous-Paleogene or Tertiary period extinction. The Triassic-Jurassic extinction event, which took place 201 million years ago, saw the extinction of possibly one-third of marine species, plus many amphibians and reptile species on land. The fifth mass extinction event, the Cretaceous-Paleogene, happened relatively recently, at 65 million years ago, the primary cause thought to have been asteroid impact. This extinction event led to the loss of between 67 and 75 per cent of species, including the extinction of non-avian dinosaurs.[5] This is the era many of us think of when we grapple with the history and scope of extinction.

It is thought that we present-day humans are living in the sixth mass extinction time, known as the Holocene, part of the next era, the Cenozoic ('new life'). The Holocene era of extinction dates from the end of the most recent Ice Age, when the last of the continental glaciers began its retreat approximately 11,700 million years ago, which allowed a milder climate to settle. The Holocene became part of the human story about 50,000 years ago, with *Homo sapiens* activity. Disagreement surrounds our present day: are we still living in the Holocene era or have we moved into a purely human-dominated stage, known as the Anthropocene epoch? Some scientists and conservationists propose that we entered the Anthropocene back in 2010, when climate change caused by carbon dioxide emissions from fossil fuels had (and continues to have) a major impact on many animals and plants, but the name 'Anthropocene', the era of the human, was coined back in the early 1980s by biologist Eugene F. Stoermer and popularized in 2000 by atmospheric chemist Paul Crutzen.[6] Whether we still live in the Holocene or have entered the Anthropocene, our current epoch is one that is dominated by humans and circumstances that have arisen from human activities and inventions. This period is one of significant extinction rates.

Some aspects and causes of particular extinctions can be traced to dates. One distinct phase of the Holocene era is that of the colonization of islands. This is not a modern phenomenon: when the Caribbean islands were settled by some of America's First Peoples 6,000 years ago, hundreds of species disappeared over time. Similar events happened on other islands, such as those settled by the ancestors of the Polynesians. (It has been estimated that during this period of island settlement, one out of five bird species became extinct.[7]) Impacts on island species intensified during the Age of Exploration – also known as the Age of Discovery, which took place from the mid-fifteenth century to the beginning of the seventeenth – with its introduction of other species, such as rats, cats and pigs, and then there was an acceleration of extinction following the invention of firearms.

Islands had a unique set of circumstances that made extinctions happen more readily, with no chance of survival elsewhere. Small land size, with no means of escape, meant that single causes could lead to extinction. Species were unlikely to have survival back-ups, such as subspecies, or a group elsewhere able to keep reproducing if one island's species was gone. Islands were depleted of native fauna. For many human inhabitants, these animals and birds were a ready supply of food, often unafraid of human predators. (Having never encountered humans before, some of the creatures did not realize the danger they posed. Many colonists labelled such behaviour, this absence of fear, as evidence of them being 'stupid'.) Evolutionary adaptation, or specialization, for island life worked against many species as well. Some birds, having landed on the islands from other land masses (either deliberately, or having been blown off course), over the years evolved small wings to replace the large wings for which they no longer had any need. Unfortunately, this smart evolutionary adaptation, which conserved their energy, rendered them flightless and easy prey when humans and other introduced animals landed on these islands.

Extinction was not and is not confined to islands: the plains of Africa saw the fall of the Cape lion and the sable antelope; North America's countryside and its skies witnessed the passing of the passenger pigeon; in Australia, the thylacine and the toolache wallaby are part of the death toll, among hundreds of species. Australia's rate of extinction is high: an estimated one in every ten unique Australian mammal species are now extinct due to introduced animals such as sheep and cattle (competition for food and habitat), foxes and cats, and with settlement, new burning and clearing practices.[8]

Modern-day causes of extinction include pollution and land clearance. Competition for food for domesticated animals, plus forests and grasslands cleared for human habitation, have meant the loss of many species in the trail of fire, poisons, machinery and firearms.

According to scientists, it is estimated that 'last century between 20,000 and 2 million species may have become extinct.'[9] The grim numbers of extinction prediction continue, with an estimate of the extinction of 50 per cent of all species in the next one hundred years, mainly due to human activity.[10] A 2023 report, which noted that extinctions are preceded by progressive population declines, showed a decline of 48 per cent of all animal species in the present time.[11]

How do we know when a species is extinct? We don't know when a species can finally be deemed extinct, although calculated, informed guesses can be made. These days, the work of the IUCN (International Union for Conservation of Nature), founded in 1948 and made up of both government and civil organizations, has become the global authority, or body, for information concerning the state of the natural world. In 1964 the IUCN established what has become known as the IUCN Red List of Threatened Species, a resource that lists not only species that are thought to be extinct, but ones that are endangered or threatened. This resource is a global insight into what is happening in and to the natural world and lists sites of extinction worldwide. The IUCN determines which species are extinct, deeming extinction to have occurred after a fifty-year period of no sightings. The IUCN Red List identifies the species that have become extinct, as well as those in another six categories. Among the creatures labelled as extinct from 2023 to 2024 are the Bachman's warbler, the green-blossom pearly mussel, the San Marcos gambusia (a fish) and the Little Mariana fruit bat (also known as the Guam flying fox). The rate of extinction is high. At present, there are more than 150,300 species on the IUCN Red List, with more than 42,100 species threatened with extinction. These species include 41 per cent of amphibians, 37 per cent of sharks and rays, 27 per cent of mammals and 13 per cent of birds.[12] 'I sought a career in herpetology [a branch of zoology specializing in amphibians and reptiles] because I enjoy working with animals,' wrote Joseph R. Mendelson, a herpetologist at Zoo Atlanta. 'I did not anticipate that it would come to resemble palaeontology.'[13]

The IUCN now has a Green List which operates alongside its Red List. The Green List is a tool of assessment to help analyse conservation actions and their impact on the recovery of particular species' populations. Green Scores show current status and list how conservation efforts have affected that current status. Species on the Green List are given a score from zero (extinct in the wild) to one hundred (fully recovered).[14]

What can we do?

De-Extinction or Resurrection Science

'Noah built a boat to save the world's biodiversity; today, scientist's build freezers.'[15] Some scientists are trying to turn back, or reverse, extinction, creating a new discipline termed 'de-extinction', or 'resurrection' science. Some have associated this new science with the likes of the science-fiction novel *Jurassic Park* (1990) and its blockbuster film adaptation of 1993, directed by Steven Spielberg, which featured resurrected dinosaurs, but evolutionary biologist Beth Shapiro wonders whether the first use of the word 'de-extinction' is found in the book *The Source of Magic* (1979) by Piers Anthony. In this fantasy novel, a magician sees what was an extinct species, cats, and he 'stared at this abrupt de-extinction, unable to formulate a durable opinion'. Shapiro suggests that we might act in a similar fashion if we encountered a living creature from a species we thought was extinct.[16]

This brand of science is attempting to bring back particular species, including the mammoth, the Pyrenean ibex, the passenger pigeon, the golden toad and the thylacine. It sounds fine in principle, but there are major concerns, scientific and ethical, which need to be answered before such programmes can be deemed successful.

De-extinction is a form of bioengineering, bringing extinct species back to life, the goal being that one day they will be released back into their historical habitat. One of the pioneers is George Church, whose scientific work centres on the de-extinction of the mammoth.[17] His project hopes to construct synthetic copies via DNA sequencing that could be understood and used by cells. This technique, known as CRISPR or Cas 9, was developed in 2012. In terms of mammoths, this technique endeavours to implant artificial mammoth genes in cells from Asian elephants, the first goal being to develop a thick pelt of fur.[18] Later, genes will be needed that will alter the elephant's blood, because mammoths' haemoglobin functioned at a lower level, supplying the oxygen needed despite the extreme cold.[19] One of the problems has been the elephant cells, specifically the conversion of ordinary cells into stem cells. Researchers have been able to cultivate stem cells for many animals, but not for elephants.[20] This may be because stem cells and cancer cells are similar. Elephants appear to have strong defences against cancer, so this may be one reason for the lack of success, at least at this stage.[21]

If – and it is a big 'if' – stem cells are gathered, and an embryo develops, will it be a mammoth, or an elephant with some mammoth genes? Even if it sports a shaggy coat, cold-resistant haemoglobin and other mammoth characteristics, it is still not a clone; rather, it is an Asian elephant that resembles a mammoth in some ways due to introduced genetic components. There is talk about these creatures inhabiting the ecosystems of the tundra, as mammoths did 10,000 years ago. Their way of digging up the ground is meant to be helpful to that particular habitat. These proxies for the extinct mammoths would be part of rewilding the Siberian tundra, transforming a mostly barren region into grassland over a few seasons. The mammoths would achieve this by trampling the earth, turning the soil, recycling nutrients and fertilizing the soil. This appears to be a symbiotic relationship: research shows that when herbivores disappeared from the Siberian tundra, so did the Arctic grassland.[22] There may be other benefits. During winter, ungrazed, frozen tundra has warmer soil beneath the permafrost layers due to the covering of snow and permafrost, which insulate the soil. Before the extinction of mammoths this ground would have been trampled and dug up by them, so the soil would have been colder than it is today. As global temperatures rise, the permafrost is melting, and releasing trapped carbon.[23] Some scientists propose that the introduction of mammoths (or cold-tolerant Asian elephants) into the Siberian tundra could actually reduce the accumulation of greenhouse gases in the atmosphere and slow the rate of global warming.

There is a fine line between being a visionary and hubris. George Church has put forward the possibility of adding characteristics from other animals, such as polar bears or penguins, to help the 'mammoths' develop new characteristics that they didn't receive during their creation or evolution, saying, 'We might be able to do even better than the mammoth did.'[24]

De-extinction is not confined to George Church's research on the mammoth. An organization called Revive & Restore was co-founded in 2012 by Stewart Brand and Ryan Phelan, with the help of the National Geographic Society and a group of scientists, to examine de-extinction. One of the goals of their de-extinction research is to increase, or expand, biodiversity. On the one hand, that sounds honourable, even noble: creating or producing an animal that is close to the original extinct species, and then releasing it into the wild, to live among the other creatures already

there. What is worth remembering though is that this new species is a genetically modified one. Putting aside the obvious questions – such as 'how
will it adapt to its environment?', 'how will it breed?' and 'what about the
other animals already living in that habitat?' – we humans might hesitate to
ask, 'what is our role, as human beings?' Is it to 'manage' nature, to tinker
with genes? Is it to build 'better' models of what were extinct species?

There are several de-extinction methods being explored. The first
is that of cloning. Cloning is the attempt to create identical copies of an
extinct species. Living cells are needed: one needs more than DNA (genes).
These cells are biopsied from living and dead (recently deceased) animals
and kept frozen until needed. Then they are transformed into either ova
or sperm to be used in living animals. If the species has been extinct for a
long time (as in the case of mammoths, the dodo and the passenger pigeon),
then cloning is not an option.[25] In order to create an identical clone of a
mammoth, a preserved living cell is required, and that will never be found.
One can resurrect a mammoth trait, such as its hairiness, but one can never
resurrect a mammoth.

Now, these genetically engineered species will inherit many of the
characteristics of their host animal: in the case of the mammoth, that
would be the Asian elephant; for the passenger pigeon, it would be the
band-tailed pigeon. The genetically engineered species will consist of new
genes and the extinct animal's original genetic make-up, but they will
also acquire adaptations from an environment to which they will need to
adjust, as it may differ significantly from that of their ancestors. All of these
will be governed by the risk card of unpredictability: which genes will dom-
inate? How will the resurrected creatures respond to new environments?
How will they 'learn' certain behaviours that would be instinctive in the
wild? Some species are governed by a biological phenomenon known as
the Allee effect, which is when a particular species needs a large number
of individuals in order to be stable.[26] When the species drops below that
threshold, the population declines rapidly, thereby leading to extinction. A
small population can mean the individual is more susceptible to predation,
it is harder for it to find a mate or to breed successfully, and it may have
trouble sourcing food. If the Allee effect occurs in captivity, then it would
certainly be a problem for a de-extinction programme that endeavours
to release animals back into the wild. One of the extinct species that

appears to have been affected by the Allee effect is the passenger pigeon; it is thought that it needed large flocks for survival.[27]

What are the financial and ethical costs? De-extinction science is not cheap, but neither are the animal lives that are intertwined within these projects. In the case of the Pyrenean ibex de-extinction project, numerous miscarriages occurred in the surrogate mothers (nanny goats). Of the 44 nanny goats implanted with clones of the last *Pyrenean ibex*, Celia, only one of them did not miscarry.[28] Unfortunately, the kid that was carried to term died soon after being birthed via a caesarean section. This outcome was in the case of a fairly close relative (the surrogate was a hybrid of a domestic goat and a different species of ibex), but it would have been an even more challenging exercise if there had not been a close, living relative.

These attempts at resurrection of extinct species may sound admirable – the wish to reverse our ancestors' mistakes, perhaps believing that humans have a moral responsibility to bring back species if they can do so – but a new set of questions might be asked. Is de-extinction science a guilt-driven process, a means of retribution for human failure to care adequately for the planet and its inhabitants? Will these efforts weaken the need to protect endangered species, the ones the planet still has? If we think we can 'replace' a species, then apathy may set in, making us less inclined to protect other species. Would successful resurrection of a once-extinct species mean that humans would look after it this time? We humans do not have a great track record for living well with other species.

Why did the species go extinct? If it was due to over-exploitation or overhunting, then that species may be less at risk. If, however, extinction was due to disease, or competition, or change in habitat, then it may be inadvisable to consider these species. If the cause is unknown, then that might also make that extinct species a high risk.

Is a de-extinct species really the same as its ancestors would have been in its former time, when that species was first alive, or is it purely a hybrid? If so, will it always remain so? Can that species be re-introduced into a habitat that has long since adjusted to its absence? What might its re-introduction mean for that ecosystem?

Finally, there is perhaps a question that underpins conservation genetics, the work and research of de-extinction science: what is the worth of a species? Is one particular species more highly regarded than another?

If so, why? What is its intrinsic value? What criterion is used to reach this conclusion? Do we try to bring back the awe-inspiring (acknowledging that these species would bring in the big bucks, so would therefore be deemed a worthy investment) or the easiest to resurrect? Perhaps those who have suffered at the hands of recent extinctions will not only be easier to bring back, but will have had fewer interruptions in their ecosystems. Is there a compelling reason to bring back these species?[29]

Does the focus on de-extinction take us away from the real work of conserving the endangered species that are still alive, their habitats and their ecosystems? Both require money, scientists and vision. Should we be prioritizing the conservation of species that are still alive? There are lots of questions and, at present, not many answers.

This book aims to capture something of the essence of 31 extinct species, knowing that this is inadequate. A larger work would still fall short of the task of saying something about – that is, remembering, or indeed 're-membering' – each and every extinct species.

What would it have been like to have seen or heard what is now an extinct creature? What would it have been like in the wild, not in a zoo? About fifteen years ago, I visited an elderly gentleman who had lived in Tasmania, the son of a logger. Near the end of my visit, I asked him what he thought about the Tasmania tiger, or the thylacine. Had his father mentioned seeing it when he was logging timber, deep in the thick forests? He grinned and said that he himself had heard its bark, late at night, in the bush. His answer brought me out in goose bumps.

Lazarus Species: A Sign of Hope?

Within the disappearing world of extinction, it is difficult to be optimistic, or, indeed, hopeful. There is, however, a slight glimmer of hope if we consider Lazarus species: species once thought to be extinct, but are no longer. This 'life' is not due to cloning, or genetic 'de-extinction', but by the simple fact of being rediscovered alive.

The most famous of these Lazarus species is the coelacanth (*Latimeria chalumnae*).[30] It is worthwhile telling its story, or portrait, because, though fascinating in and of itself, it also highlights the ways a species may be rediscovered, yet warns us about what uniqueness could vanish forever.

The coelacanth is a lobe-finned fish of the type that gave rise to the first tetrapods. Until 1938 this fish was only known as a fossil, imprinted within ancient rocks. This large fish, its closest living relative the lung fish, has been in existence since the late Devonian period. It was thought to be extinct because its fossil records abruptly end at the time of the Great Dying, near the close of the Cretaceous period, approximately 65 million years ago. In 1938 Henrick Goosen caught a coelacanth in the Indian Ocean, off the coast of South Africa, knew it was unusual and sought to have it identified. He contacted curator Marjorie Courteney-Latimer, who, after seeing it, made a sketch of the fish, which she then sent to ichthyologist James Leonard Brierley Smith. When Brierley finally set eyes on the fish, he immediately identified it as a coelacanth, because of the fish's distinctive tail flag. Its tail fin was divided into three lobes, an extra lobe compared with other fish.

It was a long wait in between specimens: it took fourteen years for the next one to be caught (and put aside), this time off the coast of the Comoro Islands, near Madagascar. At one time, the coelacanth was part of a group comprising about ninety fish species, both sea water and fresh water, but now there are only two known living species: the African coelacanth, *Latimeria chalumnae*, which lives near the Comoro Islands off the east coast of Africa, and the Indonesian coelacanth, *Latimeria menadoensis*, found in the waters off North Sulawesi, Indonesia. In 1997 the latter type was recognized by Californian biologist Mark Erdmann, who was in Indonesia on his honeymoon. He saw an odd-looking fish on a cart in a food market and identified it as a coelacanth. In 1998 Erdmann returned to the islands, spending months with the fishermen, until another coelacanth was captured. Genetic tests confirmed that it was not only a coelacanth, but a new species. The African and Indonesian coelacanths, while different from each other, are believed by some researchers to have evolved from a common ancestor.

Many scientists believe that the unique characteristics of the coelacanth represent an early step in the evolution from fish to terrestrial four-legged animals such as amphibians. The coelacanth's lobe fins (most fish are 'ray-finned') indicate that it, and fish similar to it, flourished at the time when fins and gills were evolving into feet and lungs. Its fins contain the beginnings of reptile and mammal leg bones. Many scientists acknowledge that the discovery of the coelacanth could be the greatest zoological find of the twentieth century.

Other Lazarus species include the New Holland mouse (also known as the Pookila, an Indigenous name adopted by the Australian Federal Government in 1995), Wallace's giant bee, the takahe, the Lord Howe Island stick insect and the Cuban solenodon. The New Holland mouse (*Pseudomys novaehollandiae*), first discovered in 1843, is endangered, extinct in seven of the twelve locations where it was once found in Victoria, Australia, and existing only in fragmented populations in several other locations in Australia.[31] What does it mean when a species is alive in some regions, but extinct in others? Its survival is a battle, a constant struggle because of habitat loss, predators (feral cats and foxes) and natural disasters, such as bushfires.

Similar problems face the Cuban solenodon (*Atopogale cubana*), a small, nocturnal, shrew-like rodent native to Cuba, living in the Nipe-Sagua-Baracoa mountain range.[32] It is one of the few venomous mammals in existence (its saliva is venomous). There had been no sightings from 1890 to 1974, and it had been declared extinct in 1970 before it was found again four years later. The creatures are so rare that over the years only 37 specimens have been caught. Habitat destruction and introduced predators, such as the Asian mongoose, black rats and feral dogs, have decreased their numbers and make them an endangered species.

Other Lazarus species have different stories. The takahe (*Porphyrio hochstetteri*), a beautiful New Zealand flightless swamphen, which sports dark-blue iridescent feathers, a white tail and a red beak, started to disappear around 1898. Colonists assumed it was due to predators (cats and dogs), and the takahe was presumed to be extinct until 1948, when it was found in the Murchison Mountains. Nowadays takahe numbers have increased due to breeding programmes. In recent years, a small number have been released back into the wild.

The Lord Howe Island stick insect (*Dryococelus australis*), thought to be extinct since 1930, evaded discovery until 2001, when around thirty creatures were found on a remote islet off the coast of Lord Howe Island. They were living on the world's tallest tower of volcanic rock, known as Ball's Pyramid. Once plentiful, the Lord Howe Island stick insect was thought to have become extinct due to black rats. It has the reputation of being the world's rarest insect.

The Bermuda petrel (*Pterodroma cahow*) was a casualty of predators – cats and dogs, but also of humans – who ate their eggs (which were easy to find and access because the birds were ground nesters). In 1951, eighteen breeding pairs were located on four rocky offshore islets in the Castle Harbour area. Owing to the implementation of a carefully monitored breeding programme, and intensive conservation efforts, breeding pairs have increased to 156 in 2022, producing 77 successfully fledged chicks. These rare birds can be watched, as live streaming is available from the project's webcam, called *CahowCam*.[33] This Lazarus species appears to be safe at the moment.

Two recently rediscovered species are Wallace's giant bee (*Megachile pluto*), which is the world's largest bee, and the long-beaked echidna (*Zaglossus attenboroughi*). The former is named after Alfred Russel Wallace, a prominent British entomologist, also known for his writings about evolution. Wallace discovered the giant bee when exploring the Indonesian island of Bacan. He described the female bee, which is about the length a human thumb, as 'a large black wasp-like insect, with immense jaws like a stag-beetle'.[34]

The bee wasn't seen again until 1981, when entomologist Adam Messer rediscovered it on three Indonesian islands and was able to observe some of its behaviour. Future searches were unsuccessful, so it was thought to be extinct. Then in 2018 three dead specimens of Wallace's giant bee became known. Two were sold for an enormous sum of money, together fetching more than U.S. $13,000.[35] In February 2019, having been assumed extinct for 38 years, a Wallace's giant bee was found in the wild, in a termite nest in the North Moluccas (or Malukus), an island group in Indonesia. Wallace's giant bees make their homes inside termite nests, which keep the giant bees well hidden. Its habitat is threatened by deforestation, and its rarity makes it a target for collectors. At the moment, there is no legal protection concerning trading of Wallace's giant bee.

The other recently rediscovered species I wish to mention is the long-beaked echidna, a nocturnal monotreme, also discovered in Indonesia, in this case in the Cyclops Mountains, in 2023. The long-beaked echidna (*Zaglossus attenboroughi*), named after David Attenborough, had only been scientifically recorded once before, in 1961, by a Dutch botanist. More than eighty remote cameras had been set up by a team of scientists from Oxford

University during a four-week expedition (which had taken three-and-a-half years of planning). What is remarkable is that the only image of the echidna was captured on the last memory card retrieved from the last of those eighty-plus cameras! Dr James Kempton, a biologist from Oxford University and the leader of the expedition, said that one of the main reasons for their success was securing the cooperation of the villagers of Yongsu Sapari, a settlement on the north coast of the Cyclops Mountains. The villagers believe the Cyclops Mountains to be sacred, so they were able to guide the researchers around sacred areas and informed them when they were to be silent.[36] Conservation plans include considering ways to protect both the echidna and its mountain habitat, the only place where it has been seen.[37]

There are other rediscovered, or Lazarus, species, each with its own threats. Conservationists battle to stave off second (permanent) extinctions. They must contend with low numbers, little time and limited funding, plus habitat destruction and predation, including supplying the lucrative market of collectors (usually the black market, but not always, as in the case of Wallace's giant bee).

A New Way of Viewing the World

During the 1980s, theologian, ecologist and self-described 'geologian' Thomas Berry suggested that we could enter an era which he (and Brian Swimme) called the 'Ecozoic', an age in which humans would live in harmony with all species instead of continuing on the path of destruction.[38] The etymology of the term 'Ecozoic', coined by Berry, is 'eco' (from the Greek *oikos*, meaning house, household) and 'zoic' (from *zoikos*, Greek for living beings).[39] Berry defined this period as 'the era of the house of living beings', one in which humans would live in 'a mutually enhancing way'.[40] It would also be a time in which to think and envision what the future of this planet could be. Substituting Ecozoic for the name 'Anthropocene' takes the human out of prominence and places humans alongside other species. Swimme and Berry warn that if humans are not committed to moving into the Ecozoic, during which we see the universe as a community of subjects – life systems that are to be valued, rather than mere objects or 'things' to be used or plundered – then we risk entering what could be classified as the Technozoic era, in which life will become merely an economic resource.[41]

Entomologist and biologist E. O. Wilson warned that unless we halt the destruction of Earth and its many inhabitants, we will enter another era, that of the Eremozoic, the lonely, or desolate, life. This would be an age of loneliness, less than what it should be.[42] We humans would be impoverished, many of our animal kin gone forever. Do we want to enter this era? Haven't we had a foretaste already, and don't we miss what is absent? We live in an era defined by a heavy presence of absence.

If we take to heart a new way of viewing humans, we might make a breakthrough in living in community, preserving rather than plundering the life forms that live alongside us. Swimme and Berry wrote that humans need to remember that we are a species among other species: 'We have thought about the human as nations, as cultures, as ethnic groups, as international organizations, even as global community; but none of these articulates the present human–Earth issue as precisely as thinking about the human as a species among species.'[43]

Would this way of perceiving humans, as a species living with other species, make a difference? If so, in what ways would or could it change our lives? Would we live differently, more intentionally, aware of our animal kin? Would we be content to live alongside, even on the edges, rather than desiring to be in the centre?

Another definition of extinction refers to the field of astronomy, rather than zoology. Instead of the dying of a species, extinction in the field of astronomy can mean the absorption of light from a planet or star by Earth's atmosphere. Perhaps that terminology could be applied to our extinct animal kin as well. When a species is extinct, we could imagine that it too, like the light source of a star or planet, is absorbed, not by Earth's atmosphere, but by its dirt, water and rock. It remains, in a different form, a permanent part of this planet. It is still with us, in the earth we walk on, and in the water that cleanses us.

The Dodo handing Alice a thimble, wood-engraved illustration by
John Tenniel for Lewis Carroll, *Alice's Adventures in Wonderland* (1866).

2. Memorializing Grief

'For one species to mourn the death of another is a new thing under the sun.' – Aldo Leopold[1]

'What cannot be said will be wept.' – attributed to Sappho

WE KNOW SOMETHING OF THEIR vast numbers – how passenger pigeons darkened skies, and locust clouds ripped apart terrain. Heath hens performed elaborate mating rituals; this courtship has been artistically transformed into human dance, the heath hens' twists and turns copied by Native American dancers. If we were introduced to the dodo through the reading or hearing of Lewis Carroll's *Alice's Adventures in Wonderland*, we may remember when we were surprised to learn that the dodo, a childhood literary friend, was real and had once inhabited our natural, as well as our literary, world. If camping, we might wake late at night and cocooned within its deep silence, imagine that quiet being broken by the bark of a thylacine, or disturbed by the howl of a Japanese Honshu wolf. During daylight hours, delighting in the dazzling sunshine, we search for the elusive blue of the Xerces butterfly, to complement a bright spring's palette. Knowledge of these extinct creatures may bubble to the surface during ordinary moments of our lives, refusing to be forgotten. What of the lesser known? Don't they, too, deserve to be remembered? An earwig, a pupfish, a golden toad: they once lived, members of Earth's multi-species family, and their absence leaves gaps, deep, dark, crevices in Earth's shrinking habitat, and black-ribboned gashes within our hearts.

Sculptor Todd McGrain chose to remember several extinct species by fashioning sculptures of them, a task to add substance, to 're-member' that creature, that species. Several of the sculptures are located at the site, either at the place or in the area of the sighting of the last of its species, before it went extinct. McGrain reflected on the role of his sculptures as memorials and what they mean for the future, particularly as public memorials: 'Like a locket holding the image of a lost loved one, a memorial is a touchstone for remembrance. Unlike a locket, a public memorial must speak to many.'[2] Maybe, just maybe, these portraits function as unfastened lockets, revealing the hidden, the private, to the public eye, not to be scrutinized but rather to elicit remorse, for reflection and, hopefully, for rejuvenation or re-activation, protecting other species from extinction. As McGrain was challenged to 'find form for the formless', I too searched to give voice to some who are no longer audible, to give shape to those no longer seen and texture to those now denied our gentle touch of blessing.[3]

We humans are forgetful creatures. Memorials are needed – in many cases are essential – for the deep act of remembrance. Christopher Cokinos warned that 'Histories, like species, can go extinct.'[4] Forgetfulness can happen prematurely, while the species is still living, clinging on, ghost-like, nearing the edge, still hovering on the 'critically endangered' list.[5] This lingering for a little while longer may be compared to our reactions when we assume a famous musician, writer or film star has died, but later we learn that that person is still living. That person had already been 'forgotten', consigned to the land of the dead. To forget is another form of extinction, relegating the deceased to 'darkening memory'.[6] In the film *Stand Up Guys* (2012), Al Pacino's character Val proclaimed, 'They say we die twice – once when the last breath leaves our body and once when the last person we know says our name.'[7] This also applies to our memories of our non-human kin. 'Naming' is a human construct, but it frames or references the particular. Does knowing the name of a creature, of a species, mean it will be remembered, less likely to be forgotten? If a creature has been assigned a given name – such as 'Benjamin', or 'Lonesome George' – as well as a scientific one, will that name stay fixed within our brains, passed on to future generations? Tim Dee thought so: 'Without a name made in our mouths, an animal or a place struggles to find purchase in our minds or our hearts.'[8]

Often we need to see the deceased in order to begin the process of mourning. Sometimes this includes a place or a location to visit. Many specimens reside in storage rooms and in the bowels of basements in natural history museums and in universities, preserved by various toxic substances. They may be 'let out' or be 'on loan', displayed behind glass and dimmed lights, to preserve their delicate feathers, fur or scales. Those who remain in drawers, pulled out on their trays, like a row of corpses in a morgue, have tags identifying them. These little pieces of card list a brief description, plus the locality where the creature was found, or shot – a mini biography. These dead bodies are now protected from those who wish to touch, or hold, and for the lucky few for whom this is permitted – the research biologist, the student or the curious academic – supervision and protection of the dead is carried out by curators wearing white and security in black. It's strange that these exquisite creatures, who once added their colours and notes to the palette and musical score of Earth, receive more protection now dead than when they drew breath.

'Everything is held together with stories. That is all that is holding us together, stories and compassion,' goes a sentiment oft-attributed to nature writer Barry Lopez, author of *Arctic Dreams* (1986). Animals have their own stories, their own biographies. Extinct animals have theirs, which can be harder to hear, or to acknowledge. How does one dare to speak on behalf of an extinct species? Is this human hubris, to step across a sacred border? As a human being, I do not know what my cat thinks, nor what my dog thinks; I may guess and be correct (albeit not always able to verify this, of course), but how much harder it is to do this when the creature was wild and unseen. Perhaps if we consider portraits or stories of the extinct to be love letters, they don't seem so unsettling or shocking. A love letter embodies something of the essence of the letter writer, conveyed to the reader, accompanied (usually) by reasons explaining why they are loved. Similar to human eulogies, the portraits contained in this book are framed within an outline of a life; the body of the picture then includes some of the particulars or details about the deceased. What was the deceased's essence? What made that species unique? These two questions are partially answered in the portraits.

I have been speaking of the human world, but what of the animal and its environment? The notion or concept of *umwelt* (in English, 'environment' or 'surrounding world'), coined by Jakob von Uexküll, a Baltic German biologist, speaks of each animal's environment or world. For Uexküll, every living creature inhabited its own world, each creature having or possessing its own unique sensory environment.[9] The world that the animal perceives therefore differs from the way another individual, as well as species, in that same habitat would react and intersect with it. 'Uexküll believed that organisms create and shape their own umwelt, guided by their unique evolutionary histories and individual experiences.'[10] This term has been adopted by ethologists to speak of animal behaviour and the importance of their environment. It is a reminder that, as hard as we may try, we will never understand how an animal feels, or know everything about its personal interaction with its world, which is a shared world, but a world viewed differently by every creature. Each animal has its own unique sensory world or universe; this is a subjective environment, which can only be understood by that animal. Gary Kowalski put it succinctly: 'Animals not only have biologies; they also have biographies.'[11] Animals inhabit their *umwelt*, their surroundings, but they also have their own *innenwelt*, their unique inner worlds. They, as do human animals, live in both. Uexküll brought this subjectivity to the fore; what had once been 'the preserve of poets and dreamers, is now at the heart of any modern scientific understanding of nature'.[12]

Animals are grounded in history, they experience history. Their emotional lives need to be acknowledged, even if we are unable to understand or interpret them accurately. Historian Brett L. Walker writes that animal emotions can be read as '"text" with which to give animals greater agency in historical narrative'.[13] Our emotional lives are an important part of our present and past experiences and histories: why should other animals be devoid of subjective experience?[14] Biographies encompass grief, loss, love, fun, joy. Wouldn't a human story seem odd without these elements, these emotions? Couldn't this apply to other animals too? I am not saying that every animal feels all of these emotions, and not in the same way that humans do, but we have learned enough about animals grieving, animals bonding, animals playing, to know they are not Descartes' mere 'automata'.

I write about animals for the simple reason that their stories need to be told. I know of ethnographers who have similarly hesitated, reluctant to transcribe stories of First Peoples, but have done so in order for their stories to be told, to be heard, to be read, to be kept. Some feel these can only be told by the Indigenous peoples themselves – but if they are not going to be told, others would argue that a non-Indigenous person respectfully records them, for the world not to be denied that gift. Animals cannot tell their stories, so animal biography has become a genre. I cannot enter a non-human animal's mind. I can imagine parts of its experience, but I am not a thylacine, a heath hen, a Rocky Mountain locust or a great auk. I draw upon the facts that we have about them and hope that by hearing and understanding part of the story of their existence and extinction, we may become more mindful of other species who need our prompt attention. I acknowledge that I am writing about a species, rather than an individual. I will never know any individual animal's social life, or its emotions, its feelings, but I try to focus the lens so that it rests upon the solitary unique individual, while refracted through the prism of the species, or subspecies.

Within the field of grief and loss, a fairly new category, with an accompanying expanding body of study, has emerged. It is not a new form of grief; it has been felt, indeed experienced, for a long time, but it hadn't been given a 'name', an identity, until recently, although conservationists, including Aldo Leopold, had noted its existence. This grief, now given form and voice, is known as 'ecological grief'. This is the heartbreak we feel, the deep grief we experience, when we lose something from our natural environment, be it place, plant or animal. This grief has accelerated because of climate change and habitat destruction. It has given birth to new words, including 'solastalgia', which means homesickness due to environmental changes, and 'terrafurie', a word that describes the rage we may feel when confronted by habitat destruction.[15]

This grief is accompanied by baggage, by guilt, because as we grieve, we realize and own the knowledge that humans have been, and continue to be, largely responsible for these losses. Rituals may aid the grieving to move through the darkness and the culpability, to search for and then scratch out seeds of hope.

Does ecological grief include the loss of language, the extinction of the languages of extinct species, as anthropology does for peoples, particularly First Peoples? I think it does, and if it doesn't, then perhaps its definition needs to be broadened. Language. We humans speak, write, manipulate words to convey meaning, to communicate. Non-human animals do the same within their own particular mode of communication. We may not know how they communicated, or what was meant, but we read of the cry of the golden toad as it mated, of the husky bark of a thylacine in the darkness of night, the *quiii quiii* of the brightly coloured Carolina parakeets as they soared through the sky. Language is one means of communication; it is multidimensional, encompassing dance, pheromones and other senses and levels of senses and activities we humans do not understand, hear or observe. All are methods of communication. When a species dies out, so too does that particular mode of communication. 'We grieve only for what we know.'[16]

In these portraits, I try to tell, to give voice to, a portion, a crumb, a morsel of the autobiographies of 31 extinct species. For some, we have details concerning the individual, and in several cases, even a name ('Martha', 'Benjamin', 'Lonesome George'), but without the living creature, with its unique life, 'remembering' will always be a 'water spilt on a page' activity: we have an outline, but then it disappears, with perhaps a faint smudge, or mark, remaining.

To know the deceased is important in order to acknowledge it had existed, it had lived out its particular life within this shared and fragile world. Only by knowing, by learning, by getting alongside, are we able to seek forgiveness and then move on to ensure that other species are spared such a fate. Sometimes knowledge awakens links to all kin, or gives us elements in which to delight, to celebrate and then to mourn, for those parts of that creature have been silenced forever. We know that by focusing on an individual, we risk lumping it together as 'the same' as others. It is a risk but a necessary one.

Todd McGrain's five large bird sculptures of extinct species (the great auk, the heath hen, the Labrador duck, the passenger pigeon and the Carolina parakeet), part of his 'Lost Bird Project', have been placed in the locations where the last of their species was shot, or, if that was not possible, then at a site that seemed appropriate for the marking of the final bird. For McGrain, these sculptures' meanings become defined by place. They 'would not mean what I intended until they were installed at those places haunted by what is missing'.[17]

If these sculptures are odes to five extinct bird species, can words serve a similar function? These may not be the large, tactile forms that point beyond themselves to that which is absent – and will always be absent – for a sculpture. A human-made model will always be lifeless, but words too can pay homage, tell stories and dare to be silent, letting the white between the ink be prayers or tears.

If McGrain has 'honed a physical intimacy' with the five birds he chose to memorialize through the medium of bronze, then why and how do I dare to achieve something similar through mere words, marks on paper or screen?[18] But then, of course, these creatures – of feather, fin, sinew, lungs – are marks on our brain's medulla, where emotion resides.

McGrain's sculptures are magnificent, and he has left them so 'they offer little information beyond the language of surface and form'.[19] He admits that this raises questions for the viewer. I hope these portraits 'flesh out', if you will, something of each creature's story as a species and, for several, of themselves as individuals. They may even raise questions for the reader. A sculpture can become 'a memorial' through the observer's or mourner's eyes, but it may need more information for it to become truly embedded in one's psyche. 'The memorials can only point to what is missing, remind us of what we are not seeing, so that we may simultaneously feel the absence and presence of these lost birds.'[20]

Photographs and paintings also serve as memorials. There are a number of individuals whose work, whether it be art, photography or words, is testimony to our lost kin.[21] Their work helps the reader, or viewer, stretch out a hand to feel the fur, scale or skin, the fin or feather, of long-lost animal brethren, to hear something of the stories humans have cobbled together about them, to imagine and then to mourn their loss, the missing faces in Earth's family tree. Joel Sartore's photograph of the last dusky seaside sparrow, interned at the Florida Museum of Natural History, his eternal resting place a glass jar, is difficult to contemplate, but it is hard to look away. When does mourning the dead become voyeurism? This tiny sparrow, named Orange, seems to stare out at the viewer, but his eye has closed, or perhaps decayed. There is no visible pupil; death has turned the sparrow's gaze inwards. There is a cardboard label affixed to the lid, with the following words: 'Dusky – "Orange". Last one. Died 16 Jun 87'.[22] It is a penned epitaph for the last dusky sea sparrow's glass tomb. Unlike in the case of Snow White, there will be no prince, no rescuer, to bring this creature, or its species, back to life.

Words can serve as memorials. They can also indicate what is missing and, hopefully, tell enough about the creature that the reader is not only informed but is already in the process of mourning. I pray that my words elicit recognition of kin, kindle a sense of wonder, yet also bring the darkness of grief for all that this planet – their world, their *umwelt* and their own *innenwelt* – and we have lost. Most of all, though, I hope that these portraits blow on the sparks of love.

Accounts of extinction can educate, confront, paralyse, break – and inspire. Within these pages of feather, fin, sinew and blood, may the family tree that connects you to all living beings write you in so that *your* story includes helping to save other animal kin from extinction. This narrative continues; we know some of what has gone before, but the open book points forwards to the future, an unfinished tale.

— PART TWO —

THE PORTRAITS

Aurochs (*Bos primigenius*), engraving from Franz Xaver Mettenleiter (and his sons), *Naturhistorisches Bilderbuch* (1875).

Cave painting of aurochs, Upper Paleolithic, reconstruction, Lascaux II, Dordogne.

The Aurochs

(*Bos primigenius*) (1627): aurochs, aurochsen. We have been dated to 2 million years ago in Asia, from where we then spread west and south, to Europe and Africa during the interglacials, travelling to these other regions during this warm spell. It is thought that we evolved in Asia, because no fossils have been found of us in Europe or Africa from the early part of the Pleistocene epoch (commonly known as the Ice Age).[1] It is thought that we became three separate subspecies: *Bos primigenius primigenius* in Europe and the Middle East; *Bos primigenius mauretanicus* in northern Africa; and *Bos primigenius namadicus* in India. We in Europe were dark brown, darkening to black as we aged. We had a white muzzle and a distinctive stripe down our spine. Our cows were reddish in hue, as were both genders of the African aurochsen. Sometimes there were variations, at least in the European subspecies, including individuals with white bodies, who were particularly revered. No one knows the colours of the Asian aurochsen though.

At the close of the Pleistocene epoch, we, the European aurochsen, continued to live, but the Asian and African races died out about 2,000 years before.[2] We lived on in the thick, cold forests of Europe, until 1627. We, the massive, magnificent aurochsen have now gone. How could such large walls of muscle disappear? We, favoured by nobility, painted on cave walls, feared and revered, atoms of concentrated power – how could *we* become extinct? How could we, who when moving made the very ground tremble, who had been hunted from prehistoric times, no longer breathe, no longer exist?

Our image was painted with strong lines, particularly in the caves at Chauvet (painted 31,000 years ago) and at Lascaux (17,000 years ago). In 1940 prehistoric artwork was discovered in the Lascaux caves. This artwork formed its own gallery, with more than six hundred wall paintings and nearly 1,500 etchings. It has been called the 'prehistoric Sistine Chapel'.[3] What was quite magnificent about it was the finding of the Hall of the Bulls: there *we* were, depicted in a 5.2-metre-long (17 ft) painting of a bull, the largest animal yet found in cave art.[4] Of course we would be the largest, the most prominent. In the gallery known as the Shaft of the Dead Man, we, alongside a bird and a bird man, form part of a mural. What is extra special about this drawing is that it is believed to be the earliest star map. Each of the three figures represents a star: Vega, Deneb and Altair.[5] If we were drawn to depict three of the brightest lights seen in the night sky during the summer, then we are part of something larger, bigger than our muscles and sinew – we were thought to be part of the cosmos. Perhaps we danced in the heavens, or were revered as representatives on Earth of a bull-god. Back in the Hall of the Bulls, the Pleiades star cluster is depicted on another painting. Why were we painted on rock? Were we worshipped? Was it to ensure a successful hunt? A fertility rite? The answers have faded, as have the mineral pigments.

We were more than mere flesh and blood; we loomed nearly 2 metres (6½ ft) at the shoulder, which terrified all but the brave, the brash or the foolhardy, because we lived in mythology and in legendary tales. We were the 'bull', the model for bull worship, in many regions of the world. Bulls were sacred, worshipped in many places in the Mediterranean. In Egypt, there was Apis, the sacred bull. In one of the oldest towns excavated in Turkey, shrines were found that had been made from aurochs horns, as well as effigies of wild bulls. We were the body that the thunder god Zeus donned in order to abduct the beautiful Europa. Our image decorated cups, chalices, frescoes on the walls of palaces, gold rings and murals; our form was captured (with varying degrees of success) in sculptures. Our heads and horns were shaped into rhyta, elaborate drinking vessels. Later these were used in ceremonies, perhaps in blood rituals or during animal sacrifices. In Crete, these were lavish, made of silver and gold. In 1500 BCE the Minoans of Crete revered us; we must put aside the word 'bull' and instead insert 'aurochs'.

The famous 'bull leaping' fresco on the palace at Knossos is of one of us. What of this bull-leaping ritual? Was it a cultural event or a sporting activity, or did it hold religious significance? Why would a human even try to leap over us, grabbing our horns during the turn? Sounds like either the kiss of death, or stupidity, or a bit of both. Perhaps the leap was also a moving display of the cosmos, of an image they saw in the stars, acted out between bull and human. Maybe I was Taurus, being tamed. There has always been tension between the wild and the tame, the untamed and the need to master it. In the end, I do not know; I am unsure whether they worshipped a bull, or a god who transformed into a bull, or just a god or goddess who rode a bull; the answers have dissipated into the ether. What can be said is that bulls, in some way, were important to the Minoans. The horns that decorated the palace at Knossos came from us. Our horns, now they were something! They were extremely long and curved forwards, above our pounding, powerful neck muscles.

We were admired by the famous, by conquerors, by the powerful. Maybe they would have liked some of our essence? Julius Caesar hunted us (he called us *urus*) and in *De Bello Gallico*, described us this way: 'In size they are a trifle smaller than elephants; in kind, color and shape they are bulls. Great is their strength and great is their speed' (*magna vis et magna velocitas*).[6]

We were admired and hunted. We continued to be used in the name of 'sport': bullfighting in the arena, to the death. You may think this sport was like the Spanish bullfights of today, but no, we were twice the size of those bulls, weighing up to a tonne. Our horns were prized, their tips coated in silver. Mastery over us was applauded and rewarded. Eventually, though, we became but a memory in much of Europe. By the fourteenth century we survived only in East Prussia, Lithuania and Poland; by the fifteenth and sixteenth centuries, we were confined to Poland, but even here, our numbers were in decline. We remained in the Jaktorów forest, south of Warsaw, where the local men of the village acted as gamekeepers, looking after us, for a little longer.[7] We were protected by Polish nobility, which meant our survival, but this protection came at a price: we were only saved in order for the privileged classes to continue to hunt us. In the 1606 edition of Conrad Gessner's book *Historiae animalium*, he describes the fights:

> The strongest are killed by hunters by the King's command. One animal is separated from the herd, and many men and hounds then hunt it, often for a long time. It falls only when pierced in the breast. Then, while it is still alive, the hide between the horns is stripped off and sent with the heart and the fresh or salted meat to the King. The King transmits the meat to various other princes as a gift.[8]

Gessner's description is accompanied by a woodcut of a hunter who has speared the massive aurochs. The hunter is behind a tree, keeping a safe distance from the dying, or perhaps only wounded, animal. And people say that animals are savages! What cruelty! This was hardly an act that promoted conservation, or love of a species.

Eventually there were few of us left; the reasons, as for many other extinct species, were overhunting, restricted habitat and, in our case, diseases transmitted by our family, domesticated cattle. Did you know that cattle were the last species to be domesticated? It took time to make them smaller, to breed out their fiery personality. Cattle needed to be smaller, to make them easier to herd, castrate and butcher; to be utilized by humans, harnessed to carts and ploughs. It is ironic that our relatives helped change the environment: our habitat of forests, abundant with trees, was cut down to provide fields, to provide for agriculture. Wild nature, aurochsen and plants were being restrained, tamed. By 1564 there were eight bulls, twenty-two mature cows and five calves, but they were thin.[9] Villagers had been using the fields that had been set aside for the aurochsen for their own livestock to graze; by 1602 there were only three bulls and a single cow, and in 1620 there was a single cow, who died in 1627, in the Jaktorów forest.[10] Did her death result from natural causes, or from the actions of a poacher? There is a monument to her and to the last of the aurochsen in the village.

We were missed though, we lived in people's dreams and set some alight with ambition. Two of these humans were brothers Lutz and Heinz Heck, naturalists in charge of zoos in Berlin and Munich.[11] In 1921 they attempted to bring us back by a process known as 'back-breeding', 'backcrossing', 'topcrossing' or 'breeding back'. It usually involves mating a hybrid offspring with either one of its parents, or with an animal of the same type. It can firm up certain traits in the bloodline, or introduce desirable new genes or characteristics. Lutz Heck wrote,

> Thus the aurochs still lives on in some primitive races of cattle maintained for their yield or their fighting spirit, and its heritable constitution has largely remained untouched in these descendants. It is inaccurate, therefore, to say that the aurochs is extinct. No creature is extinct if the elements of its heritable constitution are still to be found in living descendants.[12]

The brothers chose different breeds; at the Tierpark Hellabrunn (the Munich Zoo), Heinz Heck, wanting size, experimented with Scottish Highland cattle, Hungarian and Podolian steppe cattle (for their size and immense horns), Alpines, Corsicans and Friesians. Several years later, Lutz Heck, based at the Berlin Zoo, opted for another method. Looking to resurrect something of our wild spirit, he chose wilder breeds, mainly those from southwest Europe. Breeds included wild Corsican oxen, Spanish fighting bulls and the wild black cattle of the Camargue.[13]

Their 25 years of experiments had mixed outcomes. They did 'succeed' in back-breeding an animal that looked like us, in colour and markings, but not in height. Lutz was more successful than Heinz; the horns of his breeds were longer, the body more lithe, whereas Heinz had produced a heavier bull. Neither was able to resurrect or breed the height, weight and power of the true aurochs.

Sadly, our power and form were linked to German nationalism: we became a symbol of German greatness, power and courage. The Hecks had wanted to bring back the mythical Germanic old forests, populating their vastness with magnificent creatures to hunt – wisent, tarpan and us.

They were not aurochsen, just other cattle, commonly called 'neo-' or 'near-' aurochsen. The Hecks' creatures were released, set free in two great forest regions – the big-game preserve at Rominten, in East Prussia, and the primeval forest of Białowieża, in Poland. Białowieża, comprising old forest growth and on the border of Poland and Belarus, had been protected as hunting grounds of Polish kings and Russian tsars. These forests were now liquidated of their people, of their Jewish inhabitants, Polish resistance fighters and Soviet partisans, all under the name of German 'forest management' (the dual prong of human extermination and animal propagation). Lutz Heck chose to ignore the negative consequences of trying to back-breed the old aurochs, believing that when his neo-aurochsen were released, 'out rushed the first aurochsen of the new age, to wander once more in German forests, as in the legendary days of old.'[14]

The final days of the Second World War put an end to this experiment of back-breeding, at least for a time; bombing destroyed the animals in the Berlin Zoo, including all of Lutz Heck's near-aurochsen, but some survived in Munich, as did those that had already been released in Białowieża. Our legacy, and theirs, lives on today not in the form of resurrected aurochsen, but as 'Heck cattle', their skin tanned or tainted by controversy and prejudice. Many domestic breeds of cattle are claimed to have descended directly from we aurochs. If you look carefully at a black Spanish fighting bull you will see the light line that highlights its spine. Our stripe. Those Spanish bulls were gifted with some of our feisty spirit too. Perhaps we do live on, in the cattle of the present.[15]

As I consider my past, consigning us to ghost memory, new pro-grammes, such as 'Rewilding Europe', are starting up, and they are, again, attempting to bring us back, this time in the form of large bovines they have named 'Tauros'.[16] These cattle are to be back-bred and let loose in large European areas, to help create conditions that will aid the restoration of plant life of long ago. It is too much for me; we are extinct. Let me return to the shadows, to the cave at Lascaux. The animals with whom I share my portrait, the great deer, the cave lion – they too are extinct. We cavort among the stars (though I am still dangerous to both, even to the cave lion, one of my largest predators), now celestial bodies, forming a sky map with constellations of the extinct, to glitter in the cosmos, for eternity.

❀ ❀ ❀

The Dodo

(*Raphus cucullatus*) (1680 or 1681): the 'dodo'. What a stupid name! Sets me up as a thing of ridicule; if one is not accorded respect, it is easier to kill. Early explorers called me other unflattering names: 'wild turkey' and 'cassowary' were acceptable, even 'hooded swan', but 'booby' and 'bastard ostrich'?[17] The Dutch called us *dronte*, which means 'swollen', and *dodoor*, which translates as 'sluggard' – hardly the names given to a species one would cherish. There was even a name associated with a Dutch festival. On 19 September 1598, a Dutch ship sailed into the harbour at Mauritius. This was the day before an annual festival known as the *kermis* would have been held in Amsterdam. Maybe they were homesick, or just surprised when we emerged from the foliage. Whatever the reason, we were named *kermisgans* or '*kermis* goose', in honour of the fowl that would have been fattened for the festival.[18] Apparently, the Portuguese name for Mauritius was 'Island of Swans'; were we once mistaken for those fine waterfowl?[19]

Some propose that our name is of Portuguese origin, from *duedo*, *doudo* or *doido*, meaning 'idiot'.[20] Another unflattering name, the name that 'stuck', was the one from which you penned 'dodo': *dod-aars*, or *dod-aarse*, which is quite rude, because it refers to our fat, tufted behinds. The translation is more explicit: 'lump arse'.[21]

I was, in fact, a giant pigeon. Of course, 'dodo' could have been a rendition of the cry we made. If one listens to the cooing of a pigeon, it wouldn't be too far-fetched, would it?

Putting the giant pigeon aside for a moment, some individuals in the past and in the present have found it hard to believe that I was real, that I was not a made-up character for *Alice's Adventures in Wonderland*. I wonder when children realize that I was factual, real, rather than a creature of legend or fantasy? But fantasy doesn't exist and now neither do we. Are we the same, or different?

We had quite the history, going back to the Pleistocene epoch. It is thought that some pigeons, having lost their bearings, managed to find safety on the island of Mauritius. They would have had to be a sizeable flock, to avoid in-breeding.[22] There were no predators on that island, so the pigeons flourished and, over thousands of years, evolved (and this evolutionary history is still a mystery) into largish, flightless birds (with an absence of predators, we didn't need functioning wings), into what became known as the dodo. If you don't believe the pigeon ancestry, check out the results of our 2002 mitochondrial DNA extraction: they confirm that we were a pigeon, a giant one, but still a pigeon, our closest living relative being the Nicobar pigeon of southeast Asia.[23] Sadly, one of our other ancestors was the Rodrigues solitaire, who also became extinct.

We remained as we were for millions of years, until humans (the Portuguese) arrived in the early sixteenth century, and from then on, everything changed. Humans became our predators. Mind you, Arab travellers probably arrived before the Portuguese, but the real problem was not the Portuguese, who did not stay, but the later arrivals, the Dutch, who landed in 1598. Our fate was sealed when Cornelius van Neck made Mauritius a Dutch possession. For the next forty years, Mauritius was a refurbishment station, a handy place to throw anchor on the way to and from the East Indies. There was no permanent settlement then, so we were still safe. It was only in 1644, when the Dutch decided to settle on

Mauritius, the island becoming a Dutch colony (in response to rival traders from England and France), that we were in real trouble. For a while, we were able to inhabit remote regions of the island, protecting our breeding colonies, but once colonists settled, we were exposed, easy to kill, a ready source of fresh meat.

Humans were not our only predator: ship cargo – known and stowaways – saw us, unable to fly and without fear, as easy targets, and they were correct. Humans introduced many mammal species to the island, including black rats (they loved our eggs), goats, pigs, pet dogs and cats, and monkeys. Some of these were allowed to breed in the forests, a ready food supply, as well as a recreational activity for hunters. Adult dodos,

The dodo (*Raphus cucullatus*), drawing from copper plate
in John Ray, ed., *The Ornithology of Francis Willughby* (1678).

chicks and eggs were all attacked or carried off to be eaten. These introduced species multiplied rapidly, causing great damage. Monkeys cavorted in gardens, one writer observing that 'While strolling in the garden, I had the pleasure of counting four thousand monkeys in a neighbour's garden'; rats reached plague proportions (leading some of the Dutch to leave Mauritius); and the pigs were so plentiful that during an organized hunt, 1,500 of them were killed that day.[24] Actually, these animals played a bigger role in our extinction than you humans. The pigs loved our habitat of lush undergrowth, digging up roots and trampling our nests.

Having said that, you humans were not innocent. We were easy to kill; humans could walk right up to us and club us to death. If only we had been gifted the quality of 'fear', we may have stood a small chance of survival. We were thought to be stupid, but we did not know fear; we had lived and died for thousands of years without having to protect ourselves from other species.

In our favour was our taste, or lack of: another of our names owed its etymology to our tasteless, oily flesh. The Dutch called us the *walghvogel*, 'disgusting bird', or 'sicky bird'.[25] We were near inedible but, sadly, desperate sailors will eat most things, including birds with a strange flavour.

We only laid a single egg once every two years, and this egg took approximately nine months to a year to reach maturity. When we were in decline, our low reproduction rates meant that the few squabs born could not replace the numbers that had gone. Underpopulation caused stress on the diminishing numbers. It was only a matter of time, really, before we would be gone. These changes were happening at too fast a pace for us to adapt, to have a chance of survival. We dodos, who had evolved to be without wings – for we had no enemies – ended up unable to save ourselves.

In 1599 Cornelius van Neck returned to the Netherlands. On his arrival, van Neck published his account of us (which was the first):

> There are also other birds there which are as big as our swan,
> with large heads, and on the head a veil as though they had a
> small hood on their head; they have no wings but in their place
> there are three or four black quills, and where there ought to
> be a tail; there are four or five small curled plumes of a greyish

colour. We called these birds Walghvogels [nauseous bird], partly because although we stewed them for a very long time, they were very tough to eat, yet the stomach and the breast were extremely good.[26]

During the next two years, van Neck's journal was expanded and included illustrations of us for the first time.[27]

Were his descriptions correct? Partly. Although we are now fashionable – indeed symbolic, iconic, much has been written about us – facts about us are sparse, and there are few accurate descriptions of us. We were large, between 10 and 22 kilograms (22–49 lb), the size of a turkey, swan or goose, with long necks and large rumps for fat storage, similar to turkeys. It is thought that we had light-grey to dark-grey plumage, lighter grey on our bellies. We had evolved into being flightless birds (if we didn't need to fly, that conserved our energy), so our wings were small and stumpy, about the size of chickens' wings, with yellow feathers at their edges. In the 1613 journal of Johannes Verken, a German sailor, our faces were described as being featherless. We had light-grey skin and large bills with dark tips; these bills could open widely.[28] The tip of the beak was of keratin, and this would be shed and re-grown annually. This tip aided eating and fighting and may have been incorporated into courtship displays during the breeding season.[29] We sported yellow legs and feet, and had several curled feathers on our rumps, black talons and feathered hoods. We were probably upright, standing at about 75 centimetres (2 ft 6 in.) in height. We were ground eaters, like most pigeons, and would find our food via smell, a more developed sense in us than that of vision. We dined on fallen fruit, snails, crabs and coral (we needed the calcium for our egg shells) and vegetation.

Now, what I find most interesting is that Verken also mentioned that we were fighting back against human predators.[30] Yes, we were learning that we needed to defend ourselves, and could, via our hooked beaks. This was new behaviour for us. We were no longer meek or complacent.

We were regarded as exotic, or, at least, a curio, so were sent to other parts of the world, including India, where at least two of us became part of the zoo of the Mughal emperor Jahangir.[31] One of us journeyed to Japan. Now, travel wasn't like it is nowadays – think of my poor ancestor making the trip to Japan. It took nearly eight months. Not much is known of what happened to that dodo after its arrival in Japan. People were unsure if it had arrived safely. It wasn't until 2014, when documents were discovered stating its entry into Japan, that we knew it had, indeed, made it to the islands. In India there were drawings and paintings done of the dodo by a court artist, no less. The artist, Ustad Mansur, known for his zoological illustrations and paintings, was the first artist to depict us in colour. A famous, untitled painting, executed in 1610, was discovered in the Hermitage, St Petersburg, in 1953. It is unsigned, but believed to be Mansur's work. Several other birds are depicted in it as well, but the dodo is prominent, and graces centre stage.

Unfortunately, the dodo that arrived in London in 1638 did not receive the respect it deserved. This poor thing became an exhibit in cold, foggy London, far from the warmth, greenery and sounds of its island home. English writer Sir Hamon L'Estrange's description of this unfortunate dodo is the only account of a live specimen in Europe. L'Estrange focuses on what the dodo was being fed; it was thought that it ate rocks, but that would have been a tool to aid digestion, normal for many pigeons:

> About 1638, as I walked London streets, I saw the picture of a strange looking fowle hung out upon a clothe and myself with one or two more in company went in to see it. It was kept in a chamber, and was a great fowle somewhat bigger than the largest Turkey cock . . . The keeper called it a Dodo, and in the ende of a chimney there lay a heape of large pebble stones, whereof hee gave it many in our sight, some as big as nutmegs, and the keeper told us she eats them (conducing to digestion) . . . yet I am confident that afterwards she cast them all again.[32]

Do you know that more has been written about us than about any other extinct bird species? Yes, even more than the pages penned lamenting the silence of the passenger pigeon (again, another pigeon). This is very strange, because little had been recorded about us at the time we lived, and much has been conjecture, or images that have formed in people's minds, often due to the illustrations of us by John Tenniel, which were executed for Lewis Carroll's *Alice's Adventures in Wonderland*. All you have as physical evidence that we once existed are a couple of skin fragments, some bones, some descriptions and a few illustrations, and some of these weren't treasured or preserved very well. For example, in 1755 the only complete surviving stuffed dodo, which at the time resided at the Ashmolean Museum in Oxford, was thought to be in such a dreadful state, beyond repair, that it was set aside to be destroyed. This dodo was put into a fire, but a new member of staff, a William Huddersfield, apparently rushed in and saved the specimen's head and right foot. These remnants still exist, now in care at the Oxford University Museum of Natural History. Huddersfield had the foresight to have plaster casts made of these fragments for the benefit of other museums.[33]

So that's all that's left, yet there are problems surrounding the illustrations, for some are quite faulty. The traditional image of us is that we were large, fat and clumsy. This was probably not correct; the live specimens that were drawn were captive, probably overfed – or fed an incorrect diet – or were less-than-accurate stuffed attempts at fashioning a dodo. Some of them have fluffed-up feathers, but that may have been part of our mating ritual, warding off rivals, rather than an accurate depiction of our normal appearance. The Dutch Golden Age artist Roelandt Savery was probably the artist most responsible for our plumpness. He made at least twelve paintings of us; the most famous, known as *Edward's Dodo* (because it was once owned by George Edwards, an ornithologist), of 1626, depicts a fat dodo and has been the model for many images of us.[34] This painting is displayed in the Natural History Museum, London, so viewers or admirers of this artwork may think that our Rubenesque figure was our true form.

Tangible evidence was needed. After we had died out, time passed, and gradually people started to doubt we had ever existed. We were thought to be a myth, or fantasy, a made-up creature. In 1801 one scientist wrote that we resembled a 'feathered tortoise'.[35] Facts were needed before we descended into more bizarre fantastical descriptions. The year 1865 was significant, though, because George Clark, a schoolteacher, following advice from Harry Higginson, a railway engineer, explored an area of swamp land near the south coast of Mauritius, the Mare aux Songes.[36] Here Clark unearthed dodo bones. What a precious, significant find! These subfossil remains have provided most of the knowledge about our structure and make-up.[37] Dare I say that the initial find caused some academic jealousy?

Roelandt Savery (attrib.), *The Dodo and Other Birds*, c. 1626, oil on canvas.

Although the ultimate victor was Richard Owen, superintendent and anatomist at the British Museum and the first to describe our skeleton and to present a reconstructed skeleton to the scientific community, it is thought that he acquired this knowledge by dubious means, having intercepted a shipment of bones that belonged to Alfred Newton, from the University of Cambridge.[38] Rivalry, money, prestige: all part of our story.

In the Mare aux Songes, more dodo bones were uncovered. This area became known as the 'dodo graveyard', but not all were found in these low-lands of southeast Mauritius. In 2007 an almost-complete skeleton, now known as 'Dodo Fred', was discovered in a mountain cave. Another nearly complete skeleton was found on higher ground, which demonstrated that we frequented different regions of Mauritius.

If you want to know more about us and about the way people thought about us, you have to consider dates. George Clark discovered that we were large birds, with big heads, long, hooked beaks, long necks and undeveloped wings, meaning we were incapable of flight. As with most flightless birds, our legs were strong and thick, to make up for our inability to fly. When George Clark unearthed our bones, he also unearthed controversy, because this was the era of Charles Darwin's *On the Origin of Species*, published five years before Clark's discovery.[39] Now, when Owen reconstructed our skeleton and spoke about us, he portrayed us as large and fat, which became the traditional depiction of us. It is the one featured in many of your children's books – the stuff of legend! Darwin's 'survival of the fittest' theory seemed to work against us – indeed, our size and our evolutionary development of small wings, rendering us flightless, meant we were easy to kill. But was Owen correct? Were we as big and clumsy as he thought? Owen may have been influenced by the artwork of Roelandt Savery, or heard reports from Dutch sailors about this fat bird.[40] Dodos, like many other creatures, store up fat to help them through lean times. Those hard times included seasonal tropical cyclones, which destroyed much of our food source. Anyway, the point is, we were not as fat as once thought; indeed, if we were as heavy as Owen reported, we would have had trouble walking, let alone running, and our skeleton would have collapsed under such weight![41] Even so, this controversy over our weight – whether we were fat or thin – continues, more than three hundred years since we last strolled (or struggled to stroll!) upon the earth.[42] We were not victims of natural selection. What strange ideas you humans have! What took millions of years of adaptation was undone in less than a century of contact with humans: they, and their introduced animal predators, wiped us out, 'the disgusting bird', 'the booby', 'the bastard ostrich', the *dod-aarse*.

Lewis Carroll's *Alice's Adventures in Wonderland*: should we dodos thank Charles Dodgson (the author's real name) for introducing us via his work? Was the dodo, in fact, Dodgson, whose speech impediment, a stutter, meant that on many occasions he repeated his surname, 'Do . . . do . . .'?

Let me close by moving from the plump, comical dodo, to considering our place in creation. In Savery's painting *Noah Thanking God for Saving the Creation* (date unknown), the animals have vacated the Ark and are back on dry land. Among the multitude of paired creatures, painted in the bottom right-hand corner is a single, mate-less, dodo. You could easily overlook it, because this portion of the canvas is dark – indeed, the dodo is hard to see, low to the ground, in the shadows. Was Savery prophetic?

The lone dodo. Perhaps we could interpret the darkness as foreknowledge concerning our fate: in the past, or at least in the biblical past, Noah may have saved the animals, but in the future, humans diverged from aiding salvation to destroying creation.

✿ ✿ ✿

The Rodrigues Solitaire

'They walk with so much stateliness and good Grace,
that one cannot help admiring and loving them.'
– François Leguat, 1708[43]

(*Pezophaps solitaria*, 'solitary pedestrian pigeon') (1730s–'60s): I was like my closest relative, the famous dodo; I, too, was a pigeon, or columbid, flightless and large. I, too, was island-bound, in my case restricted to the volcanic Rodrigues, the smallest of the Mascarene Islands, located in the bluest of blue waters, the Indian Ocean. Both we and the dodo were from the same common ancestor, a pigeon closely related to the Nicobar pigeon (*Caloenas nicobarica*), our closest living relative. In 2002 our DNA (mine and that of the dodo) was analysed and confirmed this relationship, as well as naming other close relatives who were also ground-dwelling island endemic pigeons (the crowned pigeon of New Guinea and the tooth-billed pigeon from Samoa). Results also confirmed our placement within the Columbidae (yes, both of us were indeed pigeons!). It is thought that a long time ago, our ancestors were able to fly, and they had reached the Mascarene Islands by island-hopping from South Asia. The lack of mammals competing for the same food sources meant that we, the Rodrigues solitaire and the dodo, could develop in size.

I was not well documented; there are several written accounts and a drawing, but nothing else, which added weight to the theory that I was just a legend, mad imaginings of a ship-stranded fellow named François Leguat. Even as late as 1921, Geoffroy Atkinson, a linguist, wrote that Leguat's 1708 memoir, *A New Voyage to the East Indies*, was not factual, but a French novel, written in the style of *Robinson Crusoe*. Atkinson even doubted the existence of Leguat himself, let alone the fauna and flora he had described

The Rodrigues solitaire (*Pezophaps solitaria*) in the only
known illustration drawn from life, from François Leguat,
*Voyage et avantures . . . en deux isles désertes
des Indes orientales* (1708), vol. 1.

in his work.[44] This has since been disproved, for Leguat had indeed lived, and most of the events, creatures and plants he described were verified as being true. My identity had also been in doubt; it took the 1786 discovery of several subfossil bones in a cave to change some minds.

I was the Rodrigues solitaire, named 'solitary' because I was usually seen on my own, or with my partner. We were monogamous, as are most pigeons. Leguat described our pairing: 'they are always together ... and tho' they happen to mingle with other Birds of the same Species, these two Companions never disunite.'[45]

This is probably a good time to introduce you to Huguenot refugee François Leguat. He was quite smitten with us, particularly with the females. In 1691 Leguat and his comrades fled to Rodrigues, where they remained for several years before sailing to Mauritius in 1693 and moving back to London eight years later. When you read Leguat's account of us, particularly his description of the female, remember that Leguat had been on Rodrigues for two years, away from female company. He was probably missing the fairer sex when he described the female Rodrigues solitaire's plumage in this fashion: 'They have two elevations upon the crop, of which the feathers are whiter than the rest, and which resemble, very marvelously, the beautiful bosom of a woman.'[46] In some editions, the original wording has been censored, changed to 'the fine neck of a beautiful woman'.[47] This breast feature is clearly illustrated in an engraving Leguat did, the only picture executed by anyone who saw us alive.

Let me describe us, in less infatuated language! Our females and males varied greatly in height and weight, the female being quite a bit shorter, at 70 centimetres (2 ft 4 in.) compared to the 90 centimetres (3 ft) of the male. One observer described us as being the size of a swan. The male was light grey, with a blackish back and black feathers on its front, whereas the females were paler, tending towards light brown, with two breast-shaped elevations (think Leguat!) on their lower necks, which were paler than the rest of their plumage. Both sexes had short, slightly hooked, sharp beaks, with peaks upon our beaks and bands of black feathers at the base of the beaks. Our necks and legs were long.

We had an interesting feature, a bony growth, or knob, on our car-pometacarpus (the equivalent of the human wrist) on our wings. This growth, known as a 'musket ball', was used in combat, for communication and in mating rituals. It was like a cauliflower in appearance, consisting of several lobes. This carpal knob was found on adults of both sexes and was the result of reaching both physical maturity and sexual readiness. This feature seems to have evolved as a measure to lessen impacts from fighting and in response to hormonal release, readying one for breeding and for acquiring territory for nest building. We were highly territorial and fought with our 'musket balls', males fighting males, and females defending their territory from other female rivals, to safeguard their mates and their nests. Leguat described our mating dances, in which we fluttered our short wings and then made a large rattling noise, created by this carpal knob. When we hit our sides, or brought our wings together, a rattle was produced: 'and for periods of four or five minutes at a time the bird would perform twenty or thirty rapid pirouettes, whirling its wings with a rattling noise which could be heard about 200 yards [183 m] away.'[48] The knobs may have created low-frequency sounds, being a means of communication with a bird's partner and perhaps serving as a warning to rivals.[49] One observer described the sound thus: 'they . . . make a great noise with their wings when angry, and the noise is something like thunder in the distance.'[50]

The carpal knob, covered in thick skin, continued to grow throughout adult life and could become quite large. This 'musket ball' was unique; no other bird has evolved a similar feature to create this sound or use as a weapon. These carpal growths also protected our bones from the sharp impact they might have sustained from frequent fighting, so I am glad of this feature, otherwise we would have lived very painful lives, especially during courting and nesting times! There were other bird species that used their wings to ward off others, or had spurs or knobs, but the way we used them as weapons, combined with the communication or sound aspect, rendered us unique.

Leguat wrote of our complex social life, our fights with one another to protect our nests with their single chicks and what he called 'marriages'. Our monogamous nature, mating for life, must have resonated with him, because his description of an annual ritual is quite beautiful:

Some days after the young one leaves the nest a Company of 30 or 40 brings another young one to it; and the new-fledged Bird with its Father and Mother joyning with the Band, march to some bye Place. We frequently followed them, and found that afterwards the old ones went each their way alone, or in Couples, and left the two young ones together, which we call a *Marriage*.[51]

The female laid a single egg that was incubated in turn by each sex.

Leguat showed his fondness for us by including several pictures of us on a map he drew of the island. We lived mainly in the forested areas, not on the shore, eating seeds and fruit. Like dodos, we swallowed large stones, which were held in the gizzards and were used to grind the hard seeds in our diet. These stones, highly valued by European settlers, were used to sharpen knives and for medicinal purposes.[52] Leguat was not our only fan. Julien Tafforet, from the island of Réunion, was sent to our island to see if it was a place suitable for human settlement (though some researchers suggest that he was marooned here and stayed longer than he had anticipated). One of the possessions that accompanied him was Leguat's book.[53] Tafforet observed, described and admired us. Unfortunately, in both Leguat's and Tafforet's accounts, they describe the giant tortoises that lived here, words of hope that attracted the attention of ship captains, who were always seeking a plentiful food source for their crews. The tortoise trade became big business, as did we. Leguat may have been fond of us, but that didn't stop him (and others) consuming us. Being flightless, we were easy to catch, plentiful and, unlike my cousin the dodo, very tasty, especially from March to September when we were particularly plump. We were hunted and eaten until we were exhausted as a food source.

Other factors hastened our extinction. European settlers brought with them cats, goats and pigs. We were ground nesters, so our eggs were easy pickings. The forests were burnt off as well, so we lost our habitat. We became extinct sometime between the 1730s and the 1760s. Much later our bones were discovered in caves. Hundreds and hundreds of bones were unearthed, enough to be sent back to museums, enough to reconstruct our now extinct skeletons, enough to see fractures caused by our musket ball growths, enough . . . enough.

In 1761, when Alexandre-Guy Pingré journeyed from France to the island of Rodrigues in order to observe the transit of Venus, he did not see us, the real stars, though he was assured we still existed. Perhaps there were a few of us left, but it was a small island, with few trees. I am sure we would have been spotted.

Star gazing. Pingré may not have seen us, but his visit did lead to us starring in the sky. We became part of the night sky, because, for a time, there was a star constellation named after us: Turdus Solitarius. Sounds romantic, doesn't it? Bright stars centre stage, shining against a black backdrop, but, even as a cluster of balls of gas, we didn't last, facts were wrong, because the name Turdus Solitarius actually means 'solitary thrush'. This constellation was introduced in 1776 by French astronomer Pierre-Charles Le Monnier, in memory of Pingré's visit back in 1761. Le Monnier described us as a 'bird of the Indies and the Philippines'.[54] He had made a mistake, not realizing these were two separate birds, not one. Adding insult to injury, Le Monnier's illustration of the constellation resembles that of the solitaire of the Philippines, the blue rock thrush (*Monticola solitaries*), not the Rodrigues (*Pezophaps solitaria*).[55] Celestial mapmakers didn't know what we looked like, so it is no surprise that other birds were depicted. In 1922 the International Astronomical Union (IAU) formed a list of 88 constellations. Many, including ours, were left out. Our stars now form part of Hydra and Libra. You will no longer find us on the earth, or in the sky, our short period of stardom was over.[56]

Although we were no longer assigned to the sky, to share the stage with mythical creatures, we did possess our own legendary element. According to the writings of Leguat, when we were caught, we made no sound; instead, we simply 'shed tears'.[57] Liquid stars.

❀ ❀ ❀

Steller's Sea Cow

(*Hydrodamalis gigas*) (1768): I was known as Steller's sea cow, a huge aquatic mammal, one of the largest mammals of the Holocene epoch. A docile sirenian, perhaps the last of the cold-water sirenians, my closest relatives were the dugong and the manatee, but I was much bigger. Strange that I was called a 'cow'; even the Russians named me that, *morskaya korova* (marine cow), and according to the writings of Georg Steller, the Dutch called me *vacca marina* (sea cow).[58] 'Elephant' would have been more accurate in terms of size and lineage. Reflecting on my name, perhaps it was appropriate – being labelled 'cow' – because we were one of six species eaten into extinction, and you humans certainly like to feast on cow, either *Bos taurus* or *Hydrodamalis gigas*. I had a nickname, which had nothing to do with the moniker 'cow'. It was 'bark animal', because of my rough skin.

I was one of the last of a relict population, living off the shore of Bering Island. Life was peaceful, I had all the kelp I needed in the warm months, and though I would become quite thin in winter with decreased supplies, my 10 centimetres (4 in.) of fat kept me going, as well as providing me with protection from the freezing waters of the Bering Sea. Cold, or more accurately, ice, was a danger though, because some of us would die of suffocation from the ice, our large dead forms washed up on the beach.

It is hard to find many descriptions of me. Only one naturalist wrote up copious notes about me: my namesake, Georg Steller. We had thick skin, to prevent injury from sharp rocks and ice and to protect exposed skin from drying out, because we were buoyant mammals, unable to submerge completely underwater. We bobbed, ducking for kelp, but needed to come up for air every four to five minutes. Our skin sometimes had white patches on it, and it tended to have little pits, or craters,

Illustration of Steller's sea cow (*Hydrodamalis gigas*), from Leopold Josef Fitzinger, *Bilder-Atlas zur wissenschaftlich-populären Naturgeschichte der Säugethiere in ihren sämmtlichen Hauptformen* (1860).

perhaps caused by parasites. We didn't have much hair on our bodies, but the insides of our flippers were covered with bristles. Although we were enormous, with forked tails like whales, our heads were small, with down-pointed snouts (to make eating kelp an easier exercise), small eyes and tongues, and strange jaws, almost reptilian in appearance. We used our front limbs to pick algae, and then we could grasp it and cut it with the interlocking bristles on our lips. We were toothless, but we had something unique: two bone chewing pads in our mouths that we used to grind the kelp. Our front limbs were without digits, or phalanges: no fingers, though many museums added them to their sea cow skeleton exhibits. We didn't need them. Our forelimbs were skilfully used, as I said, for picking or grabbing food and then holding it, for scraping algae and seaweed from rocks, for bracing ourselves, to aid walking and for hugging our companions. Stellar thought our handless forelimbs were the 'strangest feature of all'.[59] 'There are no traces of fingers, nor are there any of nails or hoofs.'[60] They were similar to 'an amputated human limb' covered in thickened skin and wire-brush-like bristles.[61]

Sometimes Steller's descriptions were less than flattering; he was able to stroke us as we floated in the shallows on the high tide, observing that our skin was 'mangy, wrinkled, rough, hard and tough' and looked like 'the bark of an ancient oak', admitting that it was so we had protection against predators, rocks and icebergs.[62]

We may have had several predators, but our size put some off, as did the difficulty they would have had trying to drown us. Floating in the shallows, among rocky kelp forests, was a deterrent for others, such as sharks. Having said that, we took no chances with our young. Being social animals, we grouped in herds; when we would swim, our young would be in the middle of us, protected on all sides. Even our mating was described as a gentle act. Steller regularly observed us 'in the sting of passion' embracing each other face to face, writing of our 'conjugal affection'.[63]

We were magnificent: a 1.8-metre-long (5 ft 11 in.) stomach, an intestinal tract of 151 metres (165 yd, more than twenty times the length of our body) and a beautiful 16-kilogram (35 lb) heart. Large, but peace loving, our days were spent grazing on the kelp canopy and then lying on our backs and resting. We communicated with snorts and sighs – a simple, contented existence – until 6 November 1741, when Captain Commander Vitus Bering and the 78 crew members of the *St Peter* were shipwrecked, castaways on a mound of land that became known as Bering Island.

We did not know we were in danger from these small beings. We were spared being a food source for a year, for they existed on foxes and sea otters, but in the following year, starving men started to wonder if we could be eaten and what we would taste like. Unfortunately, we tasted like rare beef, our young like veal; even our oil was coveted.[64] Steller wrote about its pleasing properties:

> It is glandulous, stiff, and white, but when exposed to the sun it becomes yellow like May butter . . . Its odor and flavour are so agreeable that it can not easily be compared with the fat of any other sea beast . . . Moreover, it can be kept a very long time, even in the hottest weather, without becoming rancid or strong. In flavour it approximates nearly the oil of sweet almonds and can be used for the same purposes as butter. In a lamp it burns clear, without smoke or smell. And indeed, its use in medicine is not to be despised, for it moves the bowels gently, producing no less of appetite or nausea, even when drunk from the cup.[65]

Our tasty flesh, wonderful fat and hides, which would be made into shoes and belts, led to our downfall. Because of our size, we could feed many. We were hard to kill though, and the slaughtering was careless. It is estimated that for every four harpooned, only one was captured, the others left to drift out to sea, wounded and dying.[66] The loyalty we displayed to our mates should have been touching. It was noted that if a female was caught, her mate would try to free her, even if he was repeatedly struck. If able, he would follow her to shore, and stay, even after she had been butchered. Shouldn't that have changed men's hearts and actions? Such brutality meted out on a peaceful species. We just wanted to be left to ourselves, to eat, to sleep, to care for our young. We were never a threat or a danger to anyone.

Sometimes our cousins the dugongs and manatees have been mistaken for mermaids, but we were too large for that comparison. Even though we did not feature in many stories, Rudyard Kipling wrote about us in *The Jungle Book*. Unlike the beauty associated with mermaids (even if they were dugongs or manatees), Kipling chose to describe our 'ugliness'. In his story *The White Seal*, action takes place in the Bering Sea. The rare seal had been informed of our displeasing appearance. When he finally sees us, his description is far from flattering: 'Their heads were the most foolish-looking things you ever saw, and they balanced on the end of their tails in deep water when they weren't grazing, bowing solemnly to each other and waving their front flippers as a fat man waves his arm.'[67]

Later the seal refers to this waving of our fore flipper as a 'sort of clumsy telegraphic code'.[68] He even comments on our reason for extinction, listing it as our supposed stupidity! As the seal follows a herd of us to safe haven, he passes judgement: 'such idiots as these . . . would have been killed long ago it they hadn't found out some safe island.'[69] Written in 1894, we were long gone, and sadly, not to an island safe from humans.

But let's revisit the mermaid image again. Due to our enormous girth, we may not have been mistaken for mermaids, but we are associated with them, even in the present day. Our bones are uncovered from time to time and, though we are extinct, the sale of our bones is permitted. Sometimes our bones are marketed as 'mermaid ivory', but it has been discovered that often these bones are not from the Steller's sea cow; instead they are from grey whales, a protected species. Illegal trading. When is a mermaid not a mermaid? Though it begs another question: surely an extinct creature's bones need to be carefully preserved and are as precious or as valuable as those from an endangered species?

It has been suggested that another reason for our demise was the hunting of sea otters by Indigenous peoples. The killing of sea otters led to an increase in sea urchin numbers. Sea urchins, though, feast on kelp, the main component of our diet. Abundant sea urchin numbers resulted in diminishing supplies of the plant. Perhaps.

By the time of Bering's arrival, we were restricted to Copper Island and Bering Island, where there had never been a human population. We did not fear a predator we had not met before, so we were easy to kill. It was our end. It took only 27 years, from the 'discovery' of us, to our wiping out. Think of what you humans have missed out on, learning about us. In 1754 there was a human who cared, or at least was concerned that a ready food source would not be entirely depleted. His name was Jakovleff, first name unknown. He was a Russian mining engineer, who had seen the destruction of us on Copper Island. He petitioned the authorities to protect the animals on Bering Island, but no one listened.[70]

We were of the order Sirenia – perhaps related to the siren, a mythical creature that lured seafarers to their deaths by singing to them? Should we have done that? But our bubbly puffs were hardly sweet musical notes and would not draw many. Instead, our flesh, our species, was the lure and saved this shipwrecked crew and fed many more, without being thanked or respected. Perhaps, in the end, we were 'stellar', the star of the show, giving an extraordinary performance that, with the exception of Steller's notes, was not recorded or commented on at the time. Our hearts were big, big enough to have lived at peace with humans, but you chose otherwise. The loss of our 'star' has darkened the sky, another light has been snuffed out. Our unique song of snorts and sighs will not delight again.

❄ ❄ ❄

The Great Auk

'When they are seen a great way off, in flocks, they look very much like a number of children, dressed in black, with white aprons on.' – *Child's Book of Nature*, 1830s[71]

(*Pinguinus impennis*) (last recorded 3 June 1844):[72] we used to be found in large colonies, millions of us, studded around rough, rocky, bleak islands in the mid-Atlantic, off the coasts of Greenland, Canada, Iceland and Britain. In the shallow waters, we would feed on the sea's riches of fish, crabs and plankton, and once a year, on these off-shore skerries, we strayed out of our familiar water home to scramble onto the rocks to lay our single eggs in nests formed beneath us from our droppings. These eggs were quite something, varying in colour from white to a light ochre, the shell often covered in squiggles and wriggly lines. No two patterns were the same. Our eggs were designed to last: pear shaped, they were less likely to roll or slip off the rocks and smash. Standing almost upright until the precious egg had hatched, both parents looked after their chick for about two weeks, until it was ready to go to sea on its own.[73] Oh, if you could have seen us, what a sight! Thousands of us standing on rocks that protected us from major predators, from polar bears, killer whales and white-tailed eagles, but not from humans.

We travelled great distances, through the waters, not via the skies. We were the only flightless seabird in the Northern Hemisphere. Our legs were set far back, to assist in swimming, but this made it hard for us to walk on land. We were regular little surfers, riding the waves near islands wedged with sloping ledges, which allowed us to gain somewhat clumsy access (via hopping) onto the rocky ground. We may have been ungraceful on land, but in water, we could move as quickly as birds capable of flight could soar through air, because our small wings were muscular and strong, acting as rudders when we were in the water. Our heavy bodies meant we were great divers, arguably one of the most efficient of all divers. Our slow metabolic rate meant we could stay under water for long periods and we could hold our breath for up to fifteen minutes. Each of our feathers had its own muscle, which came into play by causing the feathers to stay flat against the body, preventing air from becoming trapped. Such a design meant we were less buoyant, able to dive down to 100 metres (328 ft) or more, not being restricted by the risk of floating. It was nigh impossible to catch us in water, but oh how easy it was to kill us on land, for there, we were slow and ungainly.

What did we look like? Our backs, throats and chins were blackish brown, our chests and bellies all white. In summer, during the breeding season, we had large white spots on our faces between the bills and our eyes, but in winter this patch narrowed to a white line, and our dark throat feathers changed to white.[74] Our black bills sported a number of vertical grooves, both on the top and bottom. Our toes were webbed with small claws. We were quite large birds, about the size of geese, weighing between 4 and 5 kilograms (9–11 lb). We were thought to live for about 25 years and were monogamous. Nowadays we are labelled as 'cute', but that is a recent quality given to describe us. If we were alive today, this 'cuteness' might have saved us; we may have become a modern conservation project, but . . . well . . . most environmentalists were born too late to save us.

It is a theory – of course, just a theory – but some theories are correct: it is thought that we, *Pinguinus impennis*, the great auks, helped the Vikings navigate their way to the American continent. Icelandic Vikings would have noticed we were absent during the colder weather.[75] Perhaps during those long, bitter nights, humans ruminated over our disappearance and concluded that we made our way to lands in the west. On our migratory routes, we landed in what is now known as Newfoundland and then continued down the eastern coast. Maybe they did track our course, following our movements in the waters. Of course, none of this can be proven, but it is worth noting that Vikings did make it to Newfoundland and therefore would have been the first Europeans to hunt us in North America.[76] Our bones have been found in middens and burial mounds from Newfoundland to Norway. We may have been used in ceremonial or burial rituals, because one unearthed human was discovered surrounded by two hundred great auk beaks.[77]

Our first English name was 'garefowl', from the Icelandic *geyr* (or *geir*), meaning 'spear', and *fugl*, 'fowl'.[78] This name might have come about because of how we were hunted and killed, but another interpretation links it to our impressive beaks, which resembled spears – sharp, spear-like beaks which could not save us.[79] We had plenty of other names: 'Magellan's goose'; *anglemager* (Norwegian), named after our cry, *aangla*, which alerted fishermen (anglers) to get their hooks ready; *arponaz* (old Basque for 'spear-bill'); *agparak* (which might be an Inuit word for us); and others including 'gearbhul', 'aponar', 'binocle', 'moyack' and the descriptive 'the Wobble'.[80] Some pretty impressive-sounding names. The word 'auk' comes from old Norse *alca*, which probably describes the cry of several alcid species.[81] Up to the mid-eighteenth century, our biological name had been *Alca impennis*, but this was changed to *Pinguinus impennis*, scientists wanting to make sure we remained distinct from the razorbill (*Alca torda*).[82]

Pinguinus. What does it sound like? Correct! One of the more surprising names for us was *pingouins*, the term used by the French. This name came into being when the French travelled to Newfoundland to fish for cod.[83] The French arrival in Newfoundland in 1497 was also the first record of us being killed. *Pingouins*, or penguins. Yes, truly. I suppose in many ways, we resembled the penguin, though we were *not* penguins. This name, *grand pingouin*, is still used by the French to this day and is similar to the Spanish *pingüino grande*.[84] Why were we saddled with this name, an appellative later given to birds in the Southern Hemisphere, to whom we were not related, though we were both large and flightless, with small wings? It could have been because of our white head, because *pen gwyn*

Robert Havell, after John James Audubon, *Great Auk*,
1836, hand-coloured engraving.

is Welsh for 'white head'.[85] Having said that, our head was not perfectly white. Perhaps it was because our wings looked pinioned. Probably the most likely reason was because we were fat, and the Latin for fat is *pinguis*.[86]

Although being described as 'fat' is not flattering, it is better than the Dutch name for us: *tossefugl*, or 'stupid bird'.[87] It's not surprising to be given such an unflattering name – it seems to be the way for some extinct creatures. The dodo received some pretty awful names from the Dutch. We had a bit in common with the poor dodo: after the dodo, the great auk is probably the next most famous of extinct species.

Unfortunately, our breeding season, from May to mid-July, coincided with the fishing season. By the end of the sixteenth century, the fish-rich waters in Newfoundland were known to seafarers from a number of countries, including Spain, Portugal and England, and every year several hundred ships travelled the waters to reach the rocky island known as Funk Island, perched atop waters well stocked with marine life. It was small, about a kilometre (⅗ mi.) long and less than half a kilometre (⅕ mi.) wide, situated near the great cod fisheries of the Grand Banks. Explorations to the American continent had put this island on a map back in 1501. It was associated with bird life, most probably with us, for it was known as Y dos Aves, 'Island of Birds', and Isla de Pitigoen, 'Penguin Island'.[88] Along with the fish, we too were caught, for we were plentiful and easy to catch once on land. Our flesh and large eggs could be consumed, and our feathers used by those in the millinery trade.

There were individuals, worried that the depletion of our numbers endangered our long-term survival, who tried to help. Several, including the writer Charles Kingsley, were too late. Kingsley wrote his popular story *The Water Babies* nearly twenty years after what was then our recent extinction. We, the great auk, the gairfowl, featured in it. One of us actually narrates the story of our extinction: 'And there he saw the last of the Gairfowl, standing up on the Allalonestone, all alone. And a very grand old lady she was, full three feet (90 cm) high, and bolt upright, like some old Highland chieftainess.'[89]

The great auk continues,

> Why, we have quite gone down in the world, my dear, and have
> nothing left but our honour. And I am the last of my family . . .
> Once we were a great nation, and spread over all the Northern
> Isles. But men shot us so, and knocked us on the head, and took
> our eggs.[90]

My, if Kingsley had written the uncensored version of our fate, it would not have been deemed suitable for children. Being killed by guns was a kinder method than that which took place on some of our breeding islands, particularly on Funk Island. Until the end of the eighteenth century, this was our largest colony in the world, with more than 100,000 breeding pairs lodging here during their brief season.

This was my final place, part of my story. Large boiling pots were kept constantly alight, fuelled not by wood, for the island had no trees, but by our fat. We were boiled to aid the easy removal of our feathers. Our sleek, black back feathers adorned the hats of many, but pillows and bedding were also our downfall, our down much desired for them. When the overhunting of ducks in North America had decreased supplies of eider down, eyes turned to us to save the continent's feather industry. Each spring, crews were sent out to our breeding grounds by feather merchants.

For great auks, it was hell. This was no pretty island. As early as 1535, explorers would fill their barrels and boats with the bodies of great auks (they could load up a boat with our bodies within half an hour), as well as collecting many of our eggs. Did this island gain its name from the smell of our droppings, from the stench of ammonia or from the stink of slaughtered, boiling birds? Some individuals expressed their concern about the slaughter on Funk Island. In 1785 English adventurer and trapper George Cartwright wrote in his journal,

> A boat came in from Funk Island laden with birds . . . it has been customary of late years for crews of men to live all summer on . . . that island, for the sole purpose of killing birds for the sake of their feathers . . . the destruction which they have made is incredible . . . if a stop is not put to that practice the whole breed will be diminished to almost nothing . . . this is now the only island they have left to breed on.[91]

As early as 1533, there had been calls to protect us. Even Newfoundlanders perceived that we needed some measure of protection. In 1775 they requested that authorities in London put in some restrictions, only permitting us to be killed either for food or to be used as bait.[92] Those who took our eggs were seen as committing a crime and, in theory, could receive floggings. In 1794 London authorities banned the killing of us for our feathers, but these laws were hard to police, impossible to enforce and made no notable change to our fragile status.[93]

Soon stone pens were built to house us – house us, or confine us, imprison us. There is no way to sweeten the reality, for these were extermination camps, none of us destined to survive. We were imprisoned within these stone walls to wait until it was our turn to supply what was needed, either feathers, flesh or fat. Remains of these prison walls can still be seen today. By 1810 Funk Island was the only place in the western Atlantic where we could still be found . . . until, finally, eventually, every last one of us had been killed.

Did anyone wonder about what torture was inflicted in order for humans to be comfortable at night, as they readied themselves for sleep? Did any suffer from nightmares populated by the screams of birds? Could they smell burning flesh? Boiled for our fat, stripped of our magnificent feathers. Too dreadful to mention in any detail . . . Please . . . I will return to a more general picture of the fate of the species, not of the individual. Too, too, painful.

The three Fs (food, feathers, fat) were not the only reasons we were killed. Sometimes other elements aided our demise. We were not birds to be feared, but some of the scant number of human inhabitants of the islands we inhabited while breeding were gullible; they were a superstitious lot. In the western Hebrides, on the island of St Kilda, in Scotland, one of the last of us was captured on its own. The poor bird was caged, and it made quite a noise (as you would!). Several nights later, there was a mighty storm. The islanders were convinced the storm had been caused by this lone great auk, suspecting it of being a witch. In the morning, they beat it to death.[94]

At one stage, we were found in large numbers in Iceland, on the Geirfuglasker (Great Auk Rock), a rocky place that sparked fear in the minds of some humans. What else would you expect though, their brains already filled with images of fairies and elves?[95]

Dear Geirfuglasker. It was a safe place for us, for it was difficult for humans to access, but after a volcanic eruption in 1830 submerged the Geirfuglasker, our last stronghold was cast to the depths. About fifty of us moved to an island, known as Eldey, which was nearby, but unfortunately, humans were able to reach it on one side.[96] After some understanding of our increasing rarity, there was a rush for our now-valuable eggs and bodies. Now we were hunted to order to provide specimens, instead of being slaughtered for food, fat and feathers. Our eggs, once crushed if not needed to supplement hungry sailors on their sea voyages, were now fetching a pretty penny; you could even call the great auk egg 'the golden egg'. In 1832 an egg at auction fetched £ 15.15s 6d (the average annual income for a skilled worker was £9.10s).[97] Once we became extinct, the prices soared, with an egg in 1894 selling for £315.[98] These prices meant that people were willing to risk penalties, or even injury, eager to navigate rocks and slippery ledges, in pursuit of the golden egg.

On 3 June 1844, the last great auk hunt took place on the island of Eldey. The last of us, a pair, were killed there, beaten to death (or strangled, accounts differ, but the result was the same) by Jón Brandsson and Sigurður

Ísleifsson, because a merchant wanted specimens.[99] The last egg that the last great auks were incubating (think about the wonder and preciousness of that embryo, encased in a shell of squiggly patterning) was smashed by Ketill Ketilsson's boot. Why? What purpose did that serve?

In 2017, on Fogo Island, which is situated off Newfoundland, there was an official ceremony in order to say 'sorry'.[100] It is commonly reported that the last sighting of us was in 1844, but many on this island believe that a great auk was seen in its waters in 1852. A bronze statue of a great auk sits on the headland, staring out at what was once one of its watery habitats. 'Sorry.' Humans of today do not have to atone for our extinction – that sin is levelled at their ancestors – but humans of today are to learn from our permanent demise, in order to protect other species from suffering a similar fate. We, the great auks, were the only member of our family, Alcidae, a line of large, flightless seabirds in the Northern Hemisphere, to become extinct during historical times. We, who had been on this Earth in an ancient form, the *Pinguinus alfrednewtoni*, as far back as the Pliocene period, 5.2 –1.64 million years ago, are no more. Too late for 'sorry', too late for regrets and 'what ifs'.

Not much of us remains: 78 skins, 24 complete skeletons and about 75 eggs; that is all that is left from a time when we numbered in the millions. One of the ironies is that it was scientists who rushed to secure our skins, our eggs, before we disappeared forever. Eggs. The yolks from our large eggs were used to make pudding by the Beothuk, an Indigenous group who once inhabited Newfoundland. It is believed that they, too, are extinct.[101] Our image and name featured on early twentieth-century cigarette tins. These containers are a rare find for collectors. Our glossy, black bodies, however, can no longer be collected, except within the gentle dreams of the hopeful, the childlike, where we dive deep into the imagination, holding our breaths forever.

❊ ❊ ❊

The Spectacled Cormorant (or Pallas's Cormorant)

(Formerly *Phalacrocorax perspicillatus*, now *Urile perspicillatus*) (extinct by 1852): I am often forgotten, overlooked, my extinction pales in comparison with that of the much larger former resident of Bering Island, Steller's sea cow. Now, don't misunderstand me – we must remember the sea cow's life, and its extinction, but I too was a fatality. Another better-known creature, the great auk, became extinct in 1852, the same year that some believe I disappeared forever from a jagged rocky island in the middle of a bitterly cold, wind-swept sea. I, too, was a bird, but not as famous.

My body may be rigid and stiff, a rare specimen absent from most museum collections, but my classification continues to be fluid. I was a cormorant, a large seabird. For many years, I was *Phalacrocorax perspicillatus*. *Phalacrocorax* is Latinized Greek for 'bald raven' and *perspicillatus* means 'spectacles', but now my genus has been changed to *Urile*, a taxonomic term coined in 1855 by naturalist Charles Lucien Bonaparte. I have been reclassified as *Urile perspicillatus*, and in 2021 this change was incorporated by the International Ornithological Congress (IOC) in their World Bird Lists. According to naturalists, our genus, *Urile*, split from the genus *Phalacrocorax* 8.9–10.3 million years ago.

Relatives. I suppose, in some small way, I have living relatives, but no immediate family. It is strange to think that we, the biggest of all cormorants, have disappeared from this Earth. We were kings, weighing in at 6 kilograms (13 lb). 'In size and plumpness they exceed the allied species,' wrote Georg Steller.[102] He continued, describing us as 'a special kind of large sea raven with a callow white ring around the eyes and red skin about the beak'.[103] These rings which encircle our eyes, which prompted the name 'spectacled', have been incorrectly described and illustrated over the years. Often they have been coloured yellow or orange (seen on several taxidermy specimens, which were used for ornithological illustrations), but these circles were white, bare skin, only changing if it was an old specimen, yellowing within a museum tombed drawer.[104]

We were first seen by members of the Bering expedition, who had travelled from Siberia to Alaska. In November 1741 they were stranded on a small, inhospitable island, now known as Bering Island, which is located in the Bering Sea between Russia and North America. Steller, the expedition's zoologist, was the only naturalist to see us alive, so his field notes are of the utmost importance. It is a shame that when he described our behaviour, he did so with these words: 'From the ring around the eyes and the clown-like twistings of the head and neck, it appears quite a

GRACULUS PERSPICILLATUS.

Spectacled cormorant (*Urile perspicillatus*), drawn from nature by Joseph Wolf
for Daniel Giraud Elliot, *The New and Heretofore Unfigured Species of the Birds
of North America* (1869), vol. II.

ludicrous bird.'[105] Steller was a product of his time, and his description of us reflects that. Sadly, Steller did not live to bring news of his discovery to Europe. I think that we were impressive, rather than ludicrous. The colour at the base of our bills varied: it could be white, or scarlet, or sometimes even blue. The feathers on our bodies, necks, heads and wings were deep green, with bluish tinges. We had white patches on each flank and black tails. An outstanding feature (apart from the spectacles, which the females lacked) was the males' greenish-blue double crests, which were decorated with long, thin, lemon-coloured feathers. These fine, colourful feathers were also found on their upper necks.[106] Punk chic! Long, thin feathers and circles around the eyes made for spectacular (no pun intended!) males.

We did have several minuses though. We were ungainly when walking on land and had small wings. These little wings meant we were poor fliers (though some have wondered whether we were able to fly at all). We were not suspicious of humans – we had no cause to be; we had not encountered them before. We had no predators – apart from Arctic foxes, who were more concerned with our eggs – but these factors, combined with the fact that, unlike most fish-eating birds, we were very tasty, made us all too easy to catch for the cooking pot: 'and since the flesh of one would easily satisfy three hungry men . . . they were a great comfort.'[107] We became welcome food for shipwrecked mariners, prepared using a Kamchatka cooking technique, which was to encase us in clay, feathers and all, and place the pot over hot coals, in a pit.[108] We became an exotic dish.

Later, we became food for fur trappers and hunters. Bering Island had become so popular among whalers and sea-otter hunters that in 1826 the Russian-American Company imported Aleut Indigenous people to settle there so that seal hunting could continue all year round. We fuelled the hunters while they slaughtered otters, foxes and seals. They had already finished off the sea cow, so we became a staple, but our 'copious numbers' did not last.[109] By 1850–52 the last of us had died, most likely in a cooking pot. I would have preferred my final days to have been spent perched on rocks, tasting the salty spray as waves dashed against the jagged crags, but I didn't get to choose the nature of my death, or the race towards extinction. Less than a century after we had been 'discovered', we were extinct.

For nearly a century, Steller's description was all scientists had concerning our existence, then in 1837 (some say 1839), nearly a century after

Steller's discovery of us, there arose tangible evidence that we were real. Captain Belcher visited Sitka, Alaska, and was gifted a skin of a spectacled cormorant by a man named Kupreanof (Kuprianoff/Kupreyanov), governor of the Sitka region, which included Bering Island. Kupreanof had a number of specimens in his possession, perhaps as many as six or seven.[110] Our skins were used as gifts or money, a lucrative deal for Kupreanof. There are only seven specimens of us in museums, making us rare. Imagine – we are one of the rarest museum specimens in the world. Seven stuffed birds and two imperfect skeletons – this is all that remains of the unsuspecting birds that had watched, silent, as the *St Peter* was dashed against the rocks of Bering Island in 1741. These rare specimens can be found at Dresden, Helsinki, Leiden, St Petersburg and Tring – the last housing two – and the subfossil remains are in St Petersburg and Washington, DC. Belcher's name inks the label affixed to one of the specimens at Tring; has Belcher a similar label, a rectangle of card tied to his toe, with the words 'spectacled cormorant'?

We had several fans. The first was Steller, but then ornithologist Leonhard Stejneger fell under our spell. Much of what is known about Steller, and about us, is due to the writings of Stejneger, who, working from Steller's notes and from his own observations after visiting Bering Island, wrote several papers about us, as well as a biography of Steller. He also translated Steller's diary, which led to its publication.[111] From 1882 Stejneger spent eighteen months exploring Bering Island, and the nearby islands and islets, searching for us. Even though the locals told him we had not been seen for thirty years, he kept hoping:

> The natives . . . remember very well the time when it was plentiful on the rocks, especially on the outlying islet Are Kaen . . . About thirty years ago, they say, the last ones were seen, and the reason they give why this bird has been exterminated here on the island is that it was killed in great numbers for food. They unanimously assert that it has not been seen since, and only laughed when I offered a very high reward for a specimen.[112]

Steller had only seen us on Bering Island, but locals reported that our last refuge was an islet, or skerry, known as Ariy Kamen (or Ary Rock), part of the Commander Group of islands, which was small, but fox-free. None of our eggs were ever found on Bering Island. Maybe we were careful, for there were many Arctic foxes living there, but Ariy Kamen would have been the ideal place for breeding: it had rough terrain, making it harder for human access. The great auks were last seen (a polite way of saying 'killed') on Elderly Island. Ariy Kamen may have been similar to Elderly: a large clump of rocks, our last post. Stejneger, who thought the spectacled cormorant 'the largest and handsomest of its tribe', was disappointed that we did not rate the same outpouring of attention that was given to the great auk, whose extinction occurred around the same time.[113]

Stejneger was downhearted, as he would be, not to find us alive, but what he did find, or rather, 'unearth', were 21 of our bones on Bering Island, including a pelvis.[114] In themselves, these comprised a remarkable enough discovery, adding vital information concerning our size and flight when studied later at the Smithsonian. This discovery also led to a theory that our habitat might have been more extensive than Bering Island and its nearby islands and skerries. This theory came about due to bones found in the coastal Shiriya region of northeast Japan during the 1960s and '80s. Researchers found bones of a cormorant which were from the late Pleistocene era (129,000–11,700 years ago), but this cormorant was larger than the species that currently reside in Japan. In 2014 a scientist went to the Smithsonian to compare those bones with those of the spectacled cormorant, and they seemed to be a good match. 'Before our report, there was no evidence that the spectacled cormorant lived outside of Bering Island,' said researcher Junya Watanabe, from Kyoto University.[115] Now scientists are wondering if our distribution was wider than previously thought. It has been suggested that 20,000 years ago, during the last of the ice ages, changes in sea levels led to diminished plankton levels around the Shiriya region, so the spectacled cormorants left, travelling further in order to obtain food. Maybe, just maybe, Bering Island wasn't our original home, but the site where a relic population of spectacled cormorants settled, making it their home.

One of your writers, John Milton, mentioned a cormorant in his work, *Paradise Lost*. After Satan had entered Paradise, he took on the form of a cormorant and sat in the branches of the Tree of Life. Apparently, the cormorant symbolized greed and dishonesty. I am not convinced: our wings, when spread out to dry, resembled a crucifix, a Christian symbol of sacrifice. Of course, Satan entered Paradise, a move which led to the eviction of humans. My story was the reverse: humans entered my Paradise, my Garden of Eden, and I was the one evicted, cast out forever. In Norwegian tradition, some believe that cormorants are the spirits of those lost at sea, come to visit their families. There are no callers now.

❊ ❊ ❊

The Falkland Islands Wolf

(*Dusicyon australis*) (1876): we were the Falkland Islands wolf, or the *warrah*.

Warrah is a corruption of the word *aguará*, 'fox' from Guaraní, a South American Indigenous language. Charles Darwin called us *Canis antarcticus*. Our origins are mysterious, and even after several hundred years, they remain so. Was I a wolf, a dog, a fox or a jackal? Were we descendants of 'an abandoned prehistoric domestic dog'?[116] Louis Antoine de Bougainville, who established the first settlement on this island chain in the South Atlantic Ocean, called us a *loup-renard* ('wolf-fox'), which was a modified two-way bet. Our closest-known relative (now extinct, like us) was the *Dusicyon avus*, an extinct species of canid, native to South America. Whether I was a wolf or a fox depends on what you read, or to whom you speak, but I was definitely a canid. Most agree that we were an enigma. Recent DNA testing suggests that our closest extant relative is the maned wolf, a long-legged, fox-like canid that lives on the South American mainland. This doesn't solve the problem though, because the maned wolf is neither wolf nor fox; rather, it is the sole species in the genus *Chrysocyon*. We look quite different too; the maned wolf has very long legs and is sometimes referred to as a 'fox on stilts'. Our legs, though, were much shorter.

We lived on what are now known as the Falkland Islands, 480 kilometres (300 mi.) off the east coast of Argentina. Whichever theory – fox or wolf – wins out, one thing is definitely known and adds more weight to our mystery: we were the only terrestrial mammal on these islands; no others shared that privilege. There weren't even rats or mice! How strange that is: the only mammal was a large canid. Had we been living here for thousands of years, until European settlers? Many have puzzled over our isolation.

Falkland Islands wolf or fox (*Dusicyon australis*), hand-coloured lithograph from Charles Darwin, *The Zoology of the Voyage of* HMS *Beagle*, part II: *Mammalia* (1838).

In 1834, when naturalist Charles Darwin wrote about us (he visited these islands twice, in 1833 and 1834), he wondered how we came to be living on such a remote archipelago: 'As far as I am aware, there is no other instance in any part of the world, of so small a mass of broken land, distant from a continent, possessing so large a quadruped peculiar to itself.'[117] He thought the most likely reason was that we had made the journey to the islands with Indigenous people. Others, as I said, have thought the same. DNA analysis has helped prove otherwise by supplying another piece of the puzzle. It showed that we did not come across with an Indigenous tribe, in canoes, as hunting dogs, but had travelled to these islands long before humans journeyed to the American continent; we were here before the end of the Ice Age.

But how did we get here, if not with humans? This land has never been connected to the mainland via a land bridge, so how did we cross? Was it on floating logs, or on icebergs? Perhaps, but a current and more plausible theory is that we journeyed to these barren, windswept islands via a narrow bridge of ice which had formed on top of several submarine terraces during the Last Glacial Maximum (LGM), when ice sheets covered much of the world and when global sea levels were about 130 metres (430 ft) lower than they are today.[118] It is certainly a possibility that we crossed a narrow marine strait during this period, arriving here long before human settlement. Some have proposed that as we walked across the ice bridge, we survived the end of the Pleistocene extinctions, safe on an island. Perhaps our ancestors, as individuals or possibly in packs, had followed a rich food source – penguins maybe, or seals or seabirds, which were on the margins of the ice. Hunger was enough of an incentive to brave the ice and its chilly waters. Why didn't other South American mammals follow suit? Maybe it was atypical of their behaviour, or the icy terrain, a foreign habitat, was too much of a deterrent. Remember, we were the only mammal found on these islands.

Some suggest that we then evolved in isolation into what became known as the Falkland Islands wolf, or *warrah*. Researchers posit that the *Dusicyon avus*, our relative, was more closely related to the jackal than to a fox or wolf, suggesting that it evolved features similar to those seen in the jackal of today: a wide muzzle, jaws designed to grab and shake large prey, and a willingness to scavenge.[119] It would explain the uneasiness settlers felt when we were near their sheep.

Not much is known about our behaviour, life span, reproduction cycle or social order. In 2010 jaw and skull bones were found in a collapsed burrow, in what appeared to be an old home or breeding site.[120] Although we were not foxes, perhaps we shared some similarities or habits. Foxes will take up residence in what is known as an 'earth', the burrow of another animal, such as a rabbit, enlarging it for their use. Although we were the only mammal on the islands, other animals, such as the Magellanic penguin, nested in burrows in the sand hills in the summer, so this could have been a previous habitat of theirs. No one knows if we travelled in packs (it is thought that we did not, that we hunted alone, but that we were still social creatures), but a number of us may have lived in this burrow together, or it may have been a breeding site over several breeding seasons.

Part of my problem was that I was too trusting, but I had never had cause to be otherwise, because we had been on our own, with no predators until Europeans arrived in the seventeenth century. I was able to be tamed a little; I was certainly friendly. In 1690 one of us was befriended by the captain of HMS *Welfare*, Captain John Strong, who made the first recorded landing on the Falkland Islands. One of his officers, a Mr Stimson, was the first to mention us in writing, describing us as fox-like, but much larger than an English fox.[121] A gentle, friendly Falkland Islands wolf was taken aboard, sailing back as the ship's pet, or mascot.[122] Unfortunately, the items of man scared him off. While at sea, the crew needed to fire their cannon against the French. This noise frightened the Falkland Island's wolf so much that he jumped overboard and drowned.

Our willingness to trust led to our deaths. Sometimes we would even wade out in the ocean, to greet those on newly arrived ships. If the humans appeared to be friendly, we would sometimes enter their camps. Our habit of scavenging meant that friend could turn foe, enticing us to move closer, tempting us with some meat or a bone in one hand, but holding a hunting knife in the other.

Our diet consisted of what we could find, what we could scavenge. We were not fussy. Birds mainly, including penguins. We also feasted on seal pups when we could. The take-what-I-can-get approach to food led to our downfall: when European settlers brought in sheep, well . . . they were there, weren't they? There was no sign that we could read that said 'paws off'. But it wasn't always us; introduced dogs did more damage. The Scottish farmers on the western side of the islands embraced an intensive poisoning programme, one responsible for shocking and painful deaths. They killed us in great numbers, until . . . well, until there were none. Sheep. Those animals that contributed to our demise grace both the Falkland Islands flag and the coat of arms! Sheep! We should be on it, a reminder of the beautiful creature they lost.

The climate could be cold, and in winter there were snow falls; this was a windswept, tree-free, barren and isolated clump of islands. It was a place of mountains and hills, flat plains, rugged coast lines and cliffs – but no trees, just small shrubs. The grass heath made it an attractive option for sheep farmers. It could be a stormy location though, with lots of rainfall. We of the short, thick muzzles and short legs were the size of large foxes, but stockier, with thick tawny, tan and black fur to help us through the miserable winters. Our necks and inner legs were white. Thankfully, the summers were cool. Our beautiful pelts were topped off with bushy tails, which were brown in the middle and ended in striking white tips. Our fur was much admired, so much so that it attracted fur traders from the

United States. In the eastern Falklands, we were killed in large numbers for our skins; many ended up in New York department stores, bought and later worn by the fashionable rich.

When Charles Darwin visited the Falkland Islands, he recorded that our numbers were very low in the east of the islands, and in the west, we were more numerous, but declining. He also noted how tame and gentle we were. Darwin was surprised by our tame nature. Can I just boast a bit here and say that the slight variants in the size and markings of the Falkland Island wolves of the west and those of the east led Mr Darwin to consider our differences, which helped pave the way for his theory concerning the 'origin of species'? We made an important contribution to evolutionary science.

Darwin made the prophetic remark that we could become extinct: 'Within a few years after these islands shall have become regularly settled, in all probability this fox will be classed with the dodo, as an animal which has perished from the face of the earth.'[123] How right he was. By 1865 we were no longer on the eastern part of East Falkland, having been killed for our fur, and the last of us died in 1876 at Shallow Bay, West Falkland, after most of us had been poisoned by the Scottish settlers. Fur and sheep, fur and sheep.

For a short time we did grace London society, because two of us (we were known as Antarctic wolves) were taken to London Zoo, the first one arriving in 1868. An article soon appeared, published in the 21 November issue of the *Illustrated London News*. The account, which described the *Canis antarcticus*, mentioned that our eyes were 'of a peculiar light colour imparting a curious expression to the visage'.[124] Perhaps it was because we were in a strange place, behind bars, stared at by human beings? A second Falkland Islands wolf arrived in 1870, but neither survived for long. We made it to the United States as fur wraps, lasting longer than the living ones on the Falkland Islands, or those in the London Zoo.

Even dead, we are rare, only found in eleven museums, sometimes only as ancient, bare bones, 'incomplete' specimens. We may have escaped the Pleistocene extinctions by braving icy waters, as wolf, fox, dog or jackal, but our friendly nature had not evolved to include recognizing deception … or danger. Who knows? If treated differently, we could have been asleep at your feet, a mixture of wolf, fox, dog and jackal. We would have kept you safe, warm, eaten anything and been faithful. Your loss.

❈ ❈ ❈

The Quagga

(*Equus quagga quagga*) (1883): quagga, quagga, quagga. Our name has the ring of a cartoon character about it. We were a subspecies of the plains zebra, and our name, 'quagga', was derived from the sound of our call. We lived in southern Africa, and it was the Khoekhoe who gave us the name 'Quahah' in imitation of our shrill, neighing, barking cry ('kwa-ha-ha', 'kwa-ha-ha', which we repeated as a warning). The Khoekhoe also gave the name to Burchell's zebra (for some time, we were thought to be female Burchell's) and soon 'quagga' was the label European settlers applied to all zebras. The Boers called Burchell's zebra the 'bonte quagga' (pied or spotted quagga) because of its fuller markings in contrast to us, the true quagga.[125] Only later did 'quagga' become solely our name; quite a history of confusion. The sound may have had 'ha ha' in it, but there was nothing funny about it, the 'ha ha' now silent.

Funny how names can play an important role in being remembered. It was our strange name that caught on, if you like, similar to what happened

The Quagga (*Equus quagga quagga*), aquatint by Samuel Daniell, 1804.

with the dodo: both of us had memorable, short names. What's in a name? Names define and describe species. Names can also complicate matters. The quagga became the subject of a debate concerning what constitutes a full species and what is deemed a subspecies; our name formed part of that discussion. We had been accorded the scientific name *Equus quagga*. The plains zebra was known as *Equus burchelli*. All seemed well until our next claim to fame; in 1984 we were the first extinct animal to have its DNA analysed, and this technology launched the new field of ancient DNA analysis. Two short mitochondrial DNA sequences were extracted from a quagga museum skin. This genetic information demonstrated that we were more closely related to zebras than to horses. We were a subspecies of the plains zebra, not a species on our own, a claim backed up by examining skins and skulls in museums, so our name had to be changed. Funny how details and old laws still apply; the oldest published zoological name, even if inappropriate, is given priority. The oldest one in this case was *Equus quagga*, first used in 1778. I became *Equus quagga quagga* and the plains zebra became known as *Equus quagga burchelli*,[126] later changed to *Equus quagga*! Strange to be embroiled in a scientific debate, when extinct. Perhaps if that sort of energy or passion had been applied when we were alive, we might still breathe and move and help scientists with more than just our DNA.

Here is a piece of quagga 'ha ha':

What's black and white and eats like a horse?
A zebra.

If we were zebras, surely we would have had black and white stripes? Another 'ha ha' moment:

What does a zebra look like?
A horse behind bars.

No, in this matter we differed from other zebras because our colouration was quite distinctive: the white stripes on other zebras were typically brown on us, the only white being on our legs, underparts and tail. Our only striped parts were our head and neck, while the rest of our body consisted of non-distinct markings, more like mottled areas, more horse-like than zebra. Our mane was different too, because it looked as if it had been trimmed.[127] Our body was of a rich, chestnut brown, fading to white underneath. The distribution of stripes varied considerably between individuals.

Burchell's zebra is the southern subspecies of the plains zebra. They tend to have fewer stripes the further south they live. We, the quagga, were the most southern of the plains zebra. The function of the zebra's stripes is still under debate. It is unclear why we lacked stripes on our hind parts. Stripes may have been a way to protect zebra, because the stripes confuse predators, making it difficult for them to detect individuals in a herd. It is also possible that stripes were a means of protection from biting flies, because flies seem to be less attracted to striped objects. We lived in areas with fewer flies, so maybe we did not need as many stripes? Being the most southern of the plains zebra, we had a thick winter coat, which would moult each year.

And the horse reference? Yes, zebras are related to horses, but we are not the same species. We are both in the Equidae family, with a common ancestor, of about 55 million years ago, *Hyracotherium* (or *Eohippes*, the 'dawn horse'). Zebras and donkeys are more closely related to each other than either is to the horse. Having said that, out of all zebras we were the most 'horse-like', with smaller heads than other zebra, making us the most like a wild horse.

Why are we extinct whereas other zebra are still living? The main reason was our geographic location. We were restricted to southern Africa, to the old Cape Colony velt and, to a lesser extent, to the Orange Free State, but we were plentiful, existing in great numbers.[128] We were one of three creatures who formed a sort of protection racket, a behaviour common in the southern zebra. In the wild, across the grasslands, we were often found in the presence of hartebeest and ostriches. Our acute hearing, the ostriches' eyesight and the antelopes' keen sense of smell helped protect all of us from most predators, but not from the human.[129]

On the Cape plains we were the only zebra and a ready source of food for the Boers. We were killed for our yellow flesh, used to feed their Khoekhoe servants. Their own flocks and herds were viewed as too valuable for consumption by these groups. Our hides, used as grain sacks by the locals, were useful too, so attractive in fact that we were shot in our

Quagga at the London Zoo, 1870, the only specimen photographed alive.

thousands to supply the domestic and export markets, wagons piled high with our skins. Our skins became so popular that during the last twenty years of our existence our bones were scattered across the plains of the Free State, their whiteness bearing ghostly witness to our mass destruction for commercial gain.[130] As a money-saving exercise, bullets were cut out of carcasses for future use.[131] The additional drawcard, of course, was the trophy factor.

At one time, Dutch colonists considered domesticating us because their imported work horses found the harsh conditions difficult and were prone to African horse sickness, a highly infectious and deadly disease, but we were, like other zebra, next to impossible to domesticate, highly alert and easily spooked. Having said this, the Boers used us as guard dogs to protect their domestic stock, our shrill 'kwa-ha-ha' warning cry alerting settlers to the presence of intruders. Eventually though, our cry was not enough to protect us. When new settlers brought in sheep and cattle, we were regarded as pests, competing for the same grass, which became another reason for shooting us. The use of firearms, combined with the speed of horses, meant that huge numbers of us were killed, so many that a ban was imposed in 1886, but by then it was too late to save us.[132] Our great herds, which would prance then race across the dry grasslands during the 1840s, were silenced within thirty years. It is thought that the last wild quagga was shot in 1878.

We were quite famous overseas for a time, on view in zoos, and even kept by royalty. A quagga lived in King Louis XVI's zoo at Versailles. A 1793 painting of this quagga was executed by Nicholas Maréchal, before Louis XVI's own end in the same year. The quagga and the other animals in the royal zoo, plus those in private collections, were required to be transferred to a new zoo, located in the Jardin des Plantes.[133]

Although near impossible to domesticate, we have been used as an exotic means of transportation. In 1819 in London, Mr Joseph Wilfred Parkins, later appointed a sheriff of London, could be seen seated behind a pair of male quaggas, which were pulling a light, open carriage. One of these quaggas was the subject of a painting by Jacques Laurent Agasse.[134] We were said to have better 'mouths' for wearing a harness than Burchell's zebras, which were also fashionable for a time.[135] Sir W. Jardine backed up this claim. After going for a ride in a gig, which was drawn by a quagga, he described 'the animal showing as much temper and delicacy of mouth as any domestic horse'.[136]

That makes us sound gentle, docile, but we were easily spooked, and we could be quite fiery, vicious even. Well, we were wild, a force to be reckoned with. We have been known to be dangerous when wounded, kicking in a human's skull, biting off a hand here and there, or stripping back flesh from the fingers.[137] Don't you get angry, outraged if in pain? That fire also translated into courage, for we would attack hyenas and wild dogs. Indeed, it was said that we were the boldest of all equines.

We walked across the plains in single file, all behind the leader, but if disturbed we would still operate as though in the military, forming a circle, or wheel, to protect and ready for attack. This single-file march was commented on by military officer Major Sir William Cornwallis Harris: 'Moving slowly across the profile of the ocean-like horizon, uttering a shrill barking neigh . . . long files of quaggas continually remind the early traveller of a rival caravan on its march.'[138]

We once roamed in the thousands, but there are only five known photographs of us (the fifth photograph went missing, but was rediscovered in 1991), of the same female quagga. She was a resident (prisoner, but let's use the more polite term) at the London Zoo. When she died on 15 July 1872, she had been there for 21 years.[139] That is a long time to be away from fresh air, the feel of grass and dust beneath your feet, the searing heat on one's flanks, the sweat pooling on one's hide while running. Her skeleton, now stationary, is in the Peabody Museum at Yale University, and her taxidermy skin, protected from dirt and other damage, is imprisoned at the Royal Scottish Museum in Edinburgh. On 12 August 1883, the last captive quagga, who was female and had been at Amsterdam's Artis Magistra Zoo since 1867, died (the cause of death was not recorded), meaning that we are now extinct – either as a species or as a subspecies, it doesn't matter which. You can argue semantics all you like, but it ends up the same. We no longer exist.

There are 23 known stuffed-and-mounted quagga specimens in museums around the world. There was another known one, but that museum was bombed in Königsberg, during the Second World War. There are some skeletons and a number of types of tissue. I find it sad that one of the tissue samples is that of a foetus, an aborted entry to life.

H. A. Bryden, a nineteenth-century naturalist, wrote these moving words about us: 'It is a melancholy thing to chronicle the final disappearance from its ancient primeval habitat of one of the most beautiful forms of animal life . . . [now] numbered in the increasing catalogue of extinct creatures.'[140] Bryden also penned his disgust: 'That an animal so beautiful, so capable of domestication and of use, and to be found not long since in so great abundance, should have been allowed to be swept from the face of the earth, is surely a disgrace to our latter-day civilization.'[141]

There were certain individuals who did want to see us continue. Lord Morton tried to save the quagga from extinction by starting a captive breeding programme. He was only able to obtain a male, which he ended up breeding with a female horse. A female hybrid was born with zebra stripes on her back and on her legs. She went on to breed with a black stallion, producing an offspring with several zebra-like stripes.[142] An account of Lord Morton's breeding programme was published in 1820 by the Royal Society, and this led to new scientific ideas, including telegony (which Darwin called pangenesis). Another attempt at breeding quaggas took place in the London Zoo in the 1860s, but the stallion was so distressed at being confined that it died after crashing into the walls of its enclosure.

The Heck brothers, German zoologists Lutz and Heinz Heck, believed that the quagga could be recreated.[143] They had been experimenting with selective breeding, but the Second World War ended their efforts. Then along came German-born naturalist Reinhold Rau, who became the most important person in quagga research. He was employed as chief taxidermist for the South African Museum in Cape Town, tasked with restoring a quagga foal in the museum's collection.[144] Well, Rau fell in love with us, and in 1971 he travelled to Europe to visit museums where our specimens, bones and skins were housed. He examined 22 of the 23 known specimens in existence. He became infatuated with us, and with the dream of recreating us, surprised at the differences in stripes and colours he found on our skins.

In 1984 we found our claim to fame as the first extinct species from which genetic information was retrieved. Two short mitochondrial DNA sequences were extracted from one of the quagga museum skins, and this genetic information showed that we were more closely related to zebras than to horses. We opened up a new field of science, or genetics, the field of ancient DNA. In 1987 Rau set up the Quagga Project in South Africa, to recreate quaggas by breeding selected plains zebra.[145] Nineteen individuals, with reduced striping on their bodies and legs (deemed to be quagga characteristics), were chosen from Namibia and South Africa, and the first foal was born in 1988. By 2006, the third and fourth generation of 'Rau quaggas' (which is what these back-bred individuals are called), were considered to look like extinct quaggas. This programme has its followers and its critics. Rau quaggas resemble quaggas in their external appearance, for they have fewer stripes, but they are genetically different and will remain so. They are not true quaggas. Rau thought differently. He once told an interviewer: 'The quagga is a quagga because of the way it looked, and if you produce animals that look that way, then they are quaggas. Finished.'[146]

But could our uniqueness ever be that easily resurrected? Does selective breeding take into account millions of years of evolutionary history? Can it replicate our relationship with our environment, our ability to inhabit the semi-desert Karoo, with its extremes of temperature? Can selective breeding produce our unique call, our voice embodied in our very name? Naturalist and author Scott Weidensaul commented on this, highlighting a human weakness: 'To think that a few decades of selective breeding can bridge that chasm is the height of hubris.'[147]

The 2013 animation *Khumba* (translated as 'skin') is about a zebra (named Khumba) born with half his stripes.[148] He resembles a quagga, which is fitting, because the film is dedicated to the late Reinhold Rau. Khumba embarks on a quest to earn his stripes. He thinks he is responsible for the crippling drought, because of a superstition that if a zebra has few stripes, it is a bad omen. The healer asks Khumba a question that addresses all issues 'quagga': 'How many stripes will make you a zebra?' The release poster describes the film as being about 'half a zebra – a whole lot of adventure'. That was my adventure. I, the quagga, viewed as half a zebra, a subspecies, without its 'full' zebra stripes. Did being less than a full species make us less worthy of preservation?

Perhaps the final words need to be from a Scottish poet, Thomas Pringle, who fell in love with southern Africa and its animals. Our unique voice remains one dimensional, captured in part, in ink: 'And the timorous quagga's wild whistling neigh/ Is heard at the fountain at break of day.'[149]

We still exist . . . in the imagination, in poetry, in portraits from long ago. Half a zebra? No. A subspecies of zebra? Yes, the half-striped quagga, who had generations of adventure.

❀ ❀ ❀

The Tarpan

(*Equus ferus ferus*) (there are differences in dates of extinction – wild tarpans became extinct between 1875 and 1890, and the last one in captivity probably in 1909): we were ancient, an Ice Age mammal, ancestor of the modern-day domestic horse. I was known as 'tarpan', which means 'wild horse' in the Turkic language of Kazakh. *Equus ferus ferus*. We were also called Eurasian wild horses. There is some uncertainty about whether we were one species, or a number of subspecies, designated as 'forest tarpans' and 'steppe tarpans'. Wild horses were not mentioned by Carl Linnaeus, the father of modern taxonomy. Julius von Brincken coined the name *Equus sylvestris* in 1828, giving this name to the small, robust ponies that had once lived in Europe's forests, though they had not been seen for

Ancient rock carving of a tarpan horse (*Equus ferus ferus*),
Côa Valley Archaeological Park, Portugal.

many years and were often called 'forest tarpans'. After observing us in
the Voronezh district of Russia in 1785, Dutch naturalist Pieter Boddaert
named us *Equus ferus*.[150] So we came to be known as 'forest tarpans' (*Equus
sylvestris*) (vanished) and Boddaert's 'steppe tarpans', or just as tarpans,
wild horses. It is confusing because the term 'tarpan' has been applied to
many wild horses.

Small, but robust. Spirited. Fiery. Ill-tempered, with a reputation as
a biter. We upset humans, for we would coax and disturb their domestic
mares (how could we resist the call to mate? It was part of our nature,
our instinct), and we would eat hay that had been set aside for the winter
months. On the odd occasion when we had been semi-tamed by humans,
we were still wild, never to be trusted, for we would bite and kick against
restriction of our freedom, of our spirit.

Although we were the ancestors of all horses, we differed in looks,
for we were slight of body, with dorsal stripes, thick heads and small ears,
large eyes and short, dark, upright manes. The spirit of a stallion was once
thought to reside within his mane; therefore a strong mane meant a strong
animal. We were graceful, moving as one with the environment, the earth

beneath our hooves. Our hair would lengthen in the harsh winters. Some said our coats, which were the colour of a *grullo* (a mouse-dun horse), became paler during the winter; others put this down to legend, drawing on tales of mythical white horses. We may have been small, but we could battle animals, including other horses twice our size, and win.

Eurasian animals, our territory was extensive, from western Europe to Alaska, from the Asiatic steppes, across Ukraine and through the Gobi Desert. We had been present in Europe since the Pleistocene; our image, depicting our bold, brave nature, is etched on cave walls in Lascaux in southern France and in Spain.

In more recent times we were restricted to eastern Europe. By the 1800s we were on the verge of extinction. By 1850 most of us had died out in Ukraine, killed by farmers who considered us pests. Some remained in Askania-Nova, on Ukrainian steppes. This was a beautiful unforested area – in April and May the grasslands bloomed with flowers for miles. Over the years our numbers declined, until a solitary mare was spotted, accompanied by a domestic horse. She was pursued, and during that chase, she lost an eye. She was locked up and while confined gave birth to a foal. She remained restless and managed to escape in the spring, leaving her foal behind. Later, in the autumn, she was spotted close to 30 kilometres (24 mi.) from Askania-Nova and was again pursued by locals.[151] She outran their horses, but was caught when she fell, due to a hole that was hidden by snow. She broke her leg and suffered the added indignity of being dragged onto a sleigh and taken to the local village, where they hoped to make her a false leg.[152] I think it was a blessing for her, to die several days later, spared such a process, especially if infection had set in.[153] Think of this tragedy: the last free-ranging tarpan mare accidentally died (killed, really) because of attempts to capture her. It all went so wrong. Some of us may have survived until the early years of the twentieth century, but there is no certainty of this.

Humans do not like what they cannot control; they fear that which is unable to be 'tamed'. We were strong and seen as a threat. We were driven off cliffs, or massacred. We were condemned because we were thieves; we stole mares, interbreeding with them, which produced undesirable foals (though some appreciated the hardy, spirited offspring) and a dilution of pure tarpan. We ate food supplies of hay and other crops and, on newly cultivated land, drank from the limited water supply. We were competing, particularly because our habitat was shrinking. Newly acquired firearms hit their mark. The last one of us, perhaps a crossbreed – information is unclear – died in captivity in the Moscow Zoological Gardens in 1909.

Did you know that in the Mongolian version of chess, the most powerful piece is the horse? Several power plays are only possible with that one chess piece. Perhaps that is an analogy for experiments undertaken to 'bring us back' from extinction. Efforts were made to bring us back by a method known as 'back-breeding'. The most famous attempt began in the 1930s, in Germany, at the Tierpark Hellabrunn, the Munich Zoo, where zoologists Lutz and Heinz Heck were determined to resurrect us by back-breeding, or what they termed 'new breeding', but there had been earlier attempts. In 1904 Scottish professor J. Cossar Ewart managed to produce a horse that resembled a steppe tarpan by crossing a black Welsh pony with a Shetland.[154] In the 1920s Polish zoologist Tadeusz Vetulani surmised that the tough little mouse-grey Polish horse, with a dark stripe on its spine, the konik, could be part tarpan.[155] Vetulani gathered promising specimens and brought them to Białowieża, to the wild woodland, the former home of the last tarpans, and began a process of back-breeding. He was quite successful in producing a horse that looked like us, but its mane remained flat, not upright like ours.

At the same time, the Heck brothers were back-breeding. They used several European pony breeds, such as Polish koniks, Icelandic ponies, Swedish Gotland ponies and what were known as Polish 'primitive horses', from the preserve in the Białowieża forest. They also used a stiff-maned Przewalski's stallion from Asia, because they wanted to create the distinctive short, erect mane. Can these horses 'make' a tarpan? The Heck brothers were successful in breeding a horse that looked like us, but it wasn't a tarpan, just one in appearance. Lutz Heck wrote about a foal born during this experiment of de-extinction:

> As a young animal it was of an almost uniform grey, with a black mane and black tail and a broad black stripe along the backbone. And when it changed colour it acquired a white underside, dark fronts on the legs, and all the other markings which the old Teuton horse is known to have had – we already had our first

primeval horse! An animal had been born which no man had ever hoped to see. That sort of thing is like a fairy-tale, only very much more exciting.[156]

Perhaps the Heck brothers were tainted by their own fantasies, which had more to do with a mythical past, excited by the prospect of hunting and riding beasts from a previous, glorious era, than wanting to bring us back to life for our own sake. They (quite rightly, I think) considered us the best of the wild horses.[157] When Germany invaded Poland during the Second World War, Lutz took twenty of Vetulani's grey koniks, and also Przewalski's horses from Warsaw, so that he could continue the tarpan back-breeding programme.[158] Eventually Vetulani's own work in Poland was destroyed, and near the end of the war, the Berlin Zoo was bombed, which killed many of the Heck horses. The innocent always suffer.

The 'Cherson' tarpan at the Moscow Zoo, 1884,
the only specimen to be photographed.

We remain controversial, because of our association with the Heck brothers and their copy of a tarpan. Some 'reconstructed' specimens are in several zoos and nature parks, these horses being known as 'Heck horses'. The Heck back-breeding work continued, with Lutz's son emigrating to the United States in 1959 and setting up a farm in the Catskills where, alongside other horses, Heck horses were bred. The dream continues.[159] A couple in the United States claim that they have a new 'tarpan', which has come about by breeding mustangs that had a 'wild' feel about them. People keep dreaming . . . and hoping. There is a programme to care for the 'restoration' tarpans and to train them as therapy horses.[160] Well, if they are successful, they can't really be us, can they? We were wild – certainly not trainable – and were noted kickers and biters! Not traits one would want in a therapy horse.

These are but copies, defective copies; they are not genetically tarpans, so the wild European horse, the untamed, spirited, tarpan, remains extinct. Some of our blood may flow in other horse lines, but our spirit? Ah, our unique spirit remains in the wild. Mongolian horsemen believe that a person's soul takes on the form of a 'wind horse'. There is only one photograph of a live adult tarpan, most likely a part-tarpan, which was taken in 1884, before the last of us died in captivity, away from our steppes, our flower-dotted grassland, our open range. In some Indigenous cultures, photographs are believed to contain the soul of a person – perhaps also that of a horse? If so, then our soul lives on, its life captured, in captivity, through the confines of a lens. Maybe our souls and those of deceased humans live on, together, not as competitors, but as partners, forever riding into the wind.[161]

❋ ❋ ❋

The Rocky Mountain Locust

(*Melanoplus spretus*) (extinct 1902?; formally declared extinct by IUCN 2014): we are mentioned in the Bible (well, our cousins are), featured in a famous children's book, carved in stone above a church door and the subject of an opera, yet we were a species no human wanted. We were important to several creatures, however, especially the Eskimo curlew. We were one of the curlew's major food sources, so our decline contributed to their demise – an unhappy partnership.

'Locust' is derived from the Latin *locus ustus*, which translates as 'burnt place'.[162] Use your imagination, consider the state of the landscape after we had devoured it – its barrenness could easily resemble a 'burnt place'. We were the fire, consuming much fuel in order to migrate long distances. Actually, when we flew in large swarms, our approach sounded like grass fires. Fire was one method used against us, but with little effect, and at times the sheer numbers of us that landed on these fires actually put them out! What about our scientific name? *Melanoplus spretus*, the Rocky Mountain locust. *Melanoplus* means 'black armoured', though we were more olive in hue, and *spretus* means 'despised'. What a name! But true, because we were despised, hated, loathed . . . and feared, thumb-sized weapons of war fitted out in exoskeletal armour.

This is a little embarrassing, but the only way scientists could definitively distinguish our species from another was by examining the male genitalia. American entomologist Theodore Huntingdon Hubbell made this ground-breaking discovery, which might sound a small thing, but it was actually a big deal. In 1959 this knowledge changed a commonly held view that we were actually a migratory phase of the *sanguinipes*, the migratory grasshopper, which would mean that we were still alive, as a biological variant.[163] Our genitalia announced once and for all that we were a species in our own right.

For centuries locusts (a type of grasshopper) have had an uneasy relationship with humans. In the Old Testament, a locust plague was used as a tool to try to persuade the pharaoh to let the Israelites leave Egypt. Apparently, we were not enough of a threat; it took death to change his mind.

Though small, we were included in the Bible as part of a scary description of the end times:

In appearance the locusts were like horses equipped for battle. On their heads were what looked like crowns of gold; their faces were like human faces, their hair like women's hair, and their teeth like lion's teeth; they had scales like iron breastplates, and the noise of their wings was like the noise of many chariots with horses rushing into battle. (Rev. 9:7–9)

Certainly this verse, and other Bible passages, were brought to mind for many settlers during our swarms. There used to be trillions of us, but now North America is the only inhabited continent without a locust species. Ponder that fact as you listen to our rich and many-layered narrative.

Although some assume our name came *after* finding specimens of us in glaciers in the Rocky Mountains, particularly from the Grasshopper Glacier, our name was known *before* our extinction. We lived along the high, dry eastern slopes of the Rocky Mountains, from the southern tip of forestland in British Columbia, Canada, through Montana, Wyoming, Idaho and the western Dakotas, in the USA, our primary habitat and breeding grounds being the river valleys of Montana and Wyoming. During the summers we hatched from egg pods laid in the ground the previous year.

We were mysterious, quite a biological marvel, a species given to rapid population increases, but we only descended from our sanctuaries, winging our way on air currents to cross the prairies as swarms, flying to lower, more fertile areas, during dry years when we needed food. When conditions became tough, we metamorphosed from the individual, which did little harm, to a tornado swarm – an appropriate metaphor, for we too destroyed like a wild wind twister. In response to chemical cues, we changed physically, our wings lengthened, our bodies darkened, we transformed into groups motivated by the need to feed over that of mating. We irrupted and migrated in swarms of abnormally large numbers, a biological method activated to help us survive. We travelled in groups as immature nymphs, and gathered together in large swarms as winged adults. As we advanced to the south and east, we would mate, and then our females would lay 'pods' of about thirty eggs at a time, deep in the soil, which would go through a process similar to hibernation.[164] Come spring, with its warmer weather, our nymphs would hatch; sometimes there were so many that the ground itself appeared to be moving. They needed fuel, and lots of it. They would march across fields, eating whatever they could find. Their full development involved five moults, the final one leading to fully developed wings: an adult at last![165] The new adults continued as the advancing swarm until conditions altered, and some of them made it back to the sanctuary of the Rockies until the next irruption.

In the 1870s, drought conditions were prevalent for several years, which spurred us into action. Hot, dry weather (dry weather decreased

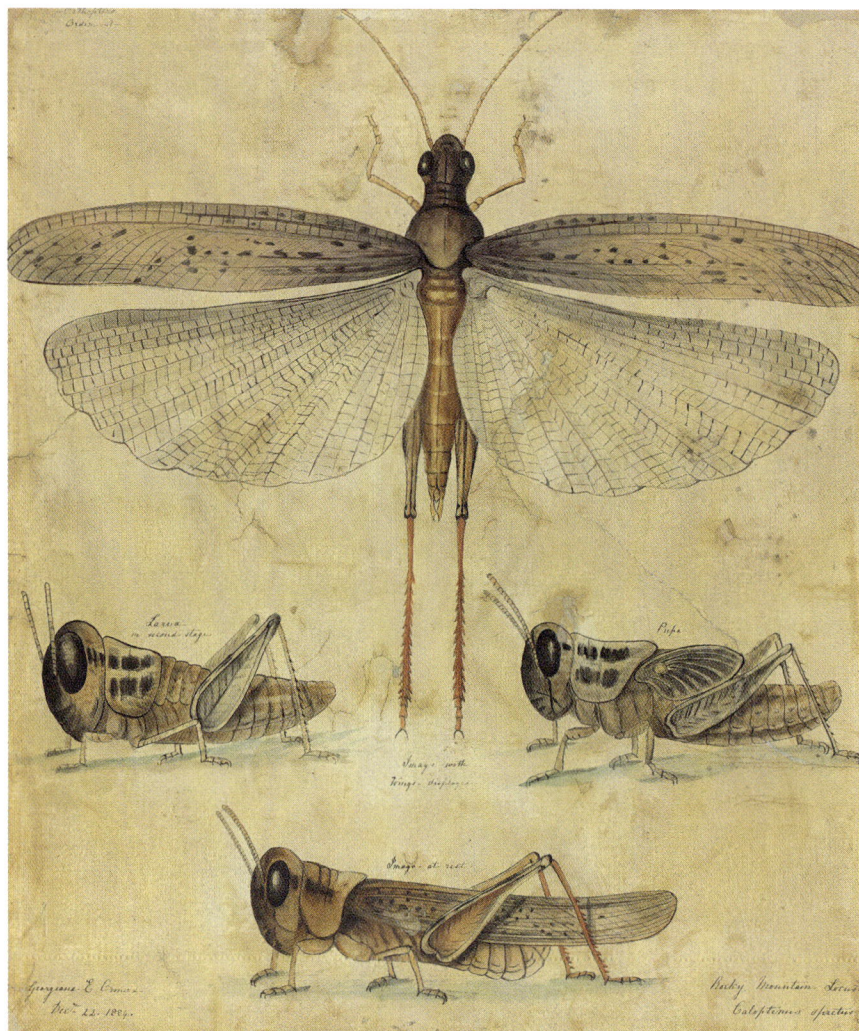

Georgiana Elizabeth Ormerod, *Rocky Mountain Locust*
(*Melanoplus spretus*), 1884, watercolour and ink on paper.

the risk of fungal infections and also increased the sugars in the crops
we ate) and the right wind currents meant that trillions of us descended
on the Great Plains during that decade. From 1873 to 1877, we devastated
the agricultural counties of the Midwest, from southern Wyoming, over
Nebraska and the Dakotas, to Iowa and Minnesota. In 1874 the extent
of our invasion included Missouri, the Canadian Prairie provinces and
central Texas. Our large, black clouds moved from field to field, county

to county, eating almost anything and everything (we weren't choosy, though we did have a fondness for the wooden handles of farm implements; marinating in sweat rendered them delectable). We destroyed crops, gardens, pasture. When we landed, our combined weight flattened trees and plants. Our bodies collected in water, which made it unsuitable for drinking, and our excrement turned ponds and streams brown. Even though chickens ate us – and that sounds like a good use for us, doesn't it? – high consumption of us made their flesh inedible, contaminated with reddish oil and accompanied by a horrible odour.[166] Sadly, it was observed that sometimes turkeys consumed too many of us, gorging themselves to death. Once we had finished with the grasslands, fields and gardens, we moved inside the homesteads, gnawing our way through furniture, curtains and clothing.

By the end of 1874, we, the tiny locusts, had caused $200 million in crop damage across the Great Plains. We had stalled progress, for we were the reason that migration to the West was put on hold, with many settlers either moving further west, or returning to the east.

We were small, individually not a threat, but collectively our influence was profound; we brought both the powerful and the humble to their knees. We destroyed livelihoods, brought on famine and even caused death via starvation. Clouds of us turned daylight to darkness. We even slowed down trains. Once the day's temperature dropped, we sheltered on railway tracks, soaking up their heat. Unfortunately, the cold made our bodies stiff, meaning we were unable to fly out of the line of oncoming trains. The oil from our crushed bodies caused the trains to slow, and at times our broken bodies created safety issues.[167] See? Even our crushed bodies wielded power!

The year 1875: ah, the one that got us a Guinness World Record. In that bumper year, one of the sightings of our swarm underwent a count (it was convoluted and difficult, and only an estimate) with an answer of 12.7 trillion locusts. Trillions, not millions or thousands, or even hundreds. Trillions. This swarm was observed during a Nebraskan summer. It was so enormous that Dr Albert Child of the u.s. Signal Corps was asked to assess the size, which he did by measuring the speed as we flew past. Then he would telegraph the towns in the area to get an idea of the extent of this swarm:

They were visible from six to seven hours of each of the successive five days, and I can see no reason to suppose that their flight was checked during the whole five days . . . 1,800 miles [3,000 km] in length, and say, at even 110 miles [177 km] in width, an area of 198,000 square miles [500,000 sq. km]! And then from one-quarter to one-half mile [0.4–0.8 km] deep.[168]

The people in the towns reported that it took five days for the swarm to pass over, and it was dark because we formed a cloud that obscured the Sun. They estimated our weight at 27 million tons, and thought that we ate our own weight in food every day – well, that was a lot of eating, of crops, bark and clothing.[169] We ate almost anything, even wool straight off a sheep's back; we were not fussy. The swarm was so large that it could be compared to the size of states or countries, this swarm being the size of Spain.[170] Child's record is the definitive one, and our collective multitude is still known as 'Albert's swarm'.

Think, pause for a moment. This wasn't just any swarm of insects, oh no; this grouping was off the record. We formed 'the largest congregation of animal life that the human race has ever known'.[171]

Alongside the term 'Albert's swarm', the fear we elicited in human beings (and in their livestock) also became part of human language. Observation of the weather conditions that favoured our arrival, the days of a long, dry autumn that came on the heels of a hot summer, were referred to as 'grasshopper weather'.[172] This term was used in Laura Ingalls Wilder's *On the Banks of Plum Creek* (1937). She described a time of no rain, no frosts and long-lasting sunshine. Her father reports that the old timers called it 'grasshopper weather'. They did not know what the term meant, the mother saying, 'Likely it's some old Norwegian saying.'[173] When merchandise was cheap, it was sometimes advertised as being 'grasshopper prices'.[174] Terms associated with us were not limited to nouns and adjectives but extended to verbs. In a letter from autumn 1876, the writer, from a Nebraskan family who had already known the destruction we caused, wrote, 'I suppose you would like to know if we have been grasshoppered again.'[175]

Not only did our behaviour lend itself to parts of speech, but to humour, which, I understand, is drawn on when circumstances and events are bleak. A common joke among those on the prairies went like this:

TEACHER: Where does all our grain go?
STUDENT: Into the hopper.
TEACHER: What hopper?
STUDENT: Grasshopper![176]

We were small, but we brought about great destruction: 'You shall carry much seed into the field but shall gather little in, for the locust shall consume it.' (Deut. 28:38)

We were described in picturesque language. A fictionalized account of the devastation we caused in the 1870s can be found within the pages of *On the Banks of Plum Creek*. Wilder's descriptions of hardship, of horror, were based on memories of what happened to her family's wheat crop in western Minnesota during the summers of 1874 and 1875. Wilder wrote about the locust swarm cloud resembling snowflakes (remember, this was in summer): 'A cloud was over the sun. It was not like any cloud they had ever seen before. It was a cloud of something like snowflakes, but they were larger than snowflakes, and thin and glittering. Light shone through each flickering particle.'[177]

A farmer in Kansas also reported that we resembled snowflakes: 'I never saw such a sight before. This morning, as we looked up toward the sun, we could see millions in the air. They looked like snowflakes.'[178] Another pioneer commented, 'It seemed as if we were in a big snowstorm . . . where the air was filled with enormous-size flakes.'[179]

We may have been small, but millions, or indeed trillions of jaws, munching on fine crops, could be heard by the human ear: 'The grasshoppers were eating. You could not hear one grasshopper eat, unless you listened very carefully while you held him and fed him grass. Millions and millions of grasshoppers were eating now. You could hear the millions of jaws biting and chewing.'[180]

The U.S. troops were called in to distribute food, clothing and blankets, and subsidies were given. In some states, able-bodied men were conscripted into 'grasshopper armies', being put to work for several days, collecting egg sacs or locusts at hatching time.[181] Many states offered bounties for sacks of us; in 1877 Missouri paid $1 a bushel for those collected in March, the bounty decreasing as the months went on. We caused the government to start funding science; in 1877 Congress established the u.s. Entomological Commission, in large part as a way to work out how to eradicate us.

What to do to save the starving settlers? Missouri state entomologist Charles Valentine Riley proposed a solution: eat us! Riley stated that livestock were devouring us and that locusts had been eaten throughout history. He wrote that when 'boiled and afterward stewed with a few vegetables and a little butter, pepper, salt and vinegar, [locusts] made an excellent fricassee'.[182] Some desperate folk were willing to try out Riley's recipes, declaring that if the locusts were fried and seasoned, they tasted like crayfish.[183] Other cooks preferred to fry them, and then add them to soups or stews. Not everyone was convinced, though. Even though Riley sang our (cooked) praises, emphasizing our nutty flavour, some settlers, probably reliving the destruction we had wrought on their homesteads, could not face seeing us eye to eye on a plate. Some even went so far as to say 'they would just as soon starve as eat those horrible creatures.'[184]

The destruction we wreaked was seen by many as a heralding of the end times. God-fearing folk prayed hard. See? We were useful – an impetus to prayer! Now, were we God-sent, part of a divine plan, or devil-sent? For the Mormons, we were viewed as a divine test, a test they had failed. The Mormons believed that they had disobeyed God by failing to observe the seventh year of Sabbath rest for the land, and for neglecting to lay up supplies.[185] If they had observed the Sabbath rest, then the land would not have been as attractive to us, for the fields would have been fallow, and we would have laid fewer eggs and moved on to better conditions. What we found, though, were crops that were ripe for us; those Mormons lost three-quarters of their grain and were in dire straits, for they had little in reserve. Their newspaper, the *Deseret News*, narrated the divine punishment: 'The destroying angels are abroad! They are coming this way. They are armed and legged and winged – as orthodox angels should be – fully equipped for war.'[186]

By the spring of 1877 our eggs covered two-thirds of Minnesota's farm land. Farmers had tried various methods, but we kept returning. In desperation, or perhaps realizing divine help was the only answer, the Minnesota governor John S. Pillsbury declared 26 April 1877 a state-wide day of prayer and fasting. Some have recorded this day as 'Grasshopper Day'. A local priest, Father Winter, encouraged people to continue their prayers, asking them to petition the Virgin Mary to intercede on their behalf to end the locust problem. Winter and his parishioners, assisted with $10,000 from Pillsbury's own pocket, decided to build a chapel in Mary's honour, on a site called Maria Hilf, 'Mary's Help', in Cold Spring, Minnesota, and offer mass and petition the Virgin Mary to intercede.[187] On 15 August 1877, the day after the chapel, which they named the Assumption Chapel – better known as the Grasshopper Chapel, because it was built to keep us at bay – was completed, mass was celebrated. By the time of the second mass, which was on 8 September, no locusts were left.

Now, I would *love* to tell you that the heartfelt prayers were an immediate success, because others have said so, telling of the cold front that eventuated, which brought snow and froze us on impact. Even Pillsbury called it a success, recollecting that 'The very next night it turned cold and froze every grasshopper in the state stiff froze them solid.'[188] That makes for a good story, but it is incorrect. The Day of Prayer was a warm and sunny one, meaning there were perfect conditions for our eggs to hatch. Over the next few days, the weather drastically changed, becoming quite cold. These conditions were not suitable for further egg laying, so we left, meaning that no new eggs were there, ready to irrupt into locusts. Most of the hatching immature insects did not survive the chill, and there was the opportunity for the farmers to plant crops again. We did not return. Perhaps the prayers had a slightly delayed reaction?

Unfortunately, the wooden Assumption Chapel was destroyed by a tornado in 1894; it was rebuilt in 1952, our story told in the stone carving above the doorway. The carving depicts Mary, and at her feet, bowing in submission, or perhaps praying, are two locusts. We are part of the architecture of a sacred building; we were the reason for a Day of Prayer.

On 19 July 1902, the last live specimens of us, a male and a female, were collected by pioneer entomologist Norman Criddle, in Manitoba, Canada. They now reside far from the grassland of the prairies, deep within the confines of the Smithsonian. It is thought that Criddle was the last man to have seen us alive.[189]

Strange. We used to number in the trillions, but within thirty years of the mightiest swarm of all, we were gone, extinct. There are only a few specimens of us in museums, safe in lined cabinets. With how many we once were, it is unsettling to think our corpses are so few. That seems to be part of the pattern of extinction, doesn't it? A creature exists in such large numbers that humans think it will always be here, and then . . . all are gone, except for the dead laid out in museums and science laboratories.

We live on, though, in *Locust: An Opera*, an 'environmental murder mystery in which solving the century-old extinction of an iconic species provides lessons for the modern world'.[190] Imagine – an opera written about *us*, the Rocky Mountain locust! In this one-hour chamber opera, the audience is also assigned a role: mimicking the sound of a locust swarm by rubbing tissue paper together.

We also live on in Grasshopper Glacier, in the Beartooth Mountains in Montana, named after us and other species of grasshopper or locust because of the millions of locusts found in the ice. Some of these corpses have been frozen for hundreds of years.

So what was the reason, or reasons, for our extinction? How did trillions of us end up as . . . none? Many methods were employed to eradicate us, from poisoning and blowing us up with gunpowder, to burning and new methods of cultivating fields. We were the mother of invention, from vacuum cleaner-like implements designed to suck us up, to the 'hopperdozer', which was a plough-like device that knocked us into a pan of poison, or shields covered with sticky tar. None of these worked very well – our numbers were too large.

Finally, though, the trouble was – to put it bluntly – people! Before the plains were settled, we were part of the natural rhythm, but by the mid-1870s the government had opened up more land. Nearly 2 million people moved to the western prairies and mountains during the 1870s, many assisted by the completion of the first transcontinental railroad in 1869. This expansion changed agricultural practices and opened up opportunities for mining. These factors created problems for our survival: westward expansion turned our sanctuaries and breeding grounds into farmland, and our breeding sites were in danger. The best land for farming was found in the river valleys of Wyoming and Montana, where we were most vulnerable. This was our habitat, our refuge, where we bred and recuperated after the long migration, much like the behaviour and instincts of the monarch butterfly.[191] Our females were fussy when it came time to lay their eggs. They would lay them in well-drained, dry, firm soils. Female locusts have two pairs of valves at the end of their abdomens, which function as earth-moving tools. They would use the valves to aid in the digging of tunnels so that their eggs could lie below the surface of the soil, out of sight of potential predators, and protected from the cold.[192] The right conditions for incubation meant successful hatching.

Settlers irrigated the prairie grasses, which drowned our egg sacs. Ploughing turned over the land, exposing our eggs to the elements and to predators. Cows altered the soil, disturbing our eggs. Progress in agriculture meant different crops were grown. Alfalfa, which was a crop we did not like, was cultivated to help feed the cattle. It was also a crop that needed irrigation, so we were deprived of both food and young. Other crops were trialled as alternatives to wheat, a crop we devoured. Winter wheat was grown, a resilient crop ready before we migrated. By the end of the last year of our invasions, less than one-sixth of the land was planted for wheat.[193] Corn, a hardier crop, was grown as well, and peas and beans, which we did not like. Waterways were changed, beavers and their dams were destroyed, flooding became more common. A delicate ecosystem was tampered with, damaged, changed forever, like us. We, the little Rocky Mountain locust, changed the face of American agriculture, and our legacy continues to the present day.

We had not been ailing; as a species, we had not been on the decline. We disappeared because our vulnerable sanctuaries in the Rocky Mountains were disturbed, permanently altered by human beings through agricultural practices such as crop changes, ploughing, irrigation and overgrazing. Considered a keystone species, we could no longer play our part. How much did our demise lead to the decline of other species, particularly birds, who relied on us for food?

Although we were viewed as a pest, surely there is a lesson or two to be gleaned from the circumstances of our extinction. The uncovering of our corpses, found during glacier melts, is courtesy of global warming, a warning for all species. Our disappearance from the Rockies, the prairies and Great Plains during hard times was not a small thing; we were tiny, but our disappearance was 'the extinction of the most abundant form of life ever to sweep across the continent'.[194] People speak of the numbers of passenger pigeons that darkened the skies; we were more numerous, but not as appealing.

Were we really destroying angels? This comparison may be closer than you think. Unlike bats and birds, insects did not forfeit the use of their front legs when wings evolved. In insects, wings emerge from the thorax.[195] Angelic? No. But did we bring people closer to God through prayer? Definitely.

Next time you see a grasshopper or a locust (I understand their numbers are on the decline), remember us, the angels of the Rockies.

❈ ❈ ❈

The Japanese Wolf (or Honshu Wolf)

(*Canis lupus hodophilax*) (1905): there were two species of wolf in Japan – note the word 'were'. Now no more, no more. The other wolf, a subspecies of grey wolf, was known as the Ezo wolf; it was larger and lived in Hokkaido. At one time, we were classified as a subspecies of grey wolf, but we were so different from them; we didn't belong, lumped together solely because we, too, were 'wolf'. We were small, not quite the world's smallest wolf, but one of them. If measured without our long, rather dog-like tails, we were approximately 84 centimetres (33 in.) in length and 39 centimetres (15 in.) in height, with a dog-like coat.[196] Our coats were short-haired, grey, white and brown, some even yellow in hue. Our likeness to dogs did not stop there, as evidenced by our short legs (most wolves have long legs). Were we more closely related to wild dogs than to wolves? An intriguing question. Before the nineteenth century, we were known by two names, *yamainu*, 'mountain dog', and *ōkami*, 'wolf'. Even those 'names' were not sufficient. We were assigned labels according to religion, region or particular social situations, including 'village dogs', 'bad dogs' or 'sick wolves', and others you will hear as I narrate my tale. Those names were superseded by the more scientific and nationalistic *Nihon ōkami*, or 'Japanese wolf'.[197]

Our origins are uncertain. Did we come to Japan as the Pleistocene wolf from the Asian mainland, where we evolved (in our case, becoming smaller in stature) to live on the islands? Or did we evolve independently from that ancient wolf? In 2022 new genetic evidence seemed to have answered this perplexing question, for it proposed that we were the last surviving wild member of the Pleistocene wolf lineage. Imagine that! We outlived the mainland Pleistocene wolf by thousands of years![198] Many years later another type of wolf arrived, probably from a continental wolf lineage. Research indicates that these two types of wolves – the ancient, giant Pleistocene wolves and the unknown variant – hybridized, leading to the formation of the Japanese wolf, in contrast to Japan's other extinct wolf, the Hokkaido wolf, whose lineage was that of the modern-day grey wolf.[199] This unknown variant may have been quite small, hence our size. In any case, our stature did not diminish our 'wolfness'.

We lived in Honshu and on the southern main islands, Shikoku and Kyushu. In northern Japan, the Ainu referred to the Ezo as the 'howling god' because that is what it did: it howled from the mountaintops! So many feared the Ezo wolves that people kept amulets to keep them at bay. That which is sacred can frighten. Reputations can create fear . . . we, the Honshu wolf, may have been wolves, but we were not a great threat to humans. Well . . . not for many years.

Our name *hodophilax* is from the Greek *hodo*, for 'path' or 'way', and *philax*, 'to guard' or 'guardian'. It may be Greek, but it honours our legends. In Japanese folklore, wolves were frequently viewed as guardians, or protectors of travellers, so though feared, we were also revered or respected. Travellers in Japan made their way on set routes from the capital. These circuits cut through mountains, with their many dangers, so we were called on for protection and guidance. We were even thought to raise and protect lost children. Guardianship extended into the sacred, for we became known as the 'okuriōkami', the 'sending (or 'escorting') wolf'.

Once revered and known as Ōguchi no Magami, or Large-Mouthed Pure God, we were believed to protect the fields from deer, boar and other grain thieves.[200] In some areas, if we were spotted, the peasants would ask, 'O lord wolf, what do you say? How about chasing the deer from our fields?'[201] We were known as 'boar deterrents', or *shishi yoke*.[202]

We were protectors of crops and of people. Our benevolence was rewarded, for in Shinto belief we were esteemed messengers of the mountain *kami*, or mountain spirits. Wolf shrines were erected, including a number on Honshu, the most famous being the Shinto wolf shrine located in the far east, in the rugged mountains of Saitama Prefecture, at Mitsumine. There is quite a history associated with the establishment of this shrine. Legend states that it was founded by Yamato Takeru no Mikoto. He had

Japanese wolf (*Canis lupus hodophilax*), plate from Philipp Franz von Siebold, *Fauna japonica*, vol. v: *Mammalia* (1842).

become lost on a mountain path but was rescued, led to safety by a guide, who was a divine white wolf.[203] Worship changed hands at the Mitsumine Shrine, from early Shintoism and Buddhism, to being a place of worship for powerful samurai.[204] Its association with wolf worship goes back to the seventeenth century, to the sacred mountains and nature worship. Even today, wolves stand guard at its gates.

Shinto wolf shrines were decked out with *ofuda*, or paper talismans. These were decorated with images of wolves and were believed to protect worshippers from disease and fire. If a talisman was taken home, that household was to leave daily offerings for the wolf, which would bring them good fortune. There were also charms that had pictures of wolves and their pups on them, being either a symbol of fertility for the farms, or for couples hoping for children.

We wolves became part of the sacred landscape. We were part of Shinto belief, Buddhist doctrine, Confucian ways and Japanese folklore and legend. Stories and poetry gifted us respect, gave us a place within the otherworldly environment in which we dwelt. We were called on by villagers. One belief was that if we howled, it meant a baby had been born. The family with the new babe would come to the shrine with offerings of food, such as red bean cake, rice and sometimes even sake. On many occasions, offerings were left at shrines and temples, outside houses and wolf dens and in fields. It is believed that we loved salt, and that precious commodity was left out for us, especially if we had guided a human home, protected him from dangers in the mountains. The fact that people would gift us such a valuable substance tells you how highly we were regarded.

We were never totally toppled as a deity, a being of sacredness. North of Kyoto there is a shrine, known as the Ōkawa Shrine. This shrine was associated with a Shinto deity known as the Daimyōjin. This deity was paired with wolves, who were his divine messengers. We were called upon to protect the crops from other animals. It is an interesting word, this Ōkawa. If you alter two letters, you get Ōkami, which means 'wolf' or 'great deity'. Some historians suggest that Ōkawa was originally Ōkami and that we, the wolf, were worshipped as the Daimyōjin deity itself, which would put us on a higher plane, from divine messenger to deity.[205] Although extinct, many believe that we still exercise some power and that this force is still felt at this wolf shrine.

But change comes – that is part of life . . . seasons, offspring, food scarcity becomes food aplenty. Change: some good, some bad. Our beautiful Japan became more industrialized, and some of those changes included the assimilation of different ideas or beliefs. In the West, in Europe and in North America, wolves were feared, believed to be predators, and were therefore hunted. They were not sacred, deities to be respected and at times to be appeased. European folk tales, fairy tales, wives' tales . . . most described the wolf as a creature to avoid, to fear, to never, ever trust.

Horse breeding was introduced in the far northeast, where poor soil made crop-growing difficult. Yes, we were sometimes a problem. Well, we were protectors of crops – horses weren't included in our list of responsibilities. Though small, we could bring a horse down. Horse depredation didn't help our image, and bounties were introduced to help control us, but these were not enacted in order to wipe us out – not then. The central player in the reversal of our benevolent image was much smaller than a horse and tinier than we are; that major character came in the form of a virus.

During the 1730s, the introduction of rabies and canine distemper sealed our fate, dramatically decreasing our numbers, yet increasing human fear. It is thought that rabies arrived in Japan via China and Korea.

This virus attacked canines, foxes, badgers and wolves. Such a dreadful disease – it destroyed not only our physical body, but our role as a spiritual entity, as a deity. We hid in the dark, lashed out at all who came near, including humans. By the nineteenth century, our image had well and truly changed. We, the wolves, went from being revered, sacred, to being hated, reviled: once benevolent deities, now demons; once honoured as 'beneficial animals' (*ekijū*), now derided as 'harmful animals' (*gaijū*) instead.[206]

Those diseases, combined with policies and laws – of persecution, rather than reverence – enacted during the Meiji Restoration, hastened our extinction. These measures included bounties, traps, organized hunts (wolf hunters from North America were brought over for their expertise and firearms), poisons such as strychnine and the use of dynamite. In the past, we were occasionally hunted, but those hunts were usually of a ceremonial nature, tied to New Year rituals of cleansing. Now the hunt, sometimes accompanied by banners and the blowing of a conch shell, rituals of the past, was designed to erase us from the landscape. The Japanese, through Shintoism, Buddhism, Neo-Confucianism and animist beliefs and practices, had respected us. Now modernization, which included 'taming' the 'wild', depleted the forests of their trees, their wolves and the lens that recognized nature as a spiritual entity. Components of 'other' were not honoured or respected, but subjugated, placed under human control. Animal spirits and their haunts were no longer revered or feared. Everything was brought under the guidance of science and technology; the mountain deity, the *yama no kami* and the wolf deity were no longer consulted, no longer believed in, now obsolete. Once we had been deconsecrated, we could be eliminated, with no concerns about possible divine revenge.

The last wild *hodophilax*, the last short-haired guardian, was killed near Washikaguchi (now called Higashi Yoshino), a small rural village near the Takami River, in Nara Prefecture, Honshu, in 1905. The wolf's beautiful pelt was stripped off its stiff, lifeless corpse and sold to zoologist Malcolm Anderson, who shipped the last wolf's coat to the British Natural History Museum. Next to the banks of the Takami River, there is a sculpture of a wolf, a memorial to the last of us. The inscription is in the form of a haiku:

I walk
with that wolf
that is no more.[207]

Each year, this last, slain wolf is remembered in a ceremony held in a local temple. For locals, human and wolf still symbolize a relationship with nature.

Only four or five of us remain, locked behind glass in museums, outside our mountainous havens and the grain fields we once guarded. There is not much we can protect from here; we are stiff models of a pre-industrial deity. Now deer strip bark from your trees, overgraze what little forest is left, strip beautiful Japan of its 'wild places'.[208]

Do you walk with me? Do you dare accompany me, a *kami* spirit, on a spirit walk? Do you smell me, revere me? Or do you hear my howl and fear me? You no longer have anything to fear: that fear is a by-product of the West, of disease . . . No fear; do not tremble, for my howl has been silenced. I am no more. Scientists suggest we, *Canis lupus hodophilax*, were the closest wild relative of the domestic dog, your household friend. Watch it as it rests, next to your feet; perhaps within its bones is the breath of a once-benevolent deity.

Honshu wolf, *kami*.
Ice Age family lineage.
Sleeps with ancestors.

❅ ❅ ❅

The Passenger Pigeon

Martha's death: 'This may be the only instance in which virtually the exact time of the extinction of a species is known, for it is most unlikely that any wild passenger pigeons survived to 1914.'[209]

There will always be pigeons in books and in museums, but these are effigies and images, dead to all hardships and to all delights. Book-pigeons cannot dive out of a cloud to make the deer run for cover, or clap their wings in thunderous applause . . . They know no urge of seasons; they feel no kiss of sun, no lash of wind and weather. They live forever by not living at all.[210]

(*Ectopistes migratorius*, 'the wandering migrator') ('Martha', 1 September 1914): I am Martha, here to speak on behalf of my species. That's what a 'spokesbird' does, or is: the voice of others, for others.

Martha. I was named after the wife of George Washington . . . but my name would have served me better if I had been given it as a nod to the biblical character Martha, the first to proclaim Jesus as Christ, recognizing his ability to breathe life into the dead. We required resurrection from the dead, we needed a miracle, to be brought back from extinction.

We were associated with religion, though, for we did serve a religious function, a resurrection of sorts, among some First Peoples. The Huron believed that during their Feast of the Dead, souls of the departed were transformed into passenger pigeons.

Strange beliefs and superstitions arose about us. Apparently, if a male passenger pigeon was buried in a garden bed, flowers that bloomed from that earth would be brighter than normal.[211] Others, though, thought we were spooky, harbingers of death and doom, an idea that could have been fuelled by the fear that accompanied witnessing our flight, because when we flew overhead as one massive, dark-winged cloud, we blocked the sun. A rather bizarre notion came from settler Cotton Mather, who thought that after roosting, passenger pigeons would migrate 'to some undiscovered Satellite, accompanying the Earth at a near distance'.[212]

The Indigenous peoples had beautiful names for us: *o-me-me-nog* to the Potawatomi and *omimi* to the Algonquin. These names were meant to echo the sounds we made. Others described us in more poetic terms: the Narragansett called us *wuscowhan* (wanderer) and the Choctaw *patchee nashoba* (lost dove).[213]

We were larger than common pigeons, 39–41 centimetres (15–16 in.) long, our slender bodies covered with soft, grey feathers on our heads and backs, which flickered blue, purple, green, bronze or magenta, depending on the light. A feathered rainbow! We charmed poets and writers. Henry David Thoreau, quite taken with our iridescent neck feathers, wrote, 'The

Robert Havell, after John James Audubon, *Passenger Pigeon*,
1827–30, hand-coloured engraving.

reflections from their necks were very beautiful, they made me think of shells cast up on a beach.'[214] Our chests were rusty pink, which faded to white on our underparts; our wings were long and pointed (streamlined); and our tails were long and graduated. Short, straight, black beaks, red legs and orange eyes completed an understated, classic look. The females were duller, more greyish-brown in hue.

Yes, we were pigeons, but we differed from other pigeons in a number of ways. Unlike most pigeons, at breeding time, we laid a single egg. During courtship, we took things a little further, surrounding our mates with our wings, which resembled giving them a hug. If we were in captivity with other species of pigeon, this extra element of courtship tended to frighten them!

Our territory stretched from the northeastern and Midwestern states into Canada and south to Texas, through the deciduous forests of North America, from the Great Plains east to the Atlantic, north to southern Canada and south to Virginia and northern Mississippi. In winter, we migrated south to the southeastern United States and Central America, sometimes to Indiana, Pennsylvania and Massachusetts.[215] We were highly migratory; through the long winter months, we flew across the southern states following warm weather and available food. Our numbers swelled as we came together for the spring migration: in late March or early April, we clouded to begin the journey to the hardwood forest of the upper Midwest and northeastern states, flying hundreds of kilometres each day.[216] Many of our northern destinations were known to us from previous breeding seasons, but we didn't always breed in the same ones. We might be in small numbers, or in large flocks. Our great migrations were probably linked to food opportunities: the congregation of large flocks in a particular locality meant there was enough food. When food sources were low, our flocks were much smaller.

Our flocks could be dense, thicker than hail clouds. In the 1830s, when flocks of us passed overhead, John James Audubon wrote that 'the light of noonday was obscured as by an eclipse.'[217] He noted that one of our flights took three days to pass, so we were – a bit of an understatement, really – an abundant bird! That was how we got our English name: from the French *passager*, 'to pass by' or 'to pass fleetingly'.[218] Our dung fell like snowflakes. We flew in layers, thick columns of grey-and-pink ribbons, fat in numbers, great flying machines with muscular breasts, pointed wings and long tails.

We could fly at speeds of up to 100 kilometres an hour (60 mph) covering great distances, often in flight from morning until evening.[219]

We were truly incredible birds. Our numbers were huge, in the billions, making us the most abundant of birds that ever lived.[220] In the eastern part of the United States, we outnumbered all the other birds combined. Even in 1870, when our numbers were declining due to continual hunting, our flocks were still impressive. A single flock flying over Cincinnati was recorded as being '1.6 km [1 mi.] . . . wide and 510 km [320 mi.] . . . long' and containing no fewer than 2 billion birds.[221]

Our chatter elicited maritime imagery: we sounded like 'a hard gale at sea, passing through the rigging of a close-reefed vessel'.[222] As we flew, the beating of thousands of wings caused us to rumble like rolling thunder, our bodies darkening the sky as if readying for a storm – our calls and flapping wings could be heard 3–4 kilometres (2–2½ mi.) away.

Our calls varied, though: when building our nests, we sounded like the croak of wood frogs; at other times, we would tweet and cluck, or make bell-like notes.[223] A 1917 account by Chief Pokagon, the last Pottawottami chief of the Pokagon band, mentions this:

> I was startled by hearing a gurgling rumbling sound, as though an army of horses laden with sleigh bells was advancing through the deep forests towards me. As I listened more intently, I concluded that instead of the tramping of horses it was distant thunder; and yet the morning was clear, calm and beautiful. Nearer and nearer came the strange commingling of sleigh bells, mixed with the rumbling of an approaching storm. While I gazed in wonder and astonishment, I beheld moving toward me in an unbroken front millions of pigeons.[224]

Maybe we would be a more apt symbol for wind, for we, too, could cause havoc. When flocks of us landed on trees, many were uprooted by our weight. Our nesting sites covered hundreds of square kilometres of forest, with dozens of us nesting in each tree, our abundant numbers causing large limbs to break and the ground to be covered in hills of droppings. If that is hard for you to imagine, think of one nesting group being 160 kilometres (100 mi.) in length. That was probably an average size.

Wind: taken for granted until it does damage. Passenger pigeon: taken for granted until we were no longer here.

Yes, our numbers did mean crop depletion – I won't deny it. We would feed on a variety of items, including nuts such as chestnuts, beech mast acorns, berries and seeds, supplemented by small insects. We ate big – well, we needed to ward off hunger, and high levels of mast needed to be consumed to ensure successful breeding. Mast was produced in autumn, but we gave birth in spring, so we needed crops to see us through these months. We would migrate to colder regions where snow had covered the mast, protecting it from being eaten by other creatures.[225]

Our throat crops could expand to the size of an orange. To give you an idea of what we could fit in, or store, when some of our throat crops were examined, one held more than one hundred corn kernels; another had seventeen acorns.[226] The American ornithologist Alexander Wilson calculated a flight of us flying to a nesting site to be approximately 2,230,272,000 birds, and the number of bushels consumed (calculating that each bird would eat half a pint of nuts and seeds a day) was about 17,424,000 each day.[227] This damage led to a bishop in Canada trying to excommunicate us because of the sin of crop depletion![228] We also had the delightful ability to regurgitate the contents of our crop if a more delicious food morsel was detected. I know, I know – wasteful, but it meant we could ingest what we preferred.

Farmers had tried scaring us off by building scarecrows, or ringing bells, but then they resorted to guns, which were more effective. Our numbers changed the face of hunting. After 1860 pigeon hunting became a full-time occupation for several thousand men. New hunting methods were netting and shooting, often combined. A place was cleared and a stool pigeon used as a decoy, with several other pigeons released as 'fliers', all to lure the large flock overhead. The stool pigeon's perch was dipped, and the flock flew down to see what was happening to the bird. Then the unfortunate birds were secured by nets, where they would be killed by the breaking of their necks or skulls.[229] Sometimes alcohol-soaked grain was used as bait, in order to make the pigeons woozy and easier to kill. Other times, large smoking pots were lit in order to produce huge black clouds. These dark, frightening clouds confused them, forcing the passenger pigeons to try to land.[230]

These successful 'methods' led to the establishment of the 'sport' of trapshooting. Live pigeons were captured and then sold as contest targets. They were transported in cramped conditions, without water. On arrival, when they were offered water, many died in the rush to quench their thirst. Others were killed by being shot, or by having their wings or necks broken, injuries sustained from being hurled from the catapult traps. Some of these poor, scared pigeons were mutilated before release, in order to make them flighty. This was a cruel sport, with the loss of thousands and thousands of pigeons. Sometimes 50,000 pigeons were used in a weekly trapshooting competition.[231] A single shooter might kill five hundred or more in a single day.[232] Our sheer numbers meant that competitions upped their stakes. In one competition, the goal was to shoot more than 30,000 in order to win – 30,000![233] And now . . .

We had become an easy and plentiful food supply. The extension of railway tracks made the availability of our fresh flesh a possibility, with hundreds of thousands of us transported to the meat markets of large cities, such as New York. In the 1850s, one New York merchant reported that he 'was selling 18,000 pigeons a day'.[234] There were many others like him in New York and in other cities and towns. By 1860 there were 48,000 kilometres (30,000 mi.) of railway track, which meant the bodies of millions of slaughtered passenger pigeons could be delivered to major destinations fairly quickly. Cookbooks were published that included a variety of recipes to help prepare us for the table. In large cities, our species graced dishes in elegant restaurants. Squabs were a delicacy. Our gizzards and blood were used in medicine, and our feathers and down filled quilts and pillows.

The sheer numbers of available passenger pigeons were staggering: in 1851 a count of birds in a nesting area at Plattsburgh, New York, yielded 1.8 million, and in 1883 in Monroe County, Wisconsin, 2 million of us were caught and transported to the cities. In April 1871, also in Wisconsin, the largest group of nesting passenger pigeons was recorded. It was estimated that '136 million birds blanketed an area of 750 square miles [1,940 km^2].'[235] Not only did the railway make us a readily available food, but these new tracks brought thousands of hunters to us, and telegraph technology meant hunters knew when and where to travel.

We wild passenger pigeons started to decline throughout the 1870s and '80s. Hunting was not the only factor that led to our extinction. Theories abound about the causes of our demise, including diseases from domestic birds, but a major reason was forest depletion. During this period, our geographic range dramatically reduced as large forests were converted to open fields for agriculture. We inhabited the eastern deciduous forest area of the United States and Canada; we had never resided in another kind of forest.[236] The social organization of our species was important for finding food; as our numbers decreased, so did opportunities for us to breed and repopulate. We abandoned our nests after hunters had removed our squabs. Thinned and fragmented populations were not as successful at finding food sources, and perhaps large numbers of us were needed for breeding success. Maybe we needed large flocks, community, in order to thrive.[237] The main reason will always be that our ruination, either through habitat destruction or through shooting, was due to humans. Hundreds of thousands of us were killed, season after season, decade after decade, which thinned our flocks and decreased our ability to breed successfully. How long could we survive against such carnage? You humans allowed – indeed caused – the passenger pigeon to 'pass by' forever.

Protective laws came too late to save us. The last record of a wild passenger pigeon shot in the open took place on 24 March 1900, in Ohio. This bird was felled by a fourteen-year-old boy, Press Clay Southworth, on his family's farm in Ohio. When the family realized it was a rare passenger pigeon, they rushed the dead bird to an amateur taxidermist, who used a black shoe button for at least one of its eyes because the taxidermist didn't have enough glass eyes.[238] This passenger pigeon, appropriately named 'Buttons', remains on display in the Ohio History Center in Columbus.

I do feel pity for that boy. Later in life, that incident haunted him somewhat. Poor, naive soul. His daughter had put two and two together, and when Southworth found out what he had done and realized the enormity of his action, he wrote a letter to a magazine, writing down his recollection of events. His letter was never printed.[239]

What about me, Martha? I became a zoo exhibit at the Cincinnati Zoo. My origins remain a bit of a mystery, with different stories told, several in order to give more prominence to the zoo and its zookeepers. In 1909 I was at the zoo with George; we were the last known pair of passenger pigeons. In the following year, George died, leaving me to a solitary, lonely existence. Of course, once it became known that I was the last passenger

Martha, the last passenger pigeon, who passed away
on 1 September 1914 at the Cincinnati Zoo.

pigeon, high prices were offered for me, but Cincinnati Zoo was not going to let their prize exhibit leave its cage, fly the coop. Strange . . . we became valuable only after we had been whittled down to our final few . . . or the last one. From billions, to one. I would love to say that my final days were happy ones, but old age . . . one does not move as quickly, as easily. On Sundays visitors were prevented from entering my enclosure because they would throw sand at me to make me move.[240] It is tragic that the area where I spent my days alive was the region where the first trapshooting club was opened in the USA, where thousands of my kin were killed, en masse.

The details of my death gave rise to fabrication of events. Did I die at 1 p.m., or at 5 p.m.? Was I 29 years old or younger? At the time of my death was I alone or surrounded by several zookeepers? In the end, these details don't really matter, and proof can no longer be found, because the zoo records were destroyed in a fire.

Old age, depression. Those factors made me moult. At least the zookeepers thought to keep my feathers, knowing they would be needed when I took my final breath, made beautiful for my eternal exhibit in a museum, the last passenger pigeon. When T. Gilbert Pearson, the head of the National Audubon Societies, received a telegram informing him of my death, he commented that it 'is a calamity of as great importance in the eyes of naturalists as the death of a kaiser to Germans throughout the world'.[241]

Did you know that within my preserved, crafted body, my heart remains? When the physician and ornithologist R. W. Shufeldt performed the autopsy, he decided not to dissect my heart; that vital organ was to be kept whole 'to preserve it in its entirety . . . as the heart of the last "Blue Pigeon" that the world will ever see alive'.[242] Shufeldt reflected on the state of other birds and the high risk of extinction. I imagine that this man handled my body with the utmost care, with compassion and perhaps tears, as he beheld my stilled heart, an icon of all passenger pigeons silenced forever.

In 1976 a bronze statue of a passenger pigeon was placed at the Cincinnati Zoo, part of the path that leads to the aviary. The large, wooden doors of the aviary are decorated with reliefs of other extinct and endangered birds. I wonder how many more species will decorate these panels of shame – or, to be a little gentler, even a touch hopeful – how many visitors will pass through them and be inspired to conserve the planet's fragile ecosystems?

One of the factors being examined is how, despite the loss of a species, it can continue to leave its mark on the landscape. We had helped spawn vegetation in the eastern states, but now that we have gone, that habitat has altered, our 'gap' has allowed another acorn-eating species to step in. Due to a plentiful food source, this culprit, the white-footed mouse, has multiplied. That might not sound like much of a problem, but this little rodent is a carrier of the bacterium *Borrelia burgdorferi*, which causes Lyme disease. Ticks bite the infected mice and later bite humans, transmitting the disease.[243]

We also left a permanent mark on the night sky. For the Mi'kmaq people, the passenger pigeon is one of the stars between the Big Dipper and the Northern Crown, affixed in the sky forever, chasing a bear.[244] Isn't that ironic? That the one once hunted is now an eternal hunter?

❀ ❀ ❀

The Carolina Parakeet

(*Conuropsis carolinensis*) ('Incas', 21 February 1918; formally declared extinct 1939): we shimmered green, unlike anything else to have graced the American skies. One pioneer described us as jewels encrusting the sky 'like an atmosphere of gems'.[245] We were emerald green, so being likened to gems was, indeed, fitting. Another wrote about us lighting up a drab tree, its white bark set off by our gleaming bodies, which resembled bright Christmas ornaments, and our orange-yellow heads shining like candles. We were given the colourful name *puzzi la née* (head of yellow) or *pot pot chee* by the Seminole and the name *kelinky* in the Chickasaw language.[246] We were admired long ago; archaeologists discovered an effigy pipe shaped like a Carolina parakeet in an ancient Native American burial mound.[247]

We were small, green parrots about twice the size of a budgerigar. Male and female were similar, sporting long tails, yellow-and-bright-orange heads, and yellow flanks and wings. We made wonderful sounds when flying. Being social birds, once in flight, we would chatter away, our cry sounding like a 'qui', which we would repeat, drawing it out until it was

Carolina Parrot

PSITTACUS CAROLINENSIS. Linn.
Males & Females 2 & 1 — Young 3.
Cockle bur Xanthium Strumarium

Robert Havell, after John James Audubon, *Carolina Parakeet*,
1827–30, hand-coloured engraving.

like 'qui-i-i-i' or 'kee-kee'. At other times, we could be heard chattering in our tree hollows, or squawking, a rather raucous sound audible from some distance away.

We were native to the United States, one of two indigenous parrots and the only one found in the eastern part of the United States.[248] We had quite the range, from the Gulf of Mexico in the south, right up north to New York and parts of the Great Lakes. We favoured the eastern deciduous forests, and we loved densely wooded river and swamp territory. We nested in hollow logs or stumps, crowding together inside, attaching ourselves to the bark with our beaks and claws. Those who were unable to get in clung to the outside. We were majestic in flight, quite beautiful to behold. We would dart in and out of the woods, and then spiral down when we had decided on a feeding area, making quite a racket! Even though we were numerous, there is still much that is unknown about us. Reports vary concerning the number of eggs we laid, and where and how we built our nests.[249]

We were remarkable, displaying unusual behaviour for a parrot, because we were able to survive in diverse (and cold) climates, even when temperatures dropped as low as -30–4°C (-22–25°F). Ponder that for a moment: a parrot in snow! Now, during the winter of 1780, the fact that we appeared in cold climates caused fear among some of the new Dutch immigrants in upstate New York. These deeply religious folk were dumbfounded, shocked. Seeing many bright bodies soaring through the grey, winter skies was thought to be an omen, signalling the end of the world, the beginnings of the apocalypse.[250] Strange that we, such a beautiful, bright bird, could cause humans to tremble, to view us as a sign of evil. Fortunately, this was not always the case; in 1847 the sight of a flock of us perched in walnut trees cheered up an army unit camped in Kansas during a snowstorm.[251] I understand that my species delighted the military during those long, grey days of winter, our bright plumage a marked contrast to the backdrop of dull, sombre sky, and our incessant chatter breaking through the muffled sound caused by snow cover.

We flew in large flocks, our numbers capable of blocking out the sun. Social creatures, we gathered in flocks of two hundred to three hundred, until humans started settling areas, cutting down our habitat, which removed many of our food sources. We had a fondness for wild plants and their seeds, including the seeds of forest trees such as cypress, beech, sycamore, elm, pine, maple and oak, but humans cleared land and planted other crops, removing our dietary staples. Fortunately (which soon turned out to be 'unfortunately'), we adapted to the new crops and fruit trees and their fruit, but that meant that we turned from 'pretty' to 'pest'. We were also attracted to ranches and farms because we were partial to salty water. If we spotted one of those lumps of salt – salt licks you call them – we would descend, and soon it would be wrapped in green and yellow! Being judged as 'pest' is highly unusual for parrots, because parrots the world over are more commonly viewed as 'pet'. That little 's' changed the focus, from survival, and the possibility of conservation, to extermination.

There was a problem – one more serious than a few crop seeds and fallen, spoiled fruit – and that was the invention of the gun and the adoption of the almost-universal notion that hunting was a sport and therefore acceptable. As well as being killed in the name of 'sport', we were hunted as part of 'pest control' initiatives, for our feathers (much prized in the millinery market) and as captive, exotic birds. As our numbers declined, we were seen as rare, coveted specimens, so we were also killed for our skins, with more than seven hundred skins in collections around the world.[252] In our favour was the notion that we might have been poisonous to eat, or at least have the potential to make a human ill, so we were not consumed very much. The famous naturalist John J. Audubon wrote that cats died after eating us. Now, we may have been viewed as a pest, eaters of crop seeds and stealers of fruits from orchards, but we consumed the seeds of the cocklebur weed, a member of the daisy family. Its spiny fruit contained seeds that were toxic to livestock and other animals, so we were doing some good. If only you humans had realized how we could have existed together, our consumption of cocklebur beneficial to ranchers and their livelihoods.

We had some supporters among the humans. Ornithologist Robert Ridgway entrusted Paul Bartsch with the care of a neglected chick. This young bird was given the name 'Doodles' – not much respect there, really. However, Bartsch and his family treated that bird well. Bartsch wrote that 'He shared our meals, was well behaved, and stuck to his own plate almost always.'[243] He wrote lovingly of Doodles, narrating the way the bird slept with him, how he chased pigeons (wondering if Doodles was seeking the company of other birds) and how he snuggled up to a pet squirrel; finally,

Bartsch wrote tenderly of Doodles's death.[254] Bartsch had a photograph of Doodles, perched high on a visitor's neck, near his mouth; dear Doodles looks as if he might be receiving a little kiss!

We, being brightly coloured parakeets, were sought after as caged birds. We were fairly easy to tame, but we did not possess the gifts of mimicry or song. If we were confined to outdoor cages, our wild brethren would visit, hanging on to the bars of the cage, seeking physical contact with each other, 'even thrusting their heads at such times, into the plumage of each other', noted ornithologist Thomas Nuttall.[255] Unfortunately, little interest was shown in helping us breed in captivity, either in homes or in zoos. If there had been, then our extinction may have been halted, and we would have continued to live, a flying paint palette dabbing colour upon the canvas skies.

As I have already said, we were a social bird, gathering in large flocks, and that, like the fate of the passenger pigeon, contributed to our downfall. We looked out for one another, even in a huge flock. When one of us was wounded, or had been killed, the rest of the flock would gather around its fallen kin.[256] Our noise and fluttering feathers would have scared away or distracted most predators, but not humans with guns. Our care for one another meant hunters could easily kill an entire flock once a single bird had been shot.

Another similarity with the passenger pigeon was that we, too, may have been a species that could only thrive, indeed survive, when we had large enough numbers. That being the case, when our numbers had decreased to a certain number, our decline could not be prevented. We probably needed a certain number in a flock to enable courtship and mating to take place.[257] When our numbers declined, so too did our genetic diversity, and with that came the increased risks of disease and sterility.[258]

We also had competition – apart from that of humans, I mean: an introduced species, brought across with European colonists. Can you guess? No, smaller, much smaller . . . honeybees! Well, that is one theory. Honeybees preferred the hollow trees that we used for roosting and nesting, so there is a theory that, combined with other pressures, honeybees forced us out of our reduced habitat.[259]

As early as 1831, Audubon wrote in his journal that our numbers were on the decline: 'Our Parakeets are very rapidly diminishing in number; and in some districts, where twenty-five years ago they were plentiful, scarcely any are now to be seen.'[260] A number of other ornithologists noted the impending threat of our demise. In 1874 one author wrote, 'There is little doubt but that their total extermination is only a matter of years.'[261] It is thought that the last wild one of us was killed near Lake Okeechobee, Florida, in 1904, but there were rumours that some of us managed to survive into the 1930s.

Now that is the primary story, the one people would read if they wanted to know what happened to the Carolina parakeet, but there is another tale, because new research has shown that the Carolina parakeet consisted of two subspecies rather than one species.[262] People spoke of our wide range, as I did at the beginning of this narrative, thinking that we were one species, or perhaps separate populations. If this recent evidence is correct, as it seems to be, then these two subspecies went extinct at *different times*, meaning there were two extinctions, not one, hence the need for a slightly amended account!

The two subspecies lived in different climatic territories that were separated by the Appalachian Mountains.[263] The eastern subspecies, *Conuropsis carolinensis*, was found in Florida but did move north along the coast to New York and also southwest to Texas. They were smaller than the other subspecies, but with brighter plumage. The Midwestern subspecies, *Conuropsis carolinensis ludovicianus*, was larger and paler and could be found from Nebraska to Ohio and down to Louisiana. These birds were more likely to move between breeding and wintering grounds. They lived in tree cavities all year round, and it is thought they probably became inert during the night, an adaptation which would have helped them survive the chilly weather.[264] There was very little overlap of territories, and this is a vital factor in this story.

Now, the reasons put forward for our extinction (of both subspecies) remain the same: deforestation, hunting (for crop protection, feathers and whole bodies for the millinery trade, and for the exotic bird industry), poultry disease and the introduction of the honey bee, but because we were two subspecies, not one species, these factors would have had a bigger impact on two isolated populations than on one wide-ranging population of one species.[265]

So, to conclude, I speak of the last captive Carolina parakeet, dear Incas. During the 1880s sixteen Carolina parakeets had arrived in Cincinnati, costing $2.50 a head, which was quite a sum back then.[266] Other zoos had

Carolina parakeets, but eventually the only surviving pair was to be found in the Cincinnati Zoo. The amazing thing is that those two, named Lady Jane and Incas, had been together since they had arrived in the 1880s. Now, the London Zoo, realizing how valuable they were, and how rare, offered to buy Lady Jane and Incas for $400, but this offer was rejected.[267] Incas died in the Cincinnati Zoo on 21 February 1918, alone except for the zookeepers, who did not say the cause of death was old age; rather, they claimed it was due to grief.[268] Incas had pined for his beloved Lady Jane, his companion of the past 32 years, who had died the year before. Did you know there are only two known photographs of Carolina parakeets?[269] Two. And they don't include a photograph of Incas or of Lady Jane.

Comparisons have been made between us and the passenger pigeon, in terms of vast numbers and common reasons for extinction. What I find intriguing is that Incas not only died in the same zoo as the last captive passenger pigeon, Martha (who died four years earlier), but in the same aviary cage. What stories of extinction that cage contains. What if it had been the same zookeeper who tended both Martha, the last passenger pigeon, and Incas, the last Caroline parakeet? He or she would have witnessed the passing of two species into extinction. We, like the passenger pigeon, once numbered in the millions, and, like them, poor souls, we disappeared at the beginning of the twentieth century. From millions in the nineteenth century, to zero not long after the turn of the twentieth century.

Martha, the last captive passenger pigeon, and Incas, the last captive Carolina parakeet. In life, they had inhabited the same cage, and after death, their stories merge as well. After Martha's death, her corpse was frozen and sent to the Smithsonian in Washington, DC, to be preserved. After Incas died, he too was frozen in a block of ice and shipped to the Smithsonian. But he failed to arrive.[270]

Another, tragic link is that sometimes Martha's date of death, 1 September 1914, is given as ours! Dear Incas died on 21 February 1918. There is a history of forgetfulness surrounding the Carolina parakeet. Did *you* know about us? Have you seen any monuments to us?[271]

Sometimes I ponder this. I hope that pigeon and parakeet met, the shimmering green of Incas, the bright foil against the bluish grey of Martha, paired up for a graceful skyward dance, chattering loudly, free of captivity's cage.

✾ ✾ ✾

The Syrian Wild Ass

(*Equus hemionus hemippus*) (1927): I will tell my story as a cautionary tale, so that the tragedy within my family tree does not extend to others . . . but it probably will. It isn't that I am a pessimist, but I know life and what happened out there, before . . .

I was an ass, the Syrian wild ass, to be more specific. *Equus hemionus hemippus*, an extinct subspecies of the onager native to the Arabian Peninsula. The word 'onager' is sometimes used to describe a military catapult. Our kicks could also render great force!

We were small, standing at about 1 metre (3 ft) high at the shoulder, with light markings. Males were hazel or pale grey in colour, lightest on the head, darker on the haunches and with pale areas on the buttocks, belly and inner legs. We had long manes and brown vertical stripes. Females were fawn to pale grey, with pure white buttocks and white lower parts. Though the smallest species of Equidae, we were wild, untameable. Perhaps that was part of the problem? Our wild nature, plus our height, didn't make us an attractive proposition as a creature to be exploited, used to pull carts or to carry people. Our size meant we ended up in the cooking pot instead, too small to be utilized as beasts of burden. Even in the early years of the twentieth century, the Bedouin were still hunting us. They would often wait until spring, for the new foals, which were easier to catch and, perhaps, tastier.[272] Our diminutive stature did not diminish our strength, though, for we were strong, beautiful and wild! We gathered in herds, running along the ground, like a cloud moving in the wind. Our coats changed colours in the seasons, a tawny one for summer, turning to a pale, sandy yellow for winter. A constantly changing, moving picture.

We could be found in Syria (of course), Palestine, Jordan, Saudi Arabia and Iraq. We could survive the harsh conditions of the Hammad desert in Syria and the Nafud desert in northern Saudi Arabia, a treacherous, dune-filled, wind-swept terrain. Rainfall in this desert was scarce, only once or twice a year, so we had to be hardy, tough. Our tenacity was depicted in artwork. When excavation work was done at Nineveh, ancient Assyria's capital, one of the bas-reliefs that was uncovered was of a Syrian wild ass being lassoed by a king's servant.[273] This must have been a pretty rare event,

Syrian wild ass (*Equus hemionus hemippus*) at Vienna Zoo in 1915,
thought to be the last surviving specimen, who died in 1929.

because on the same stone carving, the narrative continues, showing three
other wild asses outrunning the humans.

Deserts were not our only habitat – we lived in different places, able to
adapt to a variety of landscapes, from deserts and semi-deserts to mountain
steppes and grasslands. We were grazers, feeding on a range of plants,
shrubs and grasses. We liked to eat leaves too, so small tree branches featured in our diet. During the fifteenth and sixteenth centuries, we were
seen in large numbers, but over the next two hundred years, our numbers
declined. By 1850 we were becoming rare in the Syrian desert, from which
we derived our name.

We did have predators, other than humans, of course. Asiatic lions,
leopards, Caspian tigers and even striped hyenas – remember, we were
strong, but small. Ultimately, though, our fatal decline was due to war
and war machinery. The First World War took its toll on us. What were

once sparsely populated deserts were now occupied by troops, tanks and automobiles. Vehicles were numerous and fast; a hunter could lean out of a window to fire at us, which was much more efficient than riding a camel. From my point of view, though, I could often outrun a camel, even a horse, but not a motorized vehicle. All of this meant that we were overhunted.

The last sighting of a wild Syrian wild ass was recorded in 1927. It was shot near the Al Ghams oasis, at Lake Azrak, as it came down to drink water.[274] What a horrible thing: to kill a defenceless creature when it is quenching its thirst. Unprotected, off guard, fulfilling a physical need. The last captive ass died in the same year in the world's oldest zoo, the Tiergarten Schönbrunn, Vienna, so 1927 was a memorable year, the final year for our species. Mind you, some folk believe there was another Syrian wild ass at the same zoo, which lived for another few years. Either way, if you want a more conservative, yet unsubstantiated date, I suggest 1930 as the year of the death of the last captive Syrian wild ass.

We are mentioned in the Bible: 'Who has let the wild ass go free?/ Who has loosed the bonds of the swift ass,/ to which I have given the steppe for its home,/ the salt land for its dwelling place?' (Job 39:5–7). Not all my press is flattering. Sometimes the reference in Genesis to Ishmael is applied to me: 'He shall be a wild ass of a man, with his hand against everyone' (Gen. 16:12).

In the end, that was our end. Our speed and our hardiness, qualities that enabled us to withstand the harshness of the desert, did not save us from the dangers of human beings. In 1930 German zoologist T. Aharoni, lamenting the changes in the desert after the First World War, worried about our future: events 'have pushed back these extraordinarily shy, freedom-loving creatures into the heart of the desert. They appear so sporadically now that most Bedouin tribes have not seen them at all in recent years.'[275] Nicely put, even a touch poetic.

We carried on for a while, in a fashion. Some tribes had a custom of impregnating their domesticated mares with Syrian wild asses, but those lines are much diluted and can never be 'true' or 'pure' Syrian wild asses.

We will live in the eternal desert, running swiftly across a magnificent backdrop of sand, dust and freedom. Perhaps we live on in the minds of humans?

❉ ❉ ❉

The Heath Hen

(*Tympanuchus cupido cupido*) ('Booming Ben', 1932): I was an eight- or nine-year-old male heath hen, *Tympanuchus cupido cupido*, a subspecies, and now an extinct race, of the prairie chicken. (They are still around, I hear, but maybe not for long; both the greater and the lesser are endangered.) We are an incorrectly named species, because the prairie chicken is not a chicken, but a pinnated grouse. We, the heath hen, resided in the eastern regions of the United States. We preferred brushy habitat with low trees and grassy clearings, whereas those of the west, the greater prairie chicken, opted for the tallgrass of the prairies and woods of oak. No one is sure when we separated, going to dwell in different localities, but we were still related. We were about 43 centimetres (17 in.) tall, with a slightly reddish-brown hue and a mottled band which encompassed the width of our bodies. We males transformed from the fairly ordinary to being extraordinarily spectacular during our courting ritual, which I will regale you with later.

Our original range is uncertain; it is thought that we may have inhabited areas as far north as Maine and New Hampshire and as far south as the Carolinas in the USA. The truth of this is a little murky, but what is known with certainty is that by 1885, the last heath hens were confined to Martha's Vineyard, an island off the Massachusetts coast. Even though this was our last stronghold, our final destination, it is unclear whether we were introduced there (and therefore not native to the island). Prior to 1840, we were certainly still plentiful in Massachusetts, particularly in the forests that edged the coastline, and in the valley of the Connecticut River. We were so common, in fact, that Lieutenant Governor Winthrop's servants complained about the frequency that we were served as their food! They pleaded that heath hen meat not be served to them more than 'a few times' a week.[276]

We were shot in our thousands, by settlers and by professional market hunters. There were some enlightened humans who were concerned about our declining numbers. Several public officials sought to protect the heath hens that resided on the Long Island plains, a popular habitat for us. Apparently, they tried to introduce a closed season on hunting, but the majority of attitudes could not be changed. Conservation was a new idea and hard to comprehend or enforce. In 1791, when the New York State Legislature Chair read out the title of the proposed bill 'An Act for the preservation of the heath-hen and other game' to the assembly, some representatives were astonished, and could not fathom why one should preserve 'Indians or any other heathen'.[277] Once the misunderstanding was cleared up, the bill was passed. We were one of the first birds Americans tried to save from extinction, and though their efforts did not end up doing so, the attempts did herald the beginnings of the conservation movement and the introduction of measures aimed at protecting endangered species. Other species (but not all) will be more fortunate.

This did nothing to help us, though. By the end of the nineteenth century, we were no longer seen on the mainland of Massachusetts, no longer present in the western region or in New England.[278] The last of us, a population of between 120 and 200 individuals, were confined to Martha's Vineyard.[279] A census was taken every year for twenty years to check on our declining numbers. Our population varied, due to outside circumstances. In 1906 there was a fire on the island; afterwards we were counted, and only 77 individuals were found.[280] A 650-hectare (1,600 ac) reservation was set up on the island for our protection. This worked for a number of years, with our 1916 numbers increasing to 2,000.[281] Conditions seemed right, but on 12 May, during the breeding season of that same year, another severe fire broke out and ravaged the main breeding area. We were clever, protective of our young, even if it meant our death. During this fire hens refused to vacate their nests, choosing to stay, which meant their death, rather than flying away from the flames to safety.[282] The majority of the survivors were males, and, with the decrease in the number of females, our gene pool was limited. Many died from a mysterious disease – the fatalities may have been quite high because of inbreeding.[283]

This was followed by a harsh winter and frequent visits from one of our predators, the goshawk, which depleted our numbers significantly.[284] In 1918 only 150 of us were counted.[285] We had to cope with three other dangers: poultry disease (probably from turkeys, pheasants and chickens), the deadly cat and human poachers. Our numbers rose again but we never truly recovered from these crises. Humans stepped in once more to try to save us, including employing special wardens to protect us. They set about trapping cats and catching poachers, but it didn't help our numbers.

By 1927 there were only thirteen heath hens left (mostly males); in 1928, two; and from 1930, just me.[286] One single male, alone: the last of what had once been an abundant species. Epidemic diseases, fires, inbreeding, new predators, conversion of prairie into farmland, overhunting . . . all of these were reasons for my family's decline, our extinction.

Being the last of a species meant that I became an attraction, as often happens to the last or near last of a species. Tourists and ornithologists rushed to see me while they still could. At one time in the scurry to see me, I was nearly run over![287] I could have done without the fame, would have preferred to remain anonymous, out of the public eye, living the life of an ordinary heath hen, or at least the life we had led in our heyday, which was well before my final days on this wonderful Earth. I would have preferred to have lived the life of a recluse.

Maybe it is my sacredness that harnesses that spiritual discipline that yearns for, or is called to, a quiet life. My name, *Tympanuchus cupido cupido*, speaks of music and gods: *timpani*, to describe my 'boom' and *cupido*, Cupid. Apparently, so the story goes, when the naturalist Carl Linnaeus examined a heath hen, he thought its neck feathers, which droop and then stand upright, were like wings: hence Cupid, the god of love. A god . . . and music. My booming call, or 'hypnotic moaning', has been likened to the mournful 'toot' of a tugboat, or to the noise made when blowing over the mouth of an empty glass bottle.[288] Our 'boom' was made by males, by pressure exerted from inflated cheeks. Continuing the sacred theme, perhaps our boom resembled the chanting of monks. We were mystical, we males preferring to boom or chant on cloudy, misty days and choosing silence on warm, clear mornings. The featherless air sac on the male's neck swells, enlarging to the size of an orange, its hue yellow-orange, the pigment of Buddhist monks' robes.

Our spring display and courtship behaviour combined ritual and liturgy, an intricate, sacred dance: our male neck feathers, usually flat, became erect, horn-like. We bowed forwards, spreading our olive-grey tail feathers to the sky, exposing our white rumps, pointing our wings, feathers now stiff, extended like fingers, rigid knife blades, towards the ground. Bobbing our necks, inflating our orange sacs before charging forwards, we Buddhist monks changed faiths, becoming twirling dervishes, turning half or full circles in the air and then landing . . . a divine dance, a feathered

Heath hen (*Tympanuchus cupido cupido*), Martha's Vineyard, *c.* 1916.

sacrament of movement and light; a bird prayer wheel flicking back and forth, accompanied by a drum's booming beat. And then cessation . . . stillness . . . breath . . . before another *thud* was dished out on the earthen timpani. Our display pointed to the gods. Or to courtship. Until the second half of the eighteenth century, thousands of male heath hens would gather on the open prairie, east of the Rocky Mountains. The assembly area, known as a 'lek', was the stage for our show of great passion. The earth would rumble, stirred by our gentle earthquake of booming chants and by the firm steps of our sacred dance, set to win the hearts of females, rather than allegiance from any gods. Our courting rituals were elaborate, noisy, tightly choreographed and over-the-top theatrical. If you want an idea of what the dance involved, watch the prairie chicken dance performed by members of the western Blackfoot and Cree at powwows. They strut, jerk, circle and hop. There is some resemblance, some acknowledgement of the beauty and intricacies of the courting ritual. In the past, we had been included in another celebration or ritual, but it was not to our liking, or good fortune, for it is thought that we, rather than the wild turkey, graced the table at the first Pilgrims' Thanksgiving dinner.

After we mated, our nests, where up to a dozen or so white eggs could be bedded, were carefully hidden. We were ground nesters (which meant cats caught us), but most nests were never uncovered, never found, because they were carefully camouflaged, embedded within leaves, grasses and twigs. We were good parents, protective of our young.

Fame, rather than dance. We heath hens usually only flew to lower branches of trees, but in 1929 ornithologists observed a solitary, and perhaps 'hopeful', male fly to the top of a tree on Martha's Vineyard. This male kept calling, moaning, 'booming', showing its tail feathers to the sky and waiting for a response from another heath hen; of course, no heath hen, male or female, could reply, or note his courting display, for there were no others. That lone, frustrated bird, using a branch as its lek, desperate to mate, was me. I was identified, given a name, 'Booming Ben', and became famous because I was the last heath hen. Not only that – it is thought that this was the first time in the history of ornithology that a species was watched, and noted, down to the last individual. My photo was taken on several occasions, films made, and I became a popular tourist attraction. One of my protectors and photographers was Alfred Gross. He wrote these

Heath hen (*Tympanuchus cupido cupido*), taxidermy specimen.

stirring words about me, 'Booming Ben': 'It is truly remarkable that this lone bird, subject to all the vicissitudes of the weather, to disease, and to natural enemies, has been able to live in solitude for such a long time.'[289] He called me a 'sticker', marvelling at my ability to return each spring, but I put it down to a sense of hope, that maybe, just maybe . . . there would be another heath hen to answer my call. In my final year, Gross managed to catch me, and he gifted me two glittery bracelets: on my left leg, a tiny aluminium one, with the number '407880' on it, and on my right leg, a copper band, a bracelet which matched my neck sac orange, engraved with a different number, plus a letter: 'A-634024'.[290] I saw Gross again, a year later . . . but after that . . . never again.

I, 'Booming Ben', a bird with a broken heart, a dejected spirit, no longer able to dance to impress a mate or a deity, was last seen in the evening of 11 March 1932, on Martha's Vineyard. Despite the glittery tags that Gross had decorated me with, my body was never found, claimed by the earth, sinew and feather transformed into dust by the workings of the elements, my spirit finally set free. I had outlived every other heath hen by four years.

This island, my earthy home, had been dubbed 'the Doubtful Island' by explorer Samuel de Champlain. Perhaps that was prophetic. I would have preferred the name *Capawack*, a term used by the Wampanoag people, which means 'the refuge place' or 'the haven'. Prophesies aside – for the first came true and the other was a mere wish – I was here when it was known as Martha's Vineyard. This earth was named Martha, after the daughter of Bartholomew Gosnold.[291] Gosnold was the first Englishman to set foot on this piece of land, and he had a famous friend, William Shakespeare. Could these words have been penned about this island and, more importantly, about our song, now lost, like us?

> Be not afeard; the isle is full of noises,
> Sounds, and sweet airs, that give delight and hurt not.
> Sometimes a thousand twangling instruments
> Will hum about mine ears . . . (*The Tempest*, III.2)[292]

The Thylacine

(*Thylacinus cynocephalus*) ('Benjamin', 7 September 1936): crouching tiger, hidden wolf. That's what most humans thought we were. Fierce tigers, threatening wolves, wild dogs or hyenas.

We were none of the above; though the size of a German Shepherd, we were more closely related to the kangaroo than to the tiger or dog. Unlike a dog, our tails did not wag, we didn't fight over food and we were not aggressive. We were an extraordinary creature, Australia's largest carnivorous marsupial, classified among the Australian Pleistocene megafauna. We, the thylacine, the only member of our genus and of our family Thylacinidae, of the order Dasyuroidea, sported the head of a wolf, the stripes of a tiger, the tail of a kangaroo and the backwards-opening pouch of a possum and other small marsupials. A little like the platypus perhaps . . . made up of leftovers?

Some called us a Tasmanian pouched-wolf; other names with which we were regaled were the kangaroo wolf, the zebra wolf and, occasionally, the hyena opossum.[293] Our first official, or scientific, name was given by Tasmania's Surveyor-General, George Harris. He named us *Didelphis cynocephaliu* (dog-headed opossum), but in 1834 the name was redefined as *Thylacinus cynocephalus*, 'pouched dog' (or 'pouch with a dog head' because *thylakos* is Greek for 'pouch'), though most described us as 'dog-pouched with a wolf-head', which is incorrect, because there is nothing alluding to 'wolf' in our scientific name.[294] We were known as *lagunta* or *corinna* to the Indigenous Australians on the east coast of Tasmania and as *loarrina* to the northwest tribes. The southern tribes and the Bruny Island tribes had two names for us: *laoonana* and *ka-nunnah*.[295]

We were about 1.6 metres (5 ft 3 in.) in length, with a tail about 54 centimetres (21 in.) long. Our dense, short-hair coats were yellowish brown to grey in colour, highlighted with thirteen to twenty dark stripes marking our backs, from shoulder to tail. Our stiff tails were more a continuation of our bodies than separate appendages, like those of kangaroos. Our faces were edged with short, erect ears and had long muzzles. Now wolves have long legs, of equal length, which means they can run fast and are smooth and powerful. We, on the other hand, did not have the bodies

Captured thylacine (*Thylacinus cynocephalus*) at the Hobart Zoo, Tasmania, 1936.

of runners. Like other marsupials, our hind legs were longer than our shortish front legs, and our feet were large, with non-retractable claws. We had quite a bizarre gait, which differed from that of dog or wolf; we would trot, rather than run, swaying slightly, appearing to be a little drunk. These factors slowed us down, but what we lacked in speed, we made up for in pure stamina. We could keep going, using our strong sense of smell, stalking our prey, all night if necessary. Stamina plus jaws with an almost 90-degree gape made us formidable.[296] If we had been properly studied, seen as worth saving rather than a relic, perhaps it would have been shown that we had a low metabolic rate, like our relative, the Tasmanian devil (another species baptized with an unfortunate name).

Our mating was never observed, but it was believed that our breeding season was during December, with a gestation period of a month. Both females and males had back-opening pouches, big enough to fit four pups (we produced up to this number of pups). The pouch, being backwards facing, meant the pups were protected from damage from twigs and scrub in the undergrowth, and, if the mother was facing danger, she could eject her pups if she needed to flee. What a great design! The young tended to stay in the pouch for three-to-four months. After leaving the confines of the pouch, it is thought that they stayed with their mothers until the next breeding season.[297]

It was hard to know our age; animals in captivity can either be older or younger than those fortunate to be living in the wild. I don't remember the wild, the feel of grass, the rub of shrub; I was captured as a pup and taken to the Hobart Zoo, where I lived out my days. The oldest recorded living thylacine was me, the last, at twelve years of age. One of us lived in the London Zoo for more than eight years. Zoos – it seemed that people wanted to see us in zoos. We were presented in zoos near and far, trappers always on the lookout for us, especially when we became rare. The earliest photograph of a thylacine was snapped in 1864, in a zoo, by Frank Haes.

At one time, we inhabited mainland Australia, Tasmania and regions of New Guinea. We were on the mainland until about 3,000 years ago. We are depicted in Indigenous rock art dating back 13,000 years, paintings found in the Kimberley region of Western Australia and in other regions, particularly in the north. Fossils of us have been found in a number of states. In Tasmania, we were widespread, found along the north and east coasts, as well as inland.

Bad press, that's why we disappeared from Tassie – but I'll come back to that soon. Now, our absence from the mainland was due to two factors: the dingo, or wild dog, introduced about 4,000 years ago to the mainland (but not to Tasmania), and humans, or, more specifically, the invention of the spear thrower, which made for more accurate hunting, including hunting us for meat and soft pelts. The fashioning of this tool coincided with our decline.[298]

We lived on in Tasmania; no dingoes here, but there were humans – they were the reason for our extinction. Part of it was down to lack of knowledge, or naivety. British settlers were warned we were dangerous, that we were feeding on their sheep, but the real culprits were the wild, or feral, dogs. These creatures had come to Tasmania courtesy of the early sealers, living with them at their bases, and then later with European settlement. The other factor in our extinction, though, was a calculated, organized campaign of fearmongering.

We were an example of parallel evolution. Marsupials of Australia, cut off from the rest of the world, evolved differently from the placental mammals living on the majority of the planet. Although separated by

65 million years of evolution, marsupials and placental mammals could look similar (such as my being confused with a wolf or a tiger). This was one of the problems; in the nineteenth century, naturalists thought that marsupials were inferior, a relic, destined to die out.[299] This is one of the reasons we were not studied, why we remain a 'mystery' animal, why people have to guess at aspects of our behaviour. We were viewed as primitive, labelled as 'slow' and 'stupid'. A 1909 report about me in the London Zoo included the following description:

> The Tasmanian wolf is one of the most stupid animals; its lack of intelligence is the cause of its untamableness. It never loses its ferocity. Animals are 'wild' for two reasons: 1. Because they are intelligent and know what they dread; and 2. because they are stupid and do not know what they fear; the thylacine ranks very low down in the latter category.[300]

Thought to be an 'evolutionary relic', we were not studied until after we became extinct! Strange – how does one do a comprehensive study if the species is no longer alive? Of course, there are gaps in information about our biology and behaviour. Our social grouping is unknown – it is thought that solitary thylacines were unmated individuals that wandered, not having a 'home', but . . . conjecture really . . . and I'm not telling![301]

Elderly trappers filled in some of these gaps; several researchers were smart enough to draw on the knowledge of the old, before they, too, disappeared. Many thought we were solitary hunters, but trappers told stories about us hunting with others – not in a pack, like the dog, but as an intelligent team or pair, one of us driving the creature towards an ambush, the other thylacine in waiting. We were mainly nocturnal and hunted as individuals at night, but we also hunted during the day, mostly small kangaroos, wallabies, possums, rodents and even the occasional bird, but we were not scavengers. It was rare for us to eat something we had not killed ourselves (though of course this wasn't the case in captivity).

We rarely killed imported species, such as cattle, goats and pigs.[302] So . . . were we sheep killers? Trappers and some farmers said 'no'. We fed quite differently, which gave rise to stories. We were picky, perhaps we suffered from a delicate constitution. It is believed that we only ate parts of a beast, favouring its organs, such as the liver, heart, kidneys and lungs, rather than its flesh. Occasionally though, we would eat meat from its inner thigh. We did leave a lot of the dead creature, but our relatives, the Tasmanian devils, and other scavengers, would consume the carcass, there was no waste.[303] We did tend to go for the necks of prey, but this method multiplied rumours that we were wolves . . . existing on blood. Not quite the gentle fairy tale, is it? But were we wolves? No! Our heads may have been wolf-like, but our teeth were not straight like a wolf's (which ripped); rather, they were oval-shaped, designed for crushing.

Early reports about us spoke of our tendency to flee, rather than attack. The first recorded account of us came in 1805, from a group of five escaped convicts. Poor lads. After they were captured, taken back to be flogged, the pastor wrote up their experiences as escapees. On 2 May they saw a 'large tyger' in the forest.[304] When it saw them, it went away, fleeing rather than displaying aggression, or readying for a fight. Although this account didn't depict us as a future threat, when the first of us was killed by a European, in the same year, opinion changed. Governor William Paterson notified the *Sydney Gazette*, and it was reported that 'this species is destructive.'[305] What chance did we have after that?

Our reputation wasn't helped by an 1806 description of us, sent by Tasmania's Deputy Surveyor-General, George Harris, to the famous Sir Joseph Banks, then President of the Royal Society. Banks read Harris's account to the Linnean Society, a report that was later published. Harris's words fuelled our growing reputation as a potential threat: 'Eyes large and full, black, with a nictant membrane, which gives the animal a savage and malicious appearance.'[306]

Tasmania: sold to Europeans as the perfect place to settle and raise sheep. In the early days, we were not viewed as a threat to sheep; we were rarely seen. A report from 1810 states that settlements were 'free from that destructive animal to Sheep, the Native Dog . . . the hyena opossum [thylacine], but even here they are rarely seen . . . it flies at the approach of Man, and has not been known to do any Mischief.'[307]

Those blasted sheep were our downfall, aided by stock mismanagement, poor soil, feral dogs, rustling and politics.[308] The Van Diemen's Land Company was a consortium of English businessmen who owned large land holdings in the northwest of Tasmania. The years 1828 and 1829 did nothing for our name or future; poor soil, unskilled workers, unsuitable land and the worst winter for years descended on a landscape absent of shelters fashioned to protect cattle and sheep from the elements. Hundreds of animals died due to mismanagement and neglect. How does one report back to the shareholders in England? An excuse was needed, and we were deemed the villain, despite locals identifying feral dogs as the culprit for attacks and deaths. In 1830 a private bounty was introduced by the Van Diemen's Land Company: 5 shillings for every male 'hyaena' and 7 for every female.[309]

By 1887 there were more than 1.5 million sheep in Tasmania. We may have killed some, but nothing like the numbers reported, the main culprit still being feral dogs, not us. Pressure was put on the government, and in 1888 a higher bounty of £1 a head was brought in, which encouraged trappers to go off farms and into the bush to kill 'tygers' for that money. The bounty continued until 1909; by then, more than 2,000 of us had been killed. Trumped-up charges. New research has shown that our jaws were not powerful enough to kill large animals like sheep; we existed on smaller creatures, possums and the like.

You haunt my nightmares.
Barks alert bounty hunters –
Stay hidden, tiger!

With low numbers, we probably had trouble breeding. There was also the added problem of disease; it is thought that we may have succumbed to canine distemper or pleural pneumonia, both introduced diseases for which we would have had low resistance. Indeed, on 24 January 1928 a thylacine photographed in the Hobart Zoo died from disease the following day and may have been the source of infection that killed seven others later that year.[310]

One hundred and thirty-one years after those poor convicts saw one of us, we were no longer around to be seen by anyone.

Stripes.

Stripes on our fur.

Our fur. Soft, attractive. Many of our skins were sent to England.[311] Beautiful stripes. Stripes that acted as camouflage as we weaved our way through fern thickets and tough undergrowth. Stripes on the bars of my home . . . confined to a so-called 'zoo'. Stripes of my ribs showing through a scrawny, malnourished frame.

I was the subject of a rare and priceless piece of film footage, shot by David Fleay. It features me, an unhappy, anxious creature, pacing back and forth in a bare concrete enclosure during my final sad days on this Earth.

Zoo! A prison without privileges was more like it. I was poorly fed, perhaps wrongly named (was I, Benjamin, female or male?).[312] My death was preventable. I died because an inexperienced and disinterested director of the zoo had let the place run down. I had been left outside in my cage, the door to my sheltered sleeping area locked. The tree in my compound had already shed its leaves for the winter, so I froze to death during a long, bitter Tasmanian night.[313] Negligence caused my death.

My husky, coughing bark is no longer heard.

Do you know we – I, Benjamin, the last of a species that had lived for thousands of years – became extinct 59 days after a law stating that it was illegal to hunt the thylacine came in to being? We were given legal protection; less than two months later, there were few, if any, thylacines left to protect. Pouring salt into the wounds of my hunted ancestors: in 1966, nearly thirty years after I, the last thylacine in captivity, died, the Tasmanian government set up sanctuaries to protect us, believing we still existed in the bush. Let's not rush things, folks; let's take our time so politicians can suggest things that sound promising, but in practice will never come to pass, because it is too little, too late.

Brown stripes, once hidden,
now golden-slivered hope –
thylacine icon.

We may have disappeared, but Tasmania bases a tourist trade around us. We were once despised, feared, hated – now people search for us, name beer after us, adopt us as their logo. Since 1870, we have been the 'face' of the Cascade Brewery, appearing in different forms over the years, including the famous depiction of us by John Gould (he got the markings on our tails wrong, though). Our skulls and pelts were nailed on huts as trophies. Our skins no longer evidence our captures; nowadays, we decorate glassware, our logo appears on much to do with Tasmanian tourism, from bus lines to government letterheads, and even as the mascot of the Tasmanian cricket team, known as 'the tigers' (though we were bowled out). We have been appropriated by a television station, its advertising slogan, 'we've earned our stripes'. Our image is displayed on car number plates (no need to slow down for us, though), and we have been hoisted up high, one on either side of the Tasmanian coat of arms, holding it up. Quite a rise in stature, considering our once-evil reputation. Ironic that a ram is in the centre of the banner, sheep being the main reason for our demise. Look what good press does for one. We continue to live on in Australian culture, but with a kinder, softer image; four of us, sculpted in bronze, grace the University of Tasmania's ornate mace, which is used at graduation ceremonies and other formal occasions.[314] How things change when one is no longer physically present. However, not all welcome what could be understood as the misappropriation of our image, in order to promote goods that are European in origin. Not so long ago, Rodney Dillon, a Palawa Elder from Tasmania, wrote the following:

> These native animals are part of our people and it is an insult
> the way they are being used . . . They steal our land and they
> steal our animals and then they use them as their signs.
> Cascade should use a fox on its labels instead. That's what
> they [Europeans] brought with them.[315]

We have physically gone, but we live on in the Australian public psyche. We haunt dreams and become the subject of numerous sightings, here and on the mainland. We have become the stuff of myth; perhaps the belief that we still exist appeases society's grief. Tasmania. If you study the island's outline, you may detect the outline of our head.

Stories surrounding us tend to be ones about destruction, rather than inspiring myth. We seem to be absent from creation tales from the Dreamtime, but we are present in one Indigenous tale and, as a result, also in the night sky. In this story, a young thylacine pup hears the cries of Palano, who is the son of a god. Palano is being attacked by a large kangaroo. The thylacine pup latches on to the kangaroo's throat (perhaps a reference to the way we did kill our prey) and, after some time, manages to kill the kangaroo, thereby saving Palano. Palano rewards the thylacine by gifting him with permanent stripes, stripes formed from the divine blood of Palano and from ashes of a recent fire. These stripes, or marks, are left forever, to signify courage and bravery. The pup is also gifted with a new name, Wurrawana Corinna, the 'Great Ghost Tiger'.[316]

Some Indigenous peoples may have eaten us, utilizing us as a food source, but this tale may serve to demonstrate, or at least to suggest, that for some, we were taboo.[317] More than likely, we featured in other Indigenous tales, in their dances, artwork and ceremonies, but, as we were, they were dispossessed of their land – and of their lives.

The thylacine's bravery is also remembered in a form that continues after our extinction. As Wurrawana Corinna, we are a constellation, near the region of Gemini, seen during the month of February in the Southern Hemisphere; our positive gift, that of courage, twinkles in a black velvet sky. We may not feature in many traditional myths and legends, but we have come in from the cold in modern-day society.

Would we have been left alone, not seen as such a threat, if we had been known by an Indigenous name, such as *corinna*?[318] There would not have been the wolf fear, the folklore myths, the blood libel. 'Tiger' and 'wolf' brought forth an image of the monstrous; 'hyena' one not of power but of a lowly scavenger. Did you know we were 'tameable'? Some farmers even kept us as pets; our young could be entertained with a game of chasing a string. In the Hobart Zoo, one of us was walked on a lead – we were the zookeeper's favourite creature. We could have been at your feet – not dog, not wolf, not tiger but thylacine . . . your own bond with the wild.

Still . . . we remain the best known of extinct animals in Australia. Ecologist and writer Benjamin Gray called us 'the proverbial Ned Kelly of the animal kingdom'.[319] Ned Kelly. Wasn't he the bushranger on the run, who wore a tin on his head, a makeshift helmet? Well, maybe we were alike, human–animal kin, for we, too, were on the run, trying to keep from being shot, snared or captured, and his helmet had a stripe cut in it. Both of us ended up trapped, caught. Being shot would have been preferable to starving, freezing or, in poor Ned's case, swinging in the wind.

The date 7 September 1936 (on which I, the last known thylacine, died) is commemorated in Australia as National Threatened Species Day. May today's threatened be more fortunate than we thylacines, who will always be remembered, kept alive as myth and spectre. Our stripes continue to entangle and confuse minds with ancient longing and hope during bleak Tasmanian winters in dark, thick bush, under starry skies, beneath Wurrawana Corinna, the 'Great Ghost Tiger'.

❀ ❀ ❀

The Xerces Blue Butterfly

(*Glaucopsyche xerces*) (1941): I was a butterfly, the Xerces blue butterfly, a small creature, but my dazzling blue hue made me sparkle. We were air-borne gems. A flutter, a rainbow, a flight, a wing, a rabble or – my favourite collective noun for us, which is also the 'official' word – a 'kaleidoscope': a kaleidoscope of butterflies, shining jewels of blue and the browns of the female, flitting filigree and lace.

We – the females dressed in earth tones and the males often as blue as the San Francisco sky above – lived in the sand dunes of the San Francisco Peninsula, USA. Our wings also had a black, and then white, bar: perhaps a reflection of the dunes beneath the night sky. The gold of the sand, the blue of the sky, the greens, yellows and violets of the plants we favoured, deerweed and lupins, were constantly changing patterns on our kaleido-scope. We turn, fluttering through a green, violet and gold lens, under a canopied backdrop of blue. Exquisite. Precious.

We seem to be connected to jewels, our lives linked to other precious substances. Indeed, our demise, our eclipse, was due to the gleam of an-other precious commodity: the metal gold. This substance drove humans a little crazy. We used to inhabit our sand dunes, in peace, in privacy, until the substance was found in the Sierra Nevada mountain range. This caused many to rush for a chance to either acquire some, or to live out their dreams of freedom.

Our dream of freedom was to remain where we were, untouched, unnoticed. We inhabited a region known as the 'outside lands'. Pity they didn't remain 'outside'; they eventually became 'inside', later named the Sunset District. Once the town expanded, more people came to serve the folk living here, who also needed places to live. Buildings were quickly

Samples of the Xerces blue butterfly (*Glaucopsyche xerces*).

erected, shops set up for business. On the land, introduced livestock also destroyed our environment.

During this fever of activity, in 1849 or perhaps it was as late as 1850, a gentleman, Pierre Lorquin, arrived from France. His bread and butter was in providing legal services, but his passion was entomology.[320] Lorquin set out with a special contraption which we had not seen before and therefore did not know was to be avoided. This butterfly net captured some of our clan, and after they had been killed, they were sent back to France, to one of the most famous lepidopterists in France, Jean Baptiste Boisduval. It was Boisduval who gifted us with the name Xerces.[321] We were named after a fifth-century BCE Persian ruler, Xerxes, but Boisduval chose to use the French spelling. I prefer the original spelling with the 'x', for 'x' marks the spot. The 'x' resembles the shape of some of my former family who ended up in collection drawers, pinned into place, pulled out to be displayed like brooches in jewellers' display cabinets. Most rulers capture territories and yearn for more land to conquer, but we were content with a small region. We clustered in little colonies in particular sand dunes, in Twin Peaks, in North Beach and from the Presidio south to Lake Merced. We were heralded as a new addition to the world's second-largest butterfly family, the Lycaenidae, who are gossamer-winged butterflies. What did it matter? We were not long for this earth or sky.

Urban expansion. Sprawl. You humans give it a strange term: 'development'. Development of what? Cheek-by-jowl buildings – no room for exposed sand dunes and their flying colourful butterflies, our blue and brown darting like wind-blown sand particles, dancing across the coastal line, a Native American sand painting, mirroring our life . . . and our death.

Building work also killed off our food supply. The loss of a number of plants – including deerweed (formerly classified as *Lotus scoparius* but now known as *Acmispon glaber*), a low-growing larval host plant which our young would feed on during the larval stage and which our caterpillars preferred – meant that we could no longer survive. Although we had lupin as a food source, only adult butterflies could eat it.

Another factor to be added alongside development and collecting was the introduction of a non-native, the Argentine ant (*Linepithema humile*), from South America. I am sure native ants were destroyed or displaced by this insect. This altered our intricate and delicate workings, because the native ants looked after our larvae on the host plants, protecting them from predators. In return, the ants would receive sweet nectar from the backs of the caterpillars.[322] An introduced species would not have known or been involved in developing our larvae. This is a unique behaviour and would have been worth studying in more depth if we had survived. It would have taught humans something about host behaviour and the importance of preserving not only the creature, but its complete environment, plants and other living things.

The Xerces blue is believed to be the first American butterfly species to become extinct as a result of loss of habitat caused by urban development. We would prefer to be remembered for our colour, for our beauty. If we have left a legacy, then it is the spur to action regarding conservation of existing insects. The Xerces Society has taken on our name in order to do this work, and it speaks about what the world has lost – both us and other extinct species.

Speaking of beauty, many tourists and residents of the Bay Area flock (is that the collective noun used to describe a human gathering?) to the Golden Gate Park. Beautiful views, lots of green space. It is also the site of the California Academy of Sciences, which holds the largest collection of dead Xerces blue butterflies in the world. Ironic that this park was built on our dunes, where we once were a rabble, a flight, a wing. No movement now. At least this former site has been transformed into a place of nature, unlike the last area where we were found, our last refuge, the dunes of Lobo Creek, in the Presidio area, which is now a car park. We were confined to an area of 21 metres by 46 metres (69 ft by 151 ft).[323] This is where the last of us was captured, on 23 March 1941, a glittering living jewel, until netted and killed by William Lange. Lange, an entomologist, was full of remorse for the rest of his long life. Later, interviewed at the age of 86, Lange, reflecting on his act, said, 'I always thought there would be more. I was wrong.'[324]

Although many believed that was the last of us, two years later there was a report from two scientists who were convinced they had seen some of us, but that site was soon flattened and built on when officers of the Presidio military base recommended the development of the sandy dunes to the south of San Francisco.

One of the losses to the scientific community was knowledge. The patterns on the underside of our wings were quite varied. At one stage, naturalists thought that these changes denoted different species, but that was not the case, for we could breed with each other. Now the Xerces blue butterfly's quality of mutation cannot be studied, or used as a basis for other work, particularly in the field of genetics.[325]

Perhaps the underside of our wings can reveal or tell a final story. The underside was dark grey, with a central spot. There was also a bar of additional white dots. Now sometimes, as alluded to earlier, there was a change; in this case, there was a black spot within the central white spot. This dab resembled a pupil, and those who had this mutation were known as Polyphemus, the name of a brutal, one-eyed giant, one of the Cyclopes in Greek mythology, whose name means 'abounding in songs and legends'. Maybe the hint of memory, the imaginings of our kaleidoscope, rainbow songs and stories about us: the rare and now extinct, blue periwinkle trinkets flying on gossamer wings, true Californians, living by the sand, the ocean, under blue skies. Gold shimmering blues and browns, a Lycaenidae necklace, lining drawers hidden away in the dark in cabinets, our sparkle dulled for eternity.

A specimen of the Xerces blue butterfly (*Glaucopsyche xerces*).

And no plaque anywhere, nothing to denote that 'x' marks the spot of our extinction.

❊ ❊ ❊

The Arabian Ostrich

(*Struthio camelus syriacus*) (estimated 1940–45): I was a victim of hunters, shot for my feathers, for the lucrative plume market – ostrich plumes brought in good money. Even in ancient times, I was hunted for my feathers. If you doubt me, this was depicted on an ancient Assyrian seal.

We were found in the Syrian and Arabian deserts and in the Negev and Sinai. Nowadays the ostrich is only found in Africa, but we, a distinct, smaller subspecies, the Arabian ostrich (*Struthio camelus syriacus*) (also known as the Syrian ostrich, or the Middle-Eastern ostrich), used to inhabit the Arabian Peninsula and the Middle East. We had a wide range, stretching from the Euphrates in the east, to the Sinai in the west, and into southern Saudi Arabia. Our numbers were most plentiful in northwest Saudi Arabia, near the Jordanian border. Up until about 1914, we were common in Syria and Arabia. Arabs called us the *na-ama*. The males were up to 210 centimetres (6 ft 11 in.) in height; the females were slightly smaller, their height being about 175 centimetres (5 ft 9 in.), so we were large birds.[326] Our trinomial, or three-part name, includes *camelus*. We were also known as the 'camel bird', because of our similarities to the camel: long necks, which enabled us to see for vast distances across flat desert terrain, prominent eyes, sweeping eyelashes to keep out the sand; and a particular stilted walk. The comparison included our ability to withstand high temperatures and go without water for long periods. Lucky that the camel is still around, unlike the 'camel bird'. Unlike the camel, we had red legs and red necks. We were like little flames when we ran! In a sense, we fanned the flames, because our long feathers, unique in that they were not joined to each other but were separate and strong, aided us in running swiftly and also functioned as a fan, to cool us down.

We would end up in the cooking pot too: our eggs were eaten, our fat used, but before precision firearms, we were hard to catch. We were pursued on camels, hunters assisted by falcons and dogs. But we were elusive, hard to kill, like you . . . and, like you, we too were a casualty of the First World War. No medals for us, but our plumes were used by some military personnel. Firearms, a lucrative European feather market (our feathers were considered superior for hat making compared with those from the North African subspecies) and a fast-and-efficient means of pursuing us, all contributed to our demise. Once local people realized that our plumes might relieve their poverty . . . well, we were pretty much gone by the late 1930s. There are conflicting reports concerning the 'last of us'. One states that the last was either killed and eaten between 1940 and 1945 by Arab pipeline workers in the area of Al Jubail, in northeast Saudi Arabia, or shot in 1941 in Bahrain.[327] Other reports tell of two ostriches shot in 1948 and, as late as 1966, of a female ostrich drowned in a flash flood in Jordan. Unfounded stories? Tales woven from hope rather than from facts? In the end, dates don't matter because the results are the same.

Oh, but we were beautiful! Petroglyphs of us can be found on Graffiti Rock 1, near Riyadh, in Saudi Arabia. There is a wonderful carving of a family of ostriches, an adult with eleven offspring. These carvings date from the Neolithic period (approximately 9,000–3,000 BCE). We didn't just grace rocks; our image was painted onto cups, was incorporated into

Ostrich hunt in Palestine, engraving by G. Pearson
from *Wood's Bible Animals* (1875).

mosaics and decorated the covers of precious books. Our feathers adorned robes of desert tribal chiefs, and our eggs decorated mosques. We were so highly valued that we were gladly received as tribute, as gifts, even as far away as China. After the rise of Islam, the nobles would hunt us for 'sport', using bows and arrows. If we were slaughtered in a particular way, our flesh would be considered halal, permitted to be eaten by Muslims. One of our eggs was big enough to provide a small family with an entire meal (and for the same reason our eggs were valued by troops during the war); feathers and skins were used in handicrafts and exported to other countries. The gift of our eggs featured in a famous book, T. E. Lawrence's *Seven Pillars of Wisdom*. The story is told of our eggs being brought by an Arabian tribe as a peace offering: on 2 June 1917, 'through the afternoon, we received fusillades of honour, deputations, and gifts of ostrich eggs.'[328]

Reference to us is made in the Bible's Book of Job. The first part of the citation is correct: 'The ostrich's wings flap wildly.' We would do that to ward off predators, but then, 'For it leaves its eggs to the earth,/ and lets them be warmed on the ground . . ./ It deals cruelly with its young, as if they were not its own . . ./ God has made it forget wisdom,/ and given it no share in understanding' (Job 39:13, 14, 16, 17). This is inaccurate! Sometimes we would leave the eggs for a short time, but the shells were so thick, there was little likelihood of them being cracked open by a predator. Our breeding season was in the middle of winter. We would build our nests in isolated areas. Females would each lay between 12 and 21 eggs, close together, and form them into a circle.[329] Now, the male ostrich is polygamous, and sometimes more than one female would lay eggs in one nest.[330] The major female would stay and look after the eggs, and the minor females would leave, playing no role in either the incubation of the eggs or in the raising of the young. This may partly explain the verse, 'It deals cruelly with its young, as if they were not its own,' but we were not cruel. Both male and female incubated the eggs, and both parents raised the young.

We would partly cover the eggs with sand, to help protect them from rain and heat. We would even dig a little trench, so that any heavy rain would run off the eggs (remember, this was winter time). Now, we have received some bad press concerning our egg laying, with some saying we were careless, or forgetful, because the female would leave two or three eggs outside the circle. These were not for hatching: rather, they were nutrition for the young to feed on once they had hatched. I would suggest that the female knew which eggs had less chance of hatching and selected those to be the eggs positioned outside the nest. The parents shared the nesting responsibilities: one sat on the eggs, while the other was on guard. How could this nurturing, protective behaviour give rise to this Bible verse? '[B]ut my people has become cruel,/ like the ostriches in the wilderness' (Lam. 4:3b). Humans may be cruel – actually they were cruel, and continue to be cruel. We saw much evidence of that, but us? No!

Even the noises we made were labelled as mournful. All a result of anatomy. We are the only birds who produce a 'roar'. This is due to an anatomical feature; air enters our gullet, not via the trachea. The air gets pushed down, the stomach's sphincter shuts and the air is pushed upwards, causing our neck to expand. The air is finally released (with some force!) as a large burp, which can be heard from some distance away.[331] We were classed as 'unclean' birds in the Bible (Deut. 14:15), which seems unfair, because we did not eat carrion, nor do anything that would taint us.

Humans still say that ostriches bury their heads in the sand. What rubbish! It is because we have to stretch down to the ground, and our beaks are then on the ground or in the sand when we eat. Of course, this position means we are vulnerable, which is why we frequently lift our heads and necks. There are a number of Hebrew words used to describe us. In the Bible, one of the words is *ya'anah* (close to the modern *ya-en*), which means 'greedy' – not sure why, because we were picky eaters, choosing good-quality seeds and leaves.[332] But what's the point in arguing? We ended up the same: dead, extinct.

Sadly, there may have been a solution. Apparently, Colonel Richard Meinertzhagen had been trying to raise funds to bring some captive Arabian ostriches he had seen in Amman and Damascus in 1920 to the London Zoo, so that we could be bred in captivity.[333] Our subspecies may have been saved, but I am uncertain about the truth of that story. In later years, Meinertzhagen was identified as a fraudster, linked to the stealing of many specimens, some of them from the Natural History Museum in London. There is a Syrian ostrich egg in the Natural History Museum collection that has beautiful handwriting upon its surface. The penmanship is that of Meinertzhagen, and the wording states that this egg was taken from a nest by Charles Doughty, then given to Colonel Lawrence, who

سطع من ساض العن إذا الكحل به

النعام من طمعه ان لا يعلو في الطيران

Two ostriches, miniature from Ibn Bakhtīshūʿ, *Kitāb naʿt al-ḥayawān* (Book of the Characteristics of Animals), probably Baghdad, c. 1225.

gave it to Meinertzhagen in 1922. In 1948 Meinertzhagen gifted it to Tring Museum, where it was not well received by the museum's owner, Walter Rothschild. Perhaps Rothschild doubted some of the information written on the egg? What can be believed?[334] It is a Syrian ostrich egg, and that is important. Perhaps it doesn't really matter how it came into someone's possession. Do famous people *have* to be associated with a particular object in order to make it precious? Isn't it valuable on its own, as an egg from a now-extinct subspecies of ostrich?

Humans. Do they remember us? Humans ought to be careful; the firearms that finished us off may be their own downfall.

❊ ❊ ❊

The Ivory-Billed Woodpecker

'That the Ivory-bill shall not, as a part of America's natural heritage, go the way of the Passenger Pigeon and the Great Auk, is an objective of the National Audubon Society.'
– National Audubon Society, 15 September 1942.[335]

(*Campephilus principalis*) (probably 1944–8; officially declared extinct by the U.S. Fish and Wildlife Service October 2021): I was a religious bird, yes, yessiree. How so? How so? By my very presence, presence, presence! Sightings of me would cause folk to pronounce, 'Lord God' or 'Good God!' I was rare, so difficult to find that I was referred to as 'the Holy Grail' bird. I boasted a saintly pedigree. I sported other, non-religious nicknames though, including 'King of the Woodpeckers' and 'Elvis in Feathers'. Who is Elvis?

We were flamboyant – once seen, never forgotten. We were spectacular, decked out in glossy, blue-black feathers, white patches on our wings and a white stripe on each cheek, which trailed down our necks and met in the middle of our backs. Males sported dramatic red crests at the backs of their heads, whereas the female crests remained black. We had bright-yellow eyes, which contrasted beautifully against our black legs and feet. Naturalist John James Audubon called us the 'van Dyck' of birds, because our colours were so striking, reminding him of the artwork of Flemish artist Anthony van Dyck: 'I have always imagined, that in the plumage of the beautiful Ivory-billed Woodpecker, there is something very closely allied to the style of colouring of the great VANDYKE . . . whenever I have observed one of these birds flying from one tree to another, I have mentally exclaimed, "There goes a Vandyke!"', which was high praise.[336] We were quite jittery birds, with swift, repetitive movements. We were the largest woodpeckers in North America (with an impressive 76-centimetre (30 in.) wing span and the second-largest in the world. We were also among the most powerful, with bills that were 7.5 centimetres (3 in.) long and nearly 3 centimetres (1 in.) thick at the base. That bill, our big DIY power tool, could drill up to 20 centimetres (8 in.) deep in a single blow. From beak to tail, on average (though there was nothing average about us!) we were 50 centimetres (20 in.) long: we cut an appearance, made an impression!

Our call was distinctive and haunting, a nasal 'yent, yent, yent' (or 'kent, kent, kent'). Our voice was quite the musical instrument, being compared to the sound produced on a toy trumpet.[337] American ornithologist James T. Tanner also likened the sound to that of a clarinet; another described our calls with reference to a musical instrument that transcends the common woodwind and brass: he thought our calls resembled 'the burry reed notes of a Scotch bagpipe'.[338] Yessiree, a wind instrument, but not in the same field or grouping as that of the trumpet and clarinet, you'd agree. Not a black tie, evening dress orchestral event! Hearing our call on an old tape recording, a contemporary writer described our voice as having 'the foreshortened quality of a car alarm beep as it's deactivated by its owner and therefore, for me, lacks the majesty of the bird's appearance . . . Yent, yent, yent I hear. Then the loud double rap of a bill striking wood.'[339]

That rap, that drilling – not only could it get into bark and extract our meals, but that bill meant we could wreak havoc. Back in 1809 an injured ivory-billed woodpecker was left in a hotel room in Wilmington, North Carolina, by ornithologist Alexander Wilson, while he went off to settle in his horse. When Wilson returned, he found that the bird had well and truly damaged the hotel room. If he had returned a little later, that imprisoned ivory-billed woodpecker would have escaped![340] We were birds best admired from afar! Wilson understood our magnificence and our religious links: 'his whole frame so admirably adapted for his mode

Stuffed specimen of the ivory-billed woodpecker (*Campephilus principalis*), presumed extinct despite reported sightings in the 21st century.

of life and method of procuring subsistence, as to impress on the mind of the examiner the most reverential ideas of the Creator.'[341]

Speaking of the Creator, and being a religious bird, we were accorded sacred or magical qualities. Our bills and tufts were highly prized objects of trade, used by Native Americans for crafting elaborate headdresses and belts; our feathers, bills and crests decoration on ceremonial pipes. Warriors included our heads in their sacred bundles, hoping the dead woodpeckers would transfer power to them to enable them to drill through their enemies.[342] Perhaps that power transcended death, for we were sometimes found in Native American graves, many out of area (one was found in Colorado, far from its habitat).[343]

We were unusual in that we were among the last of the birds to greet the day! Late morning was our time. We would perch on branches, using our tails to help us pivot. Our swift, repetitive movements were almost dance steps: swinging our bodies from side to side, pausing, and then peering over one shoulder; swinging back, and then looking over the other shoulder, and then another swing.[344] Swing, peer, swing. Perhaps an avian southern square dance? We loved movement, bright-red patches billowing across a dark backdrop of feathers and timber. A ship's flag on dry land? We rested in the afternoon – all that scaling and drilling takes it out of one! After that, another feeding frenzy, usually flying off in pairs to search for food, before returning to our roosts.

Our nests were in holes in living or dead trees. We could create holes in fewer seconds than you could say our name! Yessiree! We had been observed digging a 12-centimetre (4¾ in.) hole in a tree in fewer than sixty seconds.[345]

Our courtship ritual consisted of beak touching, and we paired for life. Eggs were laid during the months of January and May. Our clutch of white eggs varied in number, between one and five, but mostly it consisted of three or fewer eggs. Sadly, it was rare for more than one to survive beyond the chick stage.[346] We shared the incubation of our young, a three-week period of intensive feeding. Our young would be with us for several weeks, or longer (it varied), before leaving the nest for good, but as a pair, we stayed together all year round. This fidelity is touching, but it worked against our species. If we lost our mates, there may be some difficulty finding others due to our low numbers. If a female lost her mate during the courtship period, this would mean a loss of eggs for a year. We already had low production rates, so these other factors played a role in our dwindling numbers.

During our most plentiful period (having said that, our specific requirements meant that we were never a common bird), we could be found in a large region of the USA that extended from North Carolina to Florida, the Mississippi Valley to southern Indiana and southern Illinois, and even along the coast of Texas. Of course, our different habitats dictated variations in diet and trees for our nests: in Florida, our nests were usually in cypresses, whereas in northern Louisiana, our nests tended to be found in sweet gums, oaks or red maples.[347] Most of the landscape of our habitats included dark, swampy forest or floodplains, but we could adapt to drier territory too. Wherever we laid our heads (sounds like the words from a song . . . maybe we *are* an Elvis bird!), we tended to stay put, only venturing a few kilometres from where we had hatched.

We were a casualty of 'progress', a term used to describe humans invading our restrictive territory. We were particular about where we lived and what we ate, which made us vulnerable; when those two things disappeared, we were in trouble, for we could not adjust to change. We needed large tracts of mature timberland to sustain us. A single pair of us required a lot of habitat, 15.5 square kilometres (6 sq. mi.) of wet forest. This forest had to contain mature, dead trees for our nesting needs, as well as provide us with a plentiful supply of grubs.[348] *Campephilus* means 'lover of grubs', and we were certainly that! Choosey, though. We feasted on grubs, borers or the larvae of wood-boring beetles that lived between the bark and the sapwood of freshly dead wood, trees that had died in the past two-to-three years.[349] We didn't have a strong food competitor. Pileated woodpeckers were sometimes found in our habitat, but we fed on the borers located beneath the bark, whereas they targeted borers that lived in the sap and heart of trees that had been dead for a much longer period of time.[350] You must remember that we were built for this procuring: being large and powerful, we scaled the bark, rather than hammering it; hitting at the bark underneath, such action exposed the fat beetles. We also drilled and chiselled, our long tongues able to grasp well-hidden borers. Actually, it is thought that we aided forest growth, because we fed on the type of borer that could kill living trees. When our numbers were healthy, or stable, we prevented infestations of these borers, thereby saving forests.

We also ate some fruits, seeds, acorns and berries, but none were crop or orchard fruits, so we were not a threat or pest to farmers.

By the mid-1800s, our numbers began to decline. We started to disappear from different regions; by 1855 we were no longer seen in North Carolina or the area west of the Mississippi delta; by 1900 we were rarer than the California condor. By 1915 we were no longer seen in Texas, Arkansas and Alabama.[351] Only a few of us still hung on in swampland in Florida, Georgia and South Carolina. In 1924 Arthur Augustus Allen, an ornithologist from Cornell University, and his wife were travelling in Florida. They were shown a nest of ivory-billed woodpeckers by a nature guide; they were ecstatic! When they returned, they were saddened to learn that two taxidermists had been given permission by the State of Florida to shoot them (which they had promptly done), rather than grant them protection.[352] A sign of hope, dreams of populating that region with the Lord God bird, had gone up in gun smoke.

By 1930 only small numbers of us were sighted in South Carolina, northeast Louisiana and Florida.[353] As I have already hinted at, our decline was mostly due to 'progress'. Timber was needed, and, with the rapid development and extension of the railways, our fairly specialized trees were numbered. Logging of old growth forest in the South destroyed most of the trees we liked, those that harboured our wood-boring grub diet, trees suitable for nesting and roosting. We needed uncut, mature timber. Our final years found a small number of us living in a small area of forest in Louisiana, but this was short-lived.

As with any religious symbol, we had our devotees. We had some hard-core followers, such as T. Gilbert Pearson and J. J. Kuhn, who was the game warden at the Singer Tract, a forest in Louisiana. Another fan was James T. Tanner, who entered the ornithological field at the tail end of a time when it was still widely accepted that a specimen had to be killed in order for it to be studied. In 1935, a Cornell University team, which consisted of other fans (Doc Allen, Peter Paul Kellog, George Sutton and a young Tanner), pioneered new ways of conservation rather than collection, shooting with cameras and tape recorders, not with firearms. Some states had brought in laws to try to protect us, even before Cornell University's work, but these attempts were too little, too late; we were so attractive a proposition that hunters were willing to get caught, and, if truth be told, by this time, our numbers were so low that our decline continued.[354]

James T. Tanner. He tried to keep us going . . . oh he tried so hard! Remember how I said we were a 'religious' bird? Well, we were Tanner's Holy Grail, and he was on a quest. He devoted much of his life to us, really. He found us, of course, and sang our praises, but he was unable to save us.

Among the dryness of facts and figures, he wrote poetically about us:

> [It] has frequently been described as a dweller of dark
> and gloomy swamps, has been associated with muck and
> murk, has been called a melancholy bird, but it is not that
> at all – the ivorybill is a dweller of the tree tops and sunshine;
> it lives in the sun . . . in surroundings as bright as its
> own plumage.[355]

Dear James, in his quest to search for, observe and try to save us, he journeyed over 72,000 kilometres (45,000 mi.). Tanner took trains, drove cars, walked on foot, rode horses and even went by boat; he studied old maps, listened out for our loud double rap on a tree, attuned his ears to hear our nasal 'kent, kent, kent' – he was a true pilgrim.[356] We were the subject of his PhD dissertation, and, as a result of his field work, those meticulous records concerning our behaviour have been kept. His heart was in the right place, for he said that he would never tire of watching us.

Now, I have a bit of a story about James. After all his research findings and reports, plus some photographs, people thought that was the extent of his gift to the ornithological community, indeed, to the world at large, but no! Many years later, in 2009, another naturalist, Stephen Lyn Bales, was writing a book about Tanner, and he paid a visit to Tanner's widow, who happened to live in the same city. Well . . . Nancy Tanner showed Bales some photographic negatives, which revealed unseen images of Tanner and his colleague J. J. Kuhn and an ivory-billed woodpecker whom they had named Sonny Boy.[357] Those photographs had been taken on the same day, back in 1938. Can you imagine what a treasure these negatives were, brought to light, into focus, after sixty years?

Now when numbers are low, shooting can devastate a small, local population, yessiree. In 1939 Tanner estimated there were no more than

22 of us left. Without a captive breeding programme, and without adequate protection, this put us well and truly in the danger zone. Tanner, with the support of the National Audubon Society, hoped that the 32,000 hectares (80,000 ac) of Louisiana forest, known as the Singer Tract, could be kept intact. It was thought that we had become site-dependent, for the population there stayed within its confines and only ate the grubs that existed there. In Tanner's 1942 report for the National Audubon Society, he wrote about the importance of preserving and limiting the logging of mature forests: 'Mature forests of large, old trees have almost disappeared, and these conditions favourable for the ivory-billed woodpecker will very probably never again prevail.'[358] In another journal of that year, Tanner's message was edged in gloom: 'There is little doubt but that complete logging of the tract will cause the end of the Ivory-bills there, and since the surrounding country is young second-growth forest and cultivated lands, it will doom the woodpeckers to a vain search for suitable food and habitat.'[359] Tanner's lack of sightings of us underlines his forlornness; Tanner, our number one admirer, the one who tried to save us, had his final sighting of an ivory-billed woodpecker in December 1941.[360]

It didn't matter that our decline and the appeal from Tanner had attracted the attention of the President of the United States (presidential interest in us was not something new; Thomas Jefferson had written about us). President Franklin D. Roosevelt was optimistic and was ready to intervene, but then the Second World War presented other challenges viewed as more pressing than conservation, including the need for timber, so our preservation was put on the back burner. German prisoners of war crafted boxes that were needed for the war effort from the timber that we liked. These containers included tea boxes, which were used by tea-drinking British soldiers during the war.[361]

The last confirmed report of an ivory-billed woodpecker was in 1944, spotted in northeastern Louisiana by avian painter Don Eckelberry.[362] It seems fitting that one who admired our feathered brethren, who would pause intently, trying to capture something of our majesty on canvas, would be the last to bask in our disappearing radiance of black, red and white – the last, a lone female. There have been other reports, other sightings, but none that can be proven. Heart-thumping sightings are often of the pileated woodpecker – a fine bird – but not us.

The Singer Tract was finally cleared to make way for soya bean production, which meant our 'clearance' too. The last known population of us
had disappeared by 1948. But of course, tree logging wasn't the only factor
that killed us; we were killed by the poor for food, and our long, beautiful,
jaw-dropping bills were sold in order to fashion trinkets, carved into watch
fobs and the like. We were shot by collectors and bird enthusiasts, because
we had become a much-sought-after, rare and dazzling trophy. Now, a
piece of Southern advice: rare plus beautiful equals 'watch out!' Over
the years, the prices to acquire our creamy-white bills rose, reaching the
illustrious sum of $5 in 1887, which was a lot of money back then, and
our worth continued to rise.[363] On a July 1893 price list for taxidermist
A. T. Wayne's birds (a service tailored to collectors), a male and female
ivory-billed woodpecker were priced at $22.[364]

Until recently, it was thought that a subspecies of us resided in Cuba.
In 1863 the Cuban ivory-billed woodpecker (*Campephilus principalis bairdii*)
was described as a subspecies by ornithologist John Cassin, but in 2006
DNA gathered from tissue samples demonstrated that this bird was a distinct species. This meant that the two species diverged about 1 million
years ago; it had not been imported to Cuba. Sadly, that woodpecker has
also vanished: the last official sighting was in the late 1980s.

Rare . . . extinct, yet the quest, the search, for the bird that cried 'yent,
yent' continues to this day. Believers, bird mystics, ruffle feathers every
couple of years or so, claiming they have seen us, that we still live. This is
why some are reluctant to give us an extinction date. In 1999 an unconfirmed sighting of an ivory-billed woodpecker in southeast Louisiana led
the U.S. Fish and Wildlife Service to improve habitat and grow particular
trees in order to attract the beetle larvae that we loved. In a couple of years,
several areas were well managed but, unfortunately, a natural disaster in
the form of Hurricane Katrina devastated that region, and there have been
no more unconfirmed sightings of us there.[365] This has not stopped other
unconfirmed sightings from elsewhere, though.[366]

Even without a definitive year of extinction, we remain one of the
most pursued birds. We can still be found, in museums and in the hearts
of dreamers. Dreamers . . . one of our names was 'Elvis'. Not sure who he
was, but perhaps he, too, was from the southern regions of the United
States? I have heard it said, yes I have, I have, that some folk believe he

is still alive? Maybe, yessiree, maybe some continue to hope that is the condition of the Lord God bird too.

❀ ❀ ❀

The St Helena Earwig

(*Labidura herculeana*) (1967; declared extinct by the IUCN 2014): I am earwig. Or *was* earwig. I speak on behalf of my species, so when I say 'I', I mean 'we'. I was large, Herculean, but size did not make me loveable. Size did not alter my profile from forgettable to *un*forgettable, and yet . . . we are strange, we earwigs, so different from other insects that entomologists gave us our own taxonomic group, the order Dermaptera. I have many names: I reside in a kingdom, Animalia, my phylum is Arthropoda, my class Insecta, in the order Dermaptera; my family is Labiduridae, my genus *Labidura*, and my binomial name is *Labidura herculeana*. That is my pedigree, my Insecta family (or Labriduridae) tree.

What's in a name? Who would have thought that fear and loathing could be contained within a few letters? We non-humans do not name ourselves, yet humans feel an urge to name, to define in order to contain, a tradition narrated in their Bible, when the first human named the non-human animals. If naming is about power, then humans have power, power of life and of death, the annihilating voice, the death rattle of extinction.

My common name, 'earwig', is ancient, from the Old English *ear wicga*, meaning 'ear insect' or 'ear wriggler'. *Wicga*, 'insect or beetle', is the etymological basis of the word 'wiggle'. Our association with the ear is present in other languages, too: *perce-oreille* (ear-piercer) in French, *Ohrwurm* (ear-worm) in German and *ukhovertka* (ear-turner) in Russian.[367] Was our name a description of our supposed behaviour of crawling into the human ear canal, burrowing into the brain, where we then proceeded to lay our eggs? We small creatures apparently have the ability to drive the human mad! In the first century, Pliny the Elder wrote about this myth as though it were fact: 'If an earwig . . . be gotten into the eare . . . spit into the same, and it will come forth anon.'[368]

Extraordinary that *we* are associated with ears and brains. In ten centuries of literature, there is only one reference to an earwig being found

Male and female of the extinct giant earwig *Labidura herculeana*.

in an ear![369] That is hardly a common occurrence and therefore a strange reason for our name. You will soon learn that we are excellent mothers, so it is highly unlikely that we would lay our eggs in a place where our young would be unable to survive. Besides, earwigs rarely fly (and my particular species was without hind wings), so how would most of us get into a bedroom, and then travel across a pillow into an awaiting ear? We like the damp and musty environments of the earth outside, or, for other species, inside, snug in basements or in dark, damp cupboards, not in open, light environments like bedrooms or kitchens.

Earwig: utter that word, and many wince. Is it because of our pincers? Perhaps humans fear them. Our twin pincers were known as *forficula*, 'little shears', which is rather poetic. These 'little shears' were designed to assist us in mating, to help us grasp prey and to deter predators, not as a tool for nipping humans. Do they resemble earrings? Or our wings, ears? One explanation for our name that was put forward (it doesn't apply to my species, because we have – I mean 'had' – no hind wings) suggests that the hind wings, which are tucked underneath the short, leathery forewings, when unfolded, resemble human ears. So maybe we 'earwigs' earned our name from our looks, or structure, rather than from our function?[370] Perhaps if I had been known by my order, Dermaptera (*derma* means 'skin', and *pteron*, 'wing', so 'skin wing') or as 'battle-twig' (as earwigs are known in one region of England) I might have been slightly more endearing.

I was one of about 2,000 species distributed across twelve families (a low number for an insect, we were not particularly diverse), a species found on every continent except for Antarctica. I am an insect with a low profile, with few fans. I was known as the St Helena earwig, the St Helena giant earwig or the St Helena striped earwig. Pity that having more names doesn't guarantee survival. I may not have turned (or entered) many heads, but I was a giant, hence my name 'giant', or *herculeana*, the world's largest earwig. I was huge! The largest one ever found (7.6 centimetres (3 in.) in length, including its pincer) is now well preserved, safely housed in the AfricaMuseum, Belgium.[371] I was quite an attractive insect, with an elongated, shiny, black body, reddish legs and short elytra (anterior wings), but no hind wings. Males were larger than females. Our horny forceps-like pincers were 1.5–2.3 centimetres (⅗–1 in.) in length. The females had shorter, more serrated pincers, which were lighter in colour.

We mated between December and February, a day or two after we had reached adulthood. There was no time to waste, because we only lived for about two years. The adults, as a partnership, would construct a small cell in the soil in which to lay the eggs. There the combined work ended, because the females would drive their mates from the chamber when it was time to lay their eggs.

How many humans consider the nurturing qualities of earwigs? This is a rare trait to be found among non-social insects. Earwigs were, and those species still living remain, fiercely maternal. We regularly cleaned and groomed our eggs, because they were susceptible to fungi. If on the alert, we would move our eggs to a safer place, away from danger. After the mother had helped her nymphs to hatch, she continued to rear them, feeding them on regurgitated food. Nymphs were positioned under their mother's body for protection and warmth.[372] Would we have left our eggs within human brains? I think not!

Anyway, why would I have wanted to wriggle my way through a human ear canal when I could burrow deep within dark, damp soil? I lived here, on St Helena, one of the most isolated islands in the world, in the south Atlantic Ocean, west of Africa. This island was discovered by the Portuguese in 1502, colonized by the British in 1659 and remains a British Overseas Territory. Its mild climate suited me, trade winds blowing almost continuously. This remote volcanic tropical island, with its rugged landscape, is small, only 16 kilometres (10 mi.) long and 8 kilometres (5 mi.) wide – a dot in an ocean, but it played an important role not only in our story, but in yours as well. Napoleon was exiled here in 1815 and remained a prisoner until his death in 1821. In 1792 importation of enslaved people was made illegal here. It is a small island, with an important legacy. It is a pity that human rights did not extend to the protection of other species.

On St Helena, my species favoured several locations, all in the extreme northeast of the island: Horse Point Plain, which was dry and barren, with small bushes and tufts of grass; Prosperous Bay Plain; and the indigenous gumwood forests. We kept to ourselves, only coming out at night after it had rained, for we were nocturnal. There is a wonderful smell and texture to the air and earth following rain. We were particularly active during the summer rainy season, but once the dry season arrived, we would seek shelter underground. Our burrows were not only for raising young and for housing; they were escape routes. We would scurry to them when we sensed danger, or when soil or stones were disturbed. Our species even made it into seabirds' rocky colonies. Once the birds were gone though, so too was that habitat. We were a little like Napoleon, who was confined to Longwood House during his exile here on St Helena. We, too, were contained within a small number of areas, but I am sure we were happier and had more freedom than that important human prisoner.

One of the evolutionary trends found on islands is that some species (like us) become supersized, but the small environment tells another story of contrast, the downside, the scary tale about the vulnerability of island wildlife. When humans settled here, they identified the large rocks under which we lived as ideal construction material, so they proceeded to mine it, to clear it out. This destroyed much of our habitat, along with the removal of native plants from the area, which led to soil erosion. The removal of stones, the rocky shelters that protected our long burrows, meant we were vulnerable, exposed to light and wind, and easy targets for predators. Our extinction was aided by the animals that accompanied human settlement. Prior to 1502, I was the dominant invertebrate predator in the forest, and there were no native land mammals, but human settlement was paired with introduced creatures, which either ate us or altered our environment: cattle, cats, dogs, donkeys, rats, mice, spiders, rabbits, goats, sparrows and the little beast which wreaked much havoc on us: the introduced centipede *Scolopendra morsitans*. There was little hope of survival. Loss of habitat. Loss of home, *my* home.

We were not the only species to die out on St Helena. One of my native predators, the St Helena hoopoe (*Upupa antaios*), also known as the giant St Helena hoopoe (another giant!), disappeared not long after human settlement, due to introduced species and loss of habitat. Plants became extinct as well. St Helena is special: on this island there are an estimated 502 species, mostly invertebrates, not found anywhere else in the world. Sadly, the majority of St Helena's endemic invertebrates are on the brink of extinction, due to fragmented habitats as a result of human settlement. It was too late for me . . . I hope there is time to save them.

Part of the problem, and perhaps one reason it took so long before we were protected, was that as well as being an unpopular species, unlikely to appear on posters or be admired as pin-ups, we were a bit of a riddle. First discovered in 1798 by Danish entomologist Johan Christian Fabricius, who gave us the name *Labidura herculeana*, much later, in 1904, we were confused with a smaller and more common species, the *Labidura riparia*, and demoted to a subspecies. No one paid us much heed for many years, until 1962, when I was 'rediscovered' by two ornithologists, Douglas Dorward and Philip Ashmole, who were searching not for me, but for fossilized bird bones. They had uncovered some enormous dry-tail pincers, and these were forwarded to zoologist Arthur Loveridge. We were (again) renamed, this time as *Labidura loveridgei*. But this was still incorrect. In 1965 entomologists found live specimens of us on Horse Point Plain and realized that we were, in fact, *Labidura herculeana*, not *L. loveridgei*, so our original name was finally reinstated as our official scientific name. It's hard when your name keeps changing! I do have another name, which links me to another extinct creature: I have been called 'the dodo of the Dermaptera'.[373] Like that unfortunate bird, I too was an endemic species confined to a small area on a tiny island and found nowhere else in this vast world.

I was last seen in May 1967, after two Belgian research expeditions (one in 1965–6 and the other in 1967) had unearthed forty of us, but there have been no sightings of live specimens since. We probably survived for a while longer, because dead fragments of us were found among bird bones in 1995, with another remnant found on Horse Point Plain in 2013 and an additional one in the lair of a spider in Millennium Forest in 2014. We were declared extinct in November 2014, but even being declared extinct didn't gain us much media attention. The IUCN Report noted that the last confirmed live specimen of us had been seen in May 1967, then it listed some of the reasons for our extinction, including 'since the early 1960s, its habitat has been degraded by the removal of nearly all shelter-providing surface stones for construction purposes.' This important announcement appeared at the end of a press release from the IUCN Red List update and went largely unnoticed.[374] As I said earlier, insects don't get the 'loveable' animal label from the media, or even from many conservationists. Insects play a huge role in ecosystems, so they need to be acknowledged and protected. Even the IUCN, an organization that has evaluated 100 per cent of birds and mammals, has only classified about 0.5 per cent of the world's known insects.[375] How many others have or will become extinct, before humans know of their existence? Unfortunately, when we were last seen, it was before the era of captive breeding, so we became extinct before there was a possibility of saving us.

I may not have been a pretty pin-up, but I did end up gracing a smaller version of the poster, the postage stamp. Issued in 1982, this commemorative stamp, at the pricey sum of £1, was special, because the stamp included both my image and story. It brought attention to the need for conservation, but for my species, it was too late, though several expeditions were launched. In 1988 the London Zoo sent out an expedition known as Project Hercules. This was quite a costly venture: the London Zoo pledged £3,000 to the cause, wanting to save an endangered species from extinction. Not everyone agreed that this was a good use of money. Even Dave Clarke, the leader of the expedition, admitted that it was difficult to get people interested in insects, let alone earwigs. I'm flattered, but actually every species is fascinating – you just have to observe and wonder. In 2005 the Natural History Museum tried to find me, along with a number of other groups, but all were unsuccessful – they were too late. As a way to protect other species that were on the endangered list, plans for an airport on St Helena were shelved, but even this decision was eventually overturned.[376] The airport, along with the disturbance of habitat due to its construction, became a reality in 2015. I wonder how many species became extinct or endangered as a result of this?

In the end, though dead, we still have a function, being a flagship for endemic invertebrates. My story, our story, of extinction should serve as a warning to protect the environment and the species that live in it. This is urgent work, because St Helena has more endemic invertebrates per square mile of land than the Galápagos Islands. I know most are not considered as attractive as those living on the Galápagos, but every creature is beautiful in its own way and warrants protection, a chance at life.

I am a relic of a unique and rich history of evolution. Supersized . . . scaled down . . . now gone. We no longer burrow, wriggling through to tend our eggs, or emerge to enjoy the scent of rain and the feel of wet, moist soil. Like many insects, our decline and disappearance were scarcely noticed or noted, but then something exciting happened.

Sometimes after confirmation of a species' extinction, that creature's profile is raised. In 2023, after negotiations were undertaken by British arachnologist and research taxonomist Danniella Sherwood, the St Helena government and the St Helena National Trust, one of us was donated, repatriated from the AfricaMuseum. Imagine! Returned to its birthplace, St Helena. This was a significant event because the St Helena Museum did not have a complete specimen of us. This carefully preserved St Helena earwig isn't burrowing beneath the dark earth of its former home, on the extreme northeast of this isolated, rugged island. Instead, it resides within the walls of the museum of St Helena, protected from the island's harsh winds, safe from predators, no longer underground but above, out in the open, on display, for all visitors to admire.

I am earwig.

I was . . . earwig, 'the dodo of the Dermaptera'.

The Eskimo Curlew

(*Numenius borealis*) (early 1970s?): let's begin with a riddle:

> Q: What is the difference between a passenger pigeon and an
> Eskimo curlew?
> A: The passenger pigeon is remembered, whereas the Eskimo
> curlew is mostly forgotten, overlooked.

And another:

> Q: How were passenger pigeons and Eskimo curlews similar?
> A: Both flew in such large numbers, they darkened the skies.
> Oh – and they are both extinct. Well, sort of . . . Perhaps – there,
> another riddle for you!

Sorry, not meaning to trivialize what had been our rich, yet largely unacknowledged existence, but there are connections there, similarities and,
of course, differences. We were the Eskimo curlew (*Numenius borealis*),
in the family Scolopacidae, native to North and South America, once
one of the most numerous of shorebirds, with a population of millions.
When something is abundant, one does not expect it to disappear or to
go extinct, yet we were one of the few American species that suffered a
rapid decline. It is a stark and weighty reminder that human activity can
cause irreversible damage.

Numenius borealis. What does our name mean? Was it derived from
noumenis, 'of the new moon', a description of our thin, down-curved,
crescent-shaped bill? Or perhaps it was from *numen*, which means 'to nod'?
We did dip, or bob, our heads forwards and downwards. *Borealis* is Latin
for 'northern', so we were known as the Eskimo curlew, or the northern
curlew (which doesn't sound quite as exotic). We had additional names,
including 'dough bird', used to describe our plumpness.[377] Our girths increased during the autumn migration when we would gorge on crowberries
in Labrador, which resulted in our breast flesh being soft, pale and tasty.
We were also known as 'prairie pigeons', perhaps because on our return

each spring we ate the larvae and eggs of the Rocky Mountain locust on the prairies and Great Plains. We were not pigeons; we were one of eight species of curlew, a wader, once a common shorebird, of coast, wetlands, prairies and mudflats. Hard to believe that we were once common, isn't it?

We were smallish (29–34 centimetres (11½–13 in.)) and fairly plain, not decked out in the bright hues of parakeets or birds of paradise. We were mottled, sprinkled light brown and white, with dark streaks on our necks and faces. Our bellies were dull yellow, with 'v' and 'y' markings on our breasts and flanks.[378] Our probing beaks were 5 centimetres (2 in.) long and were dark, as were our legs and feet. Some may have dubbed us 'drab', but these colours worked as camouflage, helping us blend in among grasses and scrub.

Our calls were not well known; they were complex in their variety. They contained a rippling 'tr-tr-tr', a soft whistle 'bee bee', a low sound of chatter, a soft whistle when we would land, a chirp as we walked around, calling to others, and other whistling noises. The Inuit name for us was

Digital depiction of an Eskimo curlew (*Numenius borealis*).

pi-pi-pi-uk, in imitation of our call, and often we would be heard before we were seen.[379] In 1860 a Dr Packard wrote about our call, 'I saw a flock a mile long and nearly as broad . . . The sum total of their distant notes resembled the wind whistling through a ship's rigging or at times the jingle of many sleigh bells.'[380]

I love that description of our call resembling the ting of a sleigh bell, for it conjures up travel, and we were great travellers, avian globetrotters. We bred in northwest Canada and wintered in South America. We did not need horses though, because we flew long distances, over 15,000 kilometres (9,300 mi.) on our own flight power, winging our way, as one. Our spring migration began in April–May, flying north across mixed grass prairies, favouring recently burned areas and regions disturbed by grazing bison, arriving in our breeding areas in late May to June. Our nesting season was June–August. Our exact breeding region is still open to debate; only two confirmed areas are known, both in the Northwest Territories of Canada, at the base of Cape Bathurst.[381] During late summer we flew from our breeding grounds on the treeless tundra of the far northwestern Arctic Canada and coasts of Alaska, flying from the Yukon and the Northwest territories, to Labrador (where, in some parts, crowberries are still known as 'curlew berries', in memory of us) and Newfoundland, where we fed on blueberries, flies and their larvae, and other insects, such as grasshoppers and beetles. Then, still as one, we would fly over the Atlantic, flying along the eastern fringe of North America, heading down to South America, to winter on the Campos of Argentina, landing in pampas grasses as one single, enormous flock. As a migratory bird, we would head back in late February or March, but what made our return journey even more remarkable is that we flew an entirely different route! We followed a circular migratory route, a trip I like to call our 'circle of flight'. If you want to be technical, our twice-yearly migration routes were elliptical. If we were human, you would say that we wanted variety, or were easily bored. Our spring flight, our northward migration, took us across Texas and Louisiana, north along the Mississippi and the Missouri, flying over the Great Plains, Kansas, Iowa and Nebraska, and back to Canada.

We would land in ploughed fields, and then search for insects, favouring Rocky Mountain locusts and their larvae and eggs, beetles, flies and their larvae. When we landed, our greetings mimicked whistles tinkling in the wind. In the 1850s, observers on the prairies described flocks of calling birds that stretched for miles, sounding like sleigh bells. By late May, we would be in, or at least approaching, our breeding grounds in the far north. Our circular migratory route was quite something. Actually, it is time to tell you the truth – it could appear that I am boasting, but it is important to know that our migratory route was the most elaborate (and dangerous!) of any migration cycle known. Think about it. To travel that distance, as one flock – what does that tell you about our strength, our bond, our endurance and how we small birds were wired? As a sleigh travels as one, so did we. This epic journey, navigated twice a year, could be described as monumental. Of course, there were casualties; during our northern journey, severe storms meant some were blown off course: exhausted, they would die in the ocean. Our southern migration had fewer deaths, until settlers arrived. Ironic really, because our sheer numbers may have been responsible for settlers in the first place. We may, in fact, have been among the shorebirds that alerted Christopher Columbus to the presence of nearby land during his first voyage.

In our far-north breeding grounds, our nests were nothing remarkable – none of those elaborately crafted nests, requiring hours of work from both sexes. No, ours were quick and to the point, functional but not labour intensive, just a scrape or two in the ground, and then lined with leaves or grass. They did the job.

We once numbered in the millions, darkening skies as we migrated across the North American continent. When we were plentiful, as we were in the first part of the nineteenth century, our flock was thick and dense, but as our numbers decreased, so did the depth of our flock. Our title of 'prairie pigeon' was assigned to us by settlers, who had seen the heavy flocks of passenger pigeons which blackened the skies back east. The famous ornithologist Audubon made the same comparison back in 1833, when enchanted by a flock of curlews in Labrador.[382] When Audubon did a painting of us for the book *The Birds of America* (1827–38), he chose to depict a dead bird, or perhaps it was a wounded one.[383] Was this prophetic, a vision of our future, or was it a way to point to our care or concern for others in our flock? Digressing a bit, stop and try to imagine one enormous, single flock. It must have presented an amazing sight. Unfortunately, it also meant easy hunting! Grouping together made us easy to shoot; one shooter could fell a number of us with one bullet, so we were a cost saver. Wherever we travelled, hunters were ready. When we landed, we could cover 16–20 hectares (40–50 ac). Remember, not only did this make us easy targets, but this could have been the total world population of Eskimo curlews in the one place. How vulnerable we were, and yet . . . so beautiful! When we landed on the Labrador coast to forage for snails in the mudflats, six to eight shooters were there, ready, proceeding to fire constantly. When we landed on the beaches of Newfoundland, men would fell us when night drew in, confusing us with lantern light, killing us with sticks, salting our numerous carcasses in barrels for the long winter.[384] During storms and gales, we were often blown off course, and then shot. On one occasion, we landed in Nantucket, in huge (and storm-exhausted) numbers – so many, in fact, that the island's supply of gunpowder ran out. Our killing had to be 'interrupted'.[385]

After we had landed on the prairies and across the Great Plains, professional market hunters, using the field glass (which had been developed in Nebraska), could approach us within 23 metres (25 yd), without much difficulty. As one shot rang out, the rest of the flock rose as one. One shot was reported to have killed 28 of us. We would fly on, pursued by hunters on horses or riding horse and buggy. Wagons or buggies were often so oversupplied with our carcasses that they were left to rot on the prairies, hunters going back to shoot more of us for 'sport'.[386] We had the habit of flying down and calling out over a wounded member, so, again, we were easy to kill. Nineteenth-century ornithologist Elliott Coues wrote about us in *Birds of the North West* (1874):

> They generally flew in so loose and straggling a manner that it is rare to kill more than half a dozen at a shot. When they wheel, however, in any of their more beautiful evolutions, they close together in a more compact body and offer a more favourable opportunity to the gunner.[387]

Large numbers and a well-known route, combined with a known time to appear in a given region, all led to easy and fruitful hunting. Once passenger pigeon numbers became small, birds scarce, we were seen as replacement meat. By the end of the nineteenth century, hundreds of thousands, if not millions, of us were killed each year. Extensive market hunting in the late nineteenth and early twentieth centuries was a reenactment of the passenger pigeon story. Again, we had so many things in common with that bird! Pity they were mostly fatal elements. By 1870 our numbers were declining fast, and by 1900 we were thought of as possibly being extinct. For example, the last sizeable bag of us made it to market on the East Coast in 1863; the last one in Nova Scotia was at a market in Halifax in 1897.[388] Uncontrolled market hunting, habitat destruction (the prairies were being destroyed by crop growing and by the suppression of wildfires that formerly burned the Great Plains with regularity, which had helped our diet of Rocky Mountain locusts' eggs and larvae), our tendency to circle within gunshot range after a flock member had been shot, and our apparent lack of fear of humans, plus our low reproductive rate, all contributed to our decline. Even after market hunting was officially banned in 1909, and the Migratory Bird Treaty Act was introduced in 1918 to protect migratory birds like us, our numbers never recovered – it was too late. Small numbers continued, but that was all. We were among the first species to be listed as endangered under the Endangered Species Preservation Act (the predecessor to the present Endangered Species Act).

Sometimes extinctions have links or connections with other extinctions, a costly reminder that we are all part of the web of life. When our migratory path took us across the prairies, we would feed on the larvae and eggs of the plentiful Rocky Mountain locust (*Melanoplus spretus*). This tasty insect was a primary food source, and we relished it. The settlers should have been grateful; the more we ate, the fewer they had to battle. In 1874 the largest locust swarm was recorded in Nebraska: nearly 3,200 kilometres (2,000 mi.) long and 180 kilometres (110 mi.) wide. A lot of fine dining! In fewer than thirty years, though, the Rocky Mountain locust was extinct. Unfortunately for us (but good news for the settlers), our principal food source during migration across the prairies ended, leaving us with little nourishment for the long flight ahead to our breeding grounds. The demise of the Rocky Mountain locust led to more aggressive moves in agriculture and crop planting. Once the grassland was converted into cornfields, it made it even more difficult for us to survive. Grass birds, like us, vanished like the locusts.

Though we were quite small in size, large in number and common in colour, we had some notoriety from the writings of Fred Bodsworth, a Canadian journalist who chose to make us the subject of his novel *The Last of the Curlews* (1954), a book which sold more than 3 million copies. The story is about a single male Eskimo curlew who meets up with the last remaining female Eskimo curlew in Patagonia. This love story has a nasty ending: on their northern migratory route, the pair fly over the Canadian prairie, where the female is shot by a farmer, and the lone male flies on. As is often the case in tragic love stories, death seems to be the only victor. Bodsworth wrote his novel at a time when many assumed that we were already extinct, or in such scant numbers that we may as well be extinct. Perhaps, like the passenger pigeon, Eskimo curlews needed large flocks in order to stimulate breeding. Once numbers dropped, we were doomed, lacking sufficient numbers and genetic variation for successful breeding.

In 1962 a pair of Eskimo curlews was photographed in Galveston, Texas, by Don Bleitz. In itself, that would be monumental, a celebratory occasion, but even here there is a riddle, a question to be asked: were these four photographs – considered to be the only photographic record of us in the wild – authentic?[389] Although we were thought to be extinct, there have been reports of other sightings. For example, in 1981 there was a report of 23 of us in Texas (a claim not accepted by the Texas Bird Records Committee), and in 1987 others were sighted in Canada. Were we the birds spotted? If we go to hard facts, the last confirmed sighting of us was on 4 September 1963, when a solitary Eskimo curlew was shot in Barbados. After examining the skin of this Eskimo curlew, writer and ornithologist Scott Weidensaul wrote, 'Was the curlew, like the pigeon and the parakeet, a thing of darkening memory? Or were there still a few out there, somewhere, making the great arc from tundra to pampas each year?'[390] This uncertainty has kept the door open, if you like, because at the moment, official bodies are not prepared to deem us officially extinct.

People do, on occasion, report seeing us, though they are probably reporting a sighting of a whimbrel (*Numenius phaeopus*) or the little curlew (*Numenius minutus*) because we do look alike, especially the juveniles of related species. A young whimbrel takes time to grow its bill long enough to differentiate it from an Eskimo curlew, and, as adults, whimbrels are larger, with longer, curving bills and white wing linings. If you couldn't get close enough to the bird, it would be easy to confuse species, particularly if you were hoping against hope that it was an Eskimo curlew. We are still listed as critically endangered (possibly extinct) by the IUCN. So, in a way, we remain the bird of hope, one highly unlikely to exist anymore, but the one no one wants to officially declare extinct. We are still fully protected in Argentina, Canada, the United States and Mexico. This seems strange to me; none of our nests have been found for more than 140 years, and the last official sighting was in 1963 . . . but we remain the subject of articles and blogs, discussions and musings.[391]

Like the passenger pigeon (again!) we live on, not only in Bodsworth's words, or in people's hopes or wrongly identified sightings, but in a bronze sculpture by Todd McGrain, part of his *The Lost Birds Project*. In March 2020, a 1.8-metre-tall (6 ft) memorial sculpture of an Eskimo curlew was installed at the Galveston Island State Park, Texas, the site of our first, and last, photographs.

To conclude with another riddle,

Q: How do you prove a negative?
A *plus* Q: Absence of evidence isn't proof of absence. If you can't prove our absence, are we extinct or not?[392]

Perhaps the answer can be found in a date, that of 21 April, which is World Curlew Day, and also the feast day of the Welsh St Beuno. A story is told of St Beuno, who accidentally dropped his book of sermons in the water when returning to Clynnog from Llanddwyn. A curlew swooped down and picked it up. When Beuno reached land, he found the book drying on a stone, guarded by the curlew. In gratitude, Beuno knelt and prayed for the protection of the curlew. This came to pass in making it nigh impossible for humans and other predators to find curlew nests.[393] Maybe, just maybe, our nests remain hidden, safe from human eyes. And maybe, just maybe, our sleigh bell cries will ring out once more before Yuletide, as birds of hope winging our way to the Arctic tundra.

The Tecopa Pupfish

(*Cyprinodon nevadensis calidae*) (1970; formally declared extinct 1981): I loved the warmth! And the salt. I hear that humans head to the south (or north, depending where they live) during winter, to be warm, and I understand that need. We were Tecopa pupfish (*Cyprinodon nevadensis calidae*), our scientific name longer than we were (we were only 2.5–4 centimetres (1–1½ in.) in length). We were an extinct subspecies of the Amargosa pupfish, of the pupfish family Cyprinodontidae. Now an interesting fact for fish fanatics: our family name is similar to that of the Cyprinidae, or carp family, but we were not closely related. We had more in common with pikes – flat heads, bi- or tricuspid teeth and large scales – and yet we were assigned to the order Cyprinodontiformes, an order of ray-finned fish and a type of killifish. Killifish sounds dangerous, doesn't it? But it is derived from the Dutch *kil*, which means 'small stream'. The eggs of most killifish can survive harsh conditions, including partial dehydration. These names may seem confusing, but it may simplify matters if we say that we were a species of killifish, which had its own common name, that is, 'pupfish'.

Members of the pupfish family are small and can be quite bright; they are found on three continents. Pupfish are known for their ability to live in tough environments, so they are often found in isolated, extreme locations. We, Tecopa pupfish, were colourful, the males a bright blue (a colour used to attract females to spawn), with black vertical stripes at the tips of their tails and silver scales, while the females were duller, of olive hue, with six-to-ten vertical stripes. We had small, blunt, oval-shaped heads, tricuspid teeth and small pelvic fins (which were sometimes absent), and, being ray fish, these pelvic fins had a set of six fin rays.

Although tiny, we could withstand temperatures of up to 43°C, or 110°F, which is the hottest water temperature ever recorded for a fish, so we were pretty special.[394] Even our surroundings spoke of heat, for we lived in the Southwest USA, in the Mojave Desert in California, spending our days in the Tecopa Hot Springs. Tecopa Hot Springs are in Inyo County, a little over 3 kilometres (2 mi.) north of Tecopa. We were confined to a small area: the North and South Tecopa Hot Springs and little salty pools were

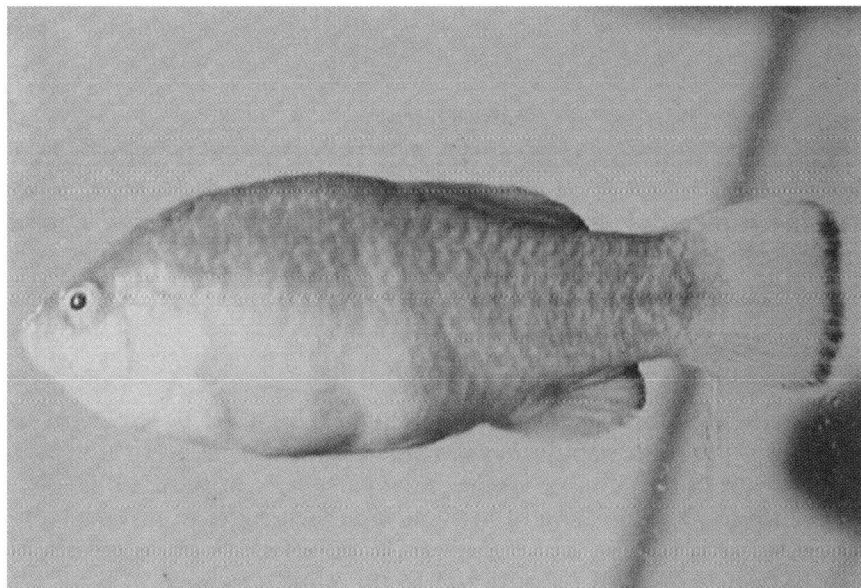

Tecopa pupfish (*Cyprinodon nevadensis calidae*).

the only places we lived. In a way, we were endangered before extinction, because we were only found in this region of the United States.

We ate blue-green algae and mosquito larvae and, if left alone, could live for two years, having produced about ten generations of fish during that time. We could produce between two and ten offspring each per breeding season, depending on the water temperature, with the offspring reaching full reproduction maturity from eight to ten weeks.

Being small and slight, we could have been viewed as insignificant, inconsequential, but our ancestral lineage was ancient and could be traced back to the Ice Age. During the mid-Pleistocene epoch, we were found in large glacial lakes, such as Lake Manly, that carved out much of the landscape. Over time, these lakes began to dry up. Evaporation changed the land to harsh desert, leaving some streams and pools – and us! It's been proposed that in prehistoric times there was only one species of pupfish, but as the climate became hotter and the lakes and rivers dried up, desert springs became isolated islands. We became geographically isolated and began to evolve to adapt to these harsh conditions. The water quality was poor in these small pockets, but we adapted. Think about it – we managed to live in environments that would have killed most fish: hot temperatures and extremely salty water. We, the Tecopa pupfish, became endemic to the outflows of what became known as the Tecopa Hot Springs.

How did we come by such a weird name? *Tecopa* is a Paiute word for 'wild cat', which was also the name given to a Paiute leader, known to be a keeper of tribal peace.[395] We were leaders in some ways too. We were named 'Tecopa' after our locality, but why 'pupfish'? 'Pupfish' was a name coined by ichthyologist Carl L. Hubbs, after observing us circling and tumbling with each other. Some have written that we 'frolic about like puppies'.[396] This could be part of male mating behaviour.

For little creatures, it took several big factors to lead to our extinction: the introduction of non-native species (perhaps I should add 'human' to that list); interference in our habitat, which led to changes in water temperature, salinity and currents; and pollution. All were caused by humans. Mosquito fish (*Gambusia affinis*) were released near the natural geysers and in marshland on the edge of the cooler sections of the hot springs, and they soon became our predators, along with bluegill, another introduced non-native species.[397] Pollution in the thermal springs outflows arose from contamination from a bathhouse and, later, from agricultural and recreational development in the area.

Altering our environment was probably the most damaging, or significant, factor that hastened our extinction. The mineral-rich waters of the Tecopa Hot Springs were believed to contain healing properties. Such claims enticed a constant flow of tourists, especially during the winter months. During the 1940s this led to the building of a bathhouse, which became a very popular destination over the next two decades. In 1965 plumbing for the bathhouse involved enlarging the springs. Both the northern and southern hot springs' outflows were rechannelled and merged. This may have been good news for the bathhouse, supplying it with warm water, but it resulted in a flow of water that was too swift for us, pushing us downstream. It also led to a steep rise in water temperature, too hot even for us, the little heat-tolerant fish, and water that was now too salty. The heat and high salt content hindered our life cycle and breeding, speeding our extinction. We were pushed to the limit, which demonstrates that even small changes to natural systems can have major effects.

Our population was low, because our habitat couldn't support large numbers, another factor that made us vulnerable to extinction. We could not survive in this changed environment. Water diversion meant that the water puddles eventually dried up . . . as did we. We were a fairly recent 'discovery', first described by Robert Rush Miller in 1948. He studied us in depth for six years, and we became the subject of his doctoral work. Miller remained fascinated by us, and he returned in 1966 to search for us, hoping against hope that we were still alive, which we were, but we were few in number.

It is thought that the last of us ended its days in an artificial pond and creek, at Jed's Motel in Tecopa Hot Springs, sometime in 1968 or thereabouts. Seems sad, doesn't it, that the little pupfish's last days were spent in an artificial, concrete environment? A motel, a place for tourists, as was the bathhouse. This information may be incorrect, though, because this pupfish may have been a hybrid, a combination of the Tecopa pupfish and the Amargosa River pupfish. The specimen had smaller scales, which suggests that it was, indeed, a hybrid. Some scientists say that the last 'pure' or confirmed Tecopa pupfish were collected on 2 February 1970.[398]

We were placed on the Endangered Species List by the u.s. Department of the Interior's Fish and Wildlife Service in 1970. The Department was concerned about our absence and in 1978 proposed that we might need to be removed from the list, which would mean we 'would no longer be afforded any protection or benefits under the Endangered Species Act of 1973'.[399] The Assistant Secretary of the Department at the time, Robert L. Herbst, said, 'The most depressing thing about this loss of life form is that it was totally avoidable. The human projects which so disrupted its habitat, if carefully planned, could have ensured its survival.'[400] On 19 November 1981, after many searches for us, the Fish and Wildlife Service declared us extinct. We were the first creature removed from the Endangered Species List, on the grounds of extinction. This removal took place after much consultation and after more than forty fruitless searches for us. Yes, we had been listed back in 1970, but even then, we were beyond rescue. Robert A. Jantzen, Director of the Fish and Wildlife Service, commented, 'It is always sad when a species becomes extinct because of human activities.'[401]

Strange . . . that we, who could withstand extreme conditions, could not survive conditions created by humans. You humans could have sat in hot springs elsewhere, or checked before altering such a sensitive habitat.

Did you really need to sit in hot springs? Or if you did, why didn't you check environmental factors before expanding the area? You did not deliberately kill us, but you invaded, conquered, extinguished. Ignorance and apathy kill. If there had been time, enough warning, would a captive breeding programme have helped the survival of our subspecies? That is uncertain. The Catarina pupfish, endemic to a spring in Nuevo León, Mexico, was declared extinct in the wild in 1994 and extinct in captivity in 2014. Its breeding programme was unsuccessful.[402]

At least we had been named, and, unlike many species that go extinct every year, we were known. Is that better? Having humans mourn for those named, and known, rather than grieve for a collective unknown, unfathomable? The mysterious remaining mysterious, unnamed?

I know I mentioned we once lived in the Mojave Desert, which is located in Death Valley, the place of our death – how fitting!

As an aside, the bathhouse, whose plumbing had contributed to our extinction, went bankrupt and is now deserted. Perhaps bankruptcy is another form of extinction?

❀ ❀ ❀

The Southern Gastric-Brooding Frog and the Northern Gastric-Brooding Frog/Eungella Gastric-Brooding Frog

(*Rheobatrachus silus*) (1981; in captivity 1983) and (*Rheobatrachus vitellinus*) (1985): frogs, amphibians. Small, unnoticed, unless you are famous, like Kermit. Well, I was noticed, but I wasn't around for much longer after that. I was a southern gastric-brooding frog, 'discovered' (I say 'discovered' because it is thought that a specimen may have been collected back in 1914) in the Blackall Range in Queensland, Australia, in 1972–3 (there is a discrepancy in dates), but by 1981 we had disappeared, become extinct. The last recorded sighting of us in the wild was in September 1981 in the Blackall Range, following a decline in our numbers from the winter of 1979. The last individual in captivity died in November 1983. My cousin, the Eungella gastric-brooding frog (for whom I will speak because it declined the opportunity to comment), sometimes known as the northern gastric-brooding frog, was even less fortunate: discovered in January

1984, our cousins were gone by 1985. The first signs of their decline were reported in January 1985, and after June that year, no more were seen. Both species inhabited Queensland – we in the south, in the Blackall and Conondale mountain ranges in the southeast, and our northern cousins in undisturbed, pristine rainforest in the Clarke Range, which includes the Eungella National Park, in mid-eastern Queensland.

We were homebodies, never located more than 4 metres (4 yd) from water. Our limited home range meant that we usually stayed within the same pool during the breeding season, only moving away if there was a flood, or a high flow of water.[403] We loved rocky streams and pools that contained leaf litter in dark, damp, sun-dappled rainforests. We used rocks and leaves to shelter from predators, birds and fish. We were most active during the warmer months, from September through to April, and it is thought (though no human can say with certainty) that we hibernated during winter in rock crevices.[404] We were active during daylight hours and at night, particularly after rain. We ate insects, from water and from the ground. We had a loud staccato call, which 'sounded like "eeeehm, eeeehm" with an upward inflection'.[405] The Eungella gastric-brooding frog had a shorter call, with a deeper pitch and fewer repeats.[406] Its call was composed of a number of 'loud staccato notes repeated in a long series', the males vocal at night during the months of September through to December.[407] Our cousins occupied waters that flowed swiftly, happy in cascades which held cool, clear water. They would hide beneath boulders, feeding on a range of creatures from the water and its edge, including small crayfish and beetles.[408] During rain, they could be seen squatting on exposed rocks.

We were both of the genus *Rheobatrachus*. We were known as gastric-brooding frogs (a reference to the unique way we incubated our young) or as platypus frogs, because we were largely aquatic in nature. We did *not* look like a platypus, but we differed in appearance from all other Australian frogs. We southern gastric-brooding frogs were medium-sized, 3–5 centimetres (1–2 in.) long, mostly brown or olive green on our backs, with dark blotches and a dark streak which went from one of our eyes to the base of one of our forelimbs. Our undersides were white or cream, with yellow markings. We had mottled webbing; large, protruding eyes; short, blunt snouts; long, unwebbed fingers; small discs on the digits;

Specimen of the southern gastric-brooding frog
(*Rheobatrachus silus*).

and complete webbing on our toes. Our bodies were moist, covered with mucus – slimy even. It is interesting to note that when our tadpoles were born, they initially lacked any skin pigmentation.

Our northern cousins' appearance was a little different. Part of their taxonomic, or scientific, name is *vitellinus*, Latin for 'of the yolk of an egg'.[409] Our cousins were larger and much more colourful. Their undersides were smooth and white or brown, but sported bright-yellow and orange colours on the lower abdomen and undersides of their limbs. We, on the other hand, were a trifle drab, brown our dominant hue. They, too, had fully webbed toes.

Our size and colours may have differed, but as species we shared the way we gave birth. We were the only two species of frog that incubated the pre-juvenile stage of our offspring in the stomach of the mother. I must say, we caused quite a stir when this was first discovered. A researcher was looking into the mouth of one of us and, to his or her shock, saw a little frog on the tongue staring back![410] How did this remarkable process happen? At some point, the female swallowed fertilized eggs, which remained in her stomach until their development was complete.[411] A chemical, the lipid prostaglandin (which has some hormone-like effects in animals) was triggered, which switched off the production of hydrochloric, or gastric, acid, providing the right environment for the developing embryos.[412] The upper intestine was then rendered inactive, so the female stopped eating. After six-to-seven weeks, when the tadpoles had developed into froglets and were ready to be released, they either were regurgitated or climbed out themselves, numbers varying from 6 to 25, exiting via the mother's mouth. Females were unlikely to breed twice in one season because of this lengthy brooding time. After the young, fully formed froglets had exited, the mother's digestive tract returned to normal, and she was able to recommence feeding within four days or so.[413]

We were the only genus to possess this ability. Imagine! A stomach functioning as a uterus! What new medical knowledge could have been gleaned by looking at ways to decrease the production of gastric acid, or deal with other issues of the stomach. Gastroenterologists were very excited and were starting their preliminary research . . . when we went extinct. What groundbreaking discoveries were forfeited? How many humans may have had a better life, if studying us in more detail had led to a breakthrough concerning ways to limit the production of gastric acid, aiding the treatment of stomach ulcers or allowing for a faster recovery following gastric surgery?[414]

Why did we go extinct? Often extinction is linked to habitat destruction, but for both species, our habitats had remained remarkably unchanged. There have been alterations in our environment since our disappearance, including timber harvesting and the sighting of feral pigs, plus a decrease in the quality and flow of water, but at the time, these were not crippling factors.

It has been suggested that climate change was the cause of our extinction.[415] Our breeding cycle occurred between October and December, and it is thought that it may have been dependent on summer rains. Climate change has brought about a marked decline in Australia's east-coast rainfall, so that may be one part of the disappearance puzzle.

Chytridiomycosis, an infectious disease caused by the chytrid fungus *Batrachochytrium dendrobatidis*, has been identified as a potential cause of the extinction of the Eungella gastric-brooding frog and for the loss of other frog species in Queensland rainforests. The decrease in rainfall due to climate change altered conditions, creating the right environment for an explosion in fungal growth.[416]

Researchers have not given up, making us the subject of a de-extinction experiment, known as the Lazarus Project.[417] These scientists hope to bring us back to life, by 'resurrection' science. Now, I understand that such projects need intact genetic material. Thanks to the research of Mike Tyler in the 1970s and '80s, there were old tissue samples of the southern gastric-brooding frog stored in a laboratory freezer at the University of Adelaide. The idea is that the DNA of the southern gastric-brooding frog will be inserted into the egg of another species, in this case, the great barred frog, which would then be the surrogate, helping to hatch an individual of the extinct species.[418] Now, apparently of all the resurrection projects, this one has been the most successful.[419] In 2013 nuclei were implanted into the donor cells of the great barred frog, and some eggs were successful. Some even managed to grow to the embryo stage, but they only survived a few days.[420] Even so, tests were able to demonstrate that our genetic material was contained within those cells.

Hmm. I am uncomfortable with this. I know such experiments aid understanding about genetics and diversity of life, but I am uncertain about the whole venture. The procedure used was somatic cell nuclear transfer. The nucleus of a fresh egg of the barred frog was destroyed and replaced with dead nuclei from us (*Rheobatrachus silus*). Was that ethical? One species of frog being deemed more important than another?

If tadpoles are ever produced, they wouldn't be fully southern gastric-brooding frogs, would they? What would you name them? What about the unique aspect of our species, stomach incubation? That can't be replicated. There is talk about making the frog resistant to the chytrid fungus – doesn't that also alter the essence of the frog, making it different from what it was? There were other unique qualities about us, too. As tadpoles, our intestines developed at a later stage from those of other aquatic tadpoles. Why, and was there a biological or environmental reason for this difference?

This concludes the 'end story' of the southern gastric-brooding frog and its close relative, the Eungella gastric-brooding frog. Did you know that *eungella* is an Indigenous term which means 'land of the clouds'? Where they used to reside is the longest continuous stretch of subtropical rainforest in Australia, a habitat known for its platypuses, but there are no more platypus frogs swimming in its creeks. This region often appears to be perched on a cloud; perhaps one day our cousin will emerge from the cloud of the infectious disease caused by the chytrid fungus, glints of yellow and orange, splashes of hope, ready to meet up with us, their kin.

In words often attributed to Chief Seattle, but more likely to be those of screenwriter Ted Perry, 'What is there to life if a man cannot hear the lonely cry of a whippoorwill or the arguments of the frogs around a pond at night?'[421]

❀ ❀ ❀

The Dusky Seaside Sparrow

(*Ammospiza maritima nigrescens*) (1987; officially declared extinct December 1990): what can be said about me, an insignificant little bird, a dusky seaside sparrow? 'Dusky seaside' sounds like I was a kind, matronly great aunt, accompanying her charges to the beach for the day, setting up a beach umbrella, bringing out sunscreen and hats. I was occasionally referred to as 'dusky', which is quite the name for a great aunt, isn't it? Like most great aunts, my plumage was a little plain: blackish, with white undersides that were heavily streaked with black. My throat and belly were white, my legs and feet grey; the only hint of colour (almost the equivalent of the donning of a bright scarf by a great aunt) was a yellow streak above my eye. Again, like many great aunts, I was non-migratory: I didn't travel far from home, home being a small geographical region. We lived on the east coast of Florida, on Merritt Island, along the upper St John's River and on the adjacent mainland, all contained within a 16-kilometre (10 mi.) radius. It is believed that we occupied the most restricted habitat of any North American bird.[422]

We lived in the salt marshes. Our nests were woven from grass stems, and they floated in cordgrass, a little above the mud. Our females were clever, protecting their nests by dropping to the ground, and then wading off, rather than flying off, to protect the location of the nests from predators.[423] The clutch would hold three or four eggs, and after twelve days, they would hatch. After they had hatched, the young, still not able to fly, would stay close to the nest, remaining on the ground on thick cordgrass.

In 1873 our dark colouration and distinct, buzz-like song led to us being listed as a species of seaside sparrow, but in 1973 I was recategorized as a subspecies of the seaside sparrow (*Ammodramus maritimus*). No reasons were given for this change, which meant that only one full species of seaside sparrow was recognized, the other nine being subspecies, including us. Strange really, because we were quite distinctive in appearance, and our song didn't resemble those of other seaside sparrows, who tended to sing 'clicks', whereas our rapid 'buzz' was unique.[424] This change in status wasn't a matter of pride; it was much more important than that because it may have contributed to our extinction. Being 'demoted' from a full species to a subspecies led to a decrease in interest in our conservation. In the end, it doesn't really matter, does it? Full or sub – neither saved me. We may have been little, overlooked, but our extinction came about as a result of the creation of two very important places: the Kennedy Space Center and Walt Disney World® 'the happiest place on Earth'. Well, it wasn't my happiest place. Let me explain.

We dusky seaside sparrows, or 'duskies', lived happy lives, flitting over and through the natural salt marshes, sharing space with insects (some on whom we dined), including mosquitoes. Between 1958 and 1962, NASA acquired all of North Merritt Island and most of the rest of Merritt Island (56,700 hectares (140,000 ac)) in order to establish the John F. Kennedy Space Center, on Cape Canaveral. Merritt Island was adjacent to Cape Canaveral. At the beginning, wildlife was not forgotten. In 1963 an agreement was forged between NASA and the U.S. Fish and Wildlife Service, which led to the establishment of the Merritt Island National Wildlife Refuge on land that was not directly needed for space programmes. These lands included our habitat on Merritt Island.[425]

Now the mosquitoes seemed to be a problem; they certainly were for us because they became another reason for our extinction. Salt-marsh mosquitoes on Merritt Island had been targeted for elimination since the early 1940s, using DDT. Aerial spraying of pesticides of various types had taken place on a regular basis for thirty years. DDT spraying continued until the early 1950s but was discontinued because mosquitoes were becoming resistant to the poison. Other pesticides and chemicals were used instead. These pesticides and poisons had an impact on our population on Merritt Island: by 1957 our population there had declined by 70 per cent.[426]

Dusky seaside sparrow (*Ammospiza maritima nigrescens*) perched on a branch.

DDT toxicity reduced our breeding pairs from 2,000 to 600, and entered our food chain.[427] The poison also affected our eggs, producing thin shells, as well as inhibiting our reproductive capability. Even a tiny amount of ingested poison can cause reproductive failure.

Those pesky mosquitoes were still congregating in large numbers in our salt marsh, too close for comfort for humans, as the site was directly opposite the Kennedy Space Center. We know humans do not like mosquitoes, or most insects, really. This area of salt marsh, which included our nesting grounds, was flooded as part of an attempt to eliminate them. This was a safer way to rid the area of mosquitoes, because flooding, plus the building of dikes, was a way to control the water levels, making them too deep for mosquitoes to breed, but this led to other problems. High salt marsh plants can only tolerate flooding for short periods, and the area was invaded by other vegetation, shrubs mostly, which differed from the cordgrass that was a crucial plant in our natural habitat. We tried to move elsewhere . . . but there was nowhere to go. Our habitat had been permanently altered, and these changed conditions provided access for new predators, such as snakes, rodents and raccoons, who had either been absent or less frequent visitors before. Our young and eggs were eaten, and then the invading shrubs became home to perching red-winged blackbirds, who chased us. Flooding had encouraged fresh-water vegetation, which did not suit us and culminated in the loss of our habitat, of our nesting grounds.

Another blow was the decision to build a road on top of the marsh. This highway, known as the Beeline, was built in order to connect the Kennedy Space Center to Walt Disney World, and it went directly through and over our habitat. The rest of the area was eventually drained and sold off as real estate. This meant that there was no programme put in place to help bring back our habitat. To be quite frank, there were individuals who did not look favourably upon the expansion of our refuge, suggesting that the area could be put to better use, such as for grazing. In 1966 we were declared an endangered species by the U.S. Fish and Wildlife Service. In the same year, the U.S. Congress passed the Endangered Species Act of 1966, and we, the dusky seaside sparrow, were on that first list of threatened and endangered species. In 1968 researchers were able to count about nine hundred of us.[428] We were officially classed as endangered under the 1973

Endangered Species Act. Sadly, our numbers continued to decline; by 1977 there were only 28 pairs, and by 1979 just 13 remained.[429]

Between 1973 and 1976, extensive wildfires in the area caused further damage. In the winter of 1973, 690 hectares (1,700 ac) were burned, and only 54 of us were counted. There were two fires in 1974, and only 37 of us could be found.[430] Fires were important in the maintenance of grasslands: natural fires started by lightning strikes in the wet season, every five to eight years or so, were sufficient to stop the encroachment of woody vegetation. Sadly, some ranchers preferred more frequent burnings, and they often lit fires adjacent to our marshes in the dry season, which damaged the marsh and caused loss of bird life.[431] In December 1975 a rancher set fire to his land near the St Johns National Wildlife Refuge. Strong winds fuelled the fire, and all 850 hectares (2,100 ac) of our habitat were incinerated. There was loss of bird life; by the following spring, only eleven of us could be counted.[432] By 1980 no pairs were left. Only small scraps of salt marsh remained on St Johns National Wildlife Refuge, and none in the Merritt Island National Wildlife Refuge. We had a small habitat; once that was gone, we had nowhere else to live.

People did try to save us – I have to mention that, but conservation efforts were small and had missed the cut-off date. The last six individuals were caught and banded: Green, Orange, Blue, White, Red and Yellow. In 1981 all but Green Band were captured (meaning he was probably the last dusky to die in the wild) and brought into captivity, taken to a breeding facility in Gainesville, Florida, away from our salt marshes, or what was left of them.[433] Red Band died soon after capture, but the others survived in captivity and were moved to a number of different locations. For a while, there was support for the breeding programme, but it was doomed to fail, because those dusky seaside sparrows were all male – a hindrance before you start. Do the maths: it wasn't going to work! The last female dusky seaside sparrow had been sighted in 1975 or 1976. In 1983 the last four living specimens were taken to Walt Disney World, in a protected environment on the Discovery Island nature reserve, to carry on crossbreeding efforts. The idea was to mate them with female Scott's seaside sparrows, which inhabited the Gulf Coast of Florida. Even though we lived in a closer geographical range to the Scott's seaside sparrow (*A. m. peninsulae*), we were more closely related to other Atlantic coastal seaside sparrows.[434]

Such a trial would have created a hybrid and should never have been attempted.[435] Support for this crossbreeding programme was withdrawn, but not before one Scott's female 'accidentally' entered the cage of a dusky, leading to the birth of three chicks.[436] Over time, these three hybrids died.

By 31 March 1986, one-eyed Orange Band was the only dusky seaside sparrow still alive. The last of us, the sole heir, an elderly dusky seaside sparrow (for he was between nine and thirteen years of age, which made him a senior, or a 'great-uncle'), died on 17 June 1987, in Walt Disney World's Discovery Island zoological park in Orlando, Florida.[437] He didn't remain at 'the happiest place on Earth'; instead, he is encased in his own capsule, not an amusement ride (for there is nothing amusing about death, and even less about extinction), but a small glass bottle in the Ornithology Collection at the Florida Museum of Natural History, his ruffled feathers almost filling the jar. Orange Band had lived at Walt Disney World; perhaps a ride at the entertainment resort could be named in his honour, maybe the 'Dusky Seaside Sparrow Shuttle'? Sorry, irony doesn't become any species. Parts of Orange Band's body tissues have been frozen, kept on ice for genetic analysis.[438]

At least we weren't eaten, or hunted. Our extinction was due solely to loss of habitat and pesticides. There is a lesson – at least one, probably more – from our story. Ecosystems are delicate, finely balanced environments; changes wreak havoc on all of the species living in a given area. We are extinct, but what about the other creatures that lived in that salt marsh? Did they disappear as well? Perhaps unacknowledged. Can one mourn that which one never knew? What ghosts haunt that region? We do have a claim to fame: it is thought that we are the most recent, well-documented extinction of a vertebrate in the United States. That may be the case, but we didn't rate a death notice in *Audubon*, the journal of the National Audubon Society.[439] The death of the last of our species did, however, prompt Brian Sharp, a former biologist who had once been stationed at Merritt Island and had fallen under our spell, to pen an epitaph to us. Its heartbreaking beauty includes these words:

It has been suggested that you might not be missed. To think that a necklace would never miss one of its pearls, or a song one of its notes. Neither this spring, nor ever again, will your exuberant performances appear on nature's stage . . . Your loss is our world and ourselves diminished.[440]

Another claim to fame is that a song was written about us, not our own buzz song but a beautiful song nonetheless, written and recorded by Ron Vaughan. This song, entitled 'One Lonely Sparrow', was dedicated to Orange Band.[441]

We may have been small, insignificant, but living across the road from NASA, we duskies were more beautiful than any rocket blasting into space. Later we were confined, captives in Walt Disney World, because our 'happiest place on Earth' no longer existed.

❀ ❀ ❀

The Golden Toad

(*Incilius periglenes*) (1989): in the family Bufonidae, classifying us as a 'true toad'. 'Toad' has been associated with the ugly, the antisocial, those on the edge. Witches, hags: we were their familiars.

Warts. Poison. The dark side of the fairy tale.

We were toads but quite different from the brown, drab-coloured ones, because we were startling, an explosion of colour!

We were once described as 'dazzling bright . . . posed like statues – jewels scattered about the dim understory'.[442] Jewels. Precious. Priceless. Treasure. Our species name *periglenes* is from the Greek, meaning 'very bright'. Bright, sparkling, shiny. We were, like many gems, a late discovery. It wasn't until 1964 that we were 'discovered' (strange term, 'discovered', isn't it? We already existed – we didn't need 'discovering' or 'finding') and then described by herpetologist Jay Savage. When he first encountered several males, he was overwhelmed: 'I must confess that my initial response when I saw them was one of disbelief and suspicion that someone had dipped the examples in enamel paint. The females proved to be equally astonishing . . . the most spectacularly colored *Bufo* known and is among the gaudiest of anurans.'[443]

We were also known as the Monte Verde toad, the golden toad of Monteverde, the Alajuela toad and the orange toad. We sounded more exotic in other languages: *gylden tudse* (Danish), *gouden pad* (Dutch), *Goldkröte* (German), *rospo d'oro* (Italian) and, the one I love most because it is so long, *sapo dorado de Monteverde* (Spanish).

We are often lauded as the pin-up, the 'poster amphibian', pointing to the decline in the amphibian population and species and at the same time highlighting the first documented 'casualty' of, or extinction due to, climate change.[444] We were thought to be Costa Rica's first extinction caused by global warming. This was different from the days following our 'discovery', when we graced posters, promoting the tourist industry and persuading people to visit Costa Rica and experience its rich plant and animal life.

I would have preferred to have just continued to dazzle the occasional observer with my bright-orange skin, which contrasted beautifully against the lush green foliage of my cloud forest home. We lived in a high-altitude (elevation of 1,500–1,620 metres (4,900–5,300 ft), wet, mountainous rainforest region on the Cordillera de Tilarán, on the divide between Puntarenas and Alajuela provinces, in northern Costa Rica.[445] Our cloud forest home was small, approximately 0.5 by 8 kilometres (0.3 by 5 mi.), within the Monteverde Cloud Forest Reserve.[446] We lived nowhere else in the world. This area had an average annual rainfall of between 3,000 millimetres (118 in.) and 6,000 millimetres (236 in.) in much of the forest region, where we lived.[447] The forest received heavy rains most days, so was shrouded in clouds or fog. The forest canopy was lush, the twisted limbs and trunks of trees dark, the soil black, covered in fallen, decomposing leaves. It was a forest of a grim fairy tale: cool, dark, dripping wet, enveloped in the stench of decaying vegetation. At night there was no light entry, so it was dark, pitch black.

We were a bright, sparkly gem in the jewel box of species. Male and female golden toads were markedly different in colour, yet both were shimmering 'bling'. We were known for our extreme sexual dimorphism: the males were a brilliant, bright orange, the females more olive to black, with scarlet smudges edged in yellow. Both male and female shone, but only when we reached adulthood could you tell the genders apart. The females were larger than the males: between 42 and 56 millimetres (1⅔–2⅕ in.) in length, whereas the males were 39–48 millimetres (1½–2 in.). We had fairly smooth skin, although we did have warts: however, these were granular, not large and unbecoming. They were mainly on the upper surface and were tipped with small, black pointed spines. Only the toes of our hind feet were webbed, near the base. We had quite a long lifespan of ten to twelve years.

The heavy rainy season, the months of April through to June, were our breeding months, and we were passionate about this activity! Enormous numbers of us (when we existed) would congregate around small pools of water in the forest. Many males would gather at the small pools or puddles, waiting for the females to arrive. There were always more males than females, often a ratio of 8:1, so there was fierce competition to win the females. Sometimes non-paired males would try to separate a mating pair – we were desperate! If mating was successful, between two hundred and four hundred eggs would be produced, and the larvae would remain in the pool of water for up to five weeks, developing. After the mating activity had finished, we would return to our burrows. Did we remain in our burrows during the other seasons of the year? We had only been studied during our breeding season, so much about our behaviour during other seasons remains unknown, including a decisive list of our dietary habits. We remain an enigma, because crucial information about our habits died with us.

We were quite vulnerable when it came to breeding: we had a narrow window of time in which to breed, but we needed the correct amount of water in order to produce and then mature our thousands of eggs. If there was too much rain, our eggs would drift away, and if too little, the eggs would dry up, or desiccate. The year 1987 brought on a 'dry' season: 'Every day the ground is drier and the pools contain less water. Today's observations are discouraging. Most of the pools have dried completely, leaving behind desiccated eggs already covered in mold.'[448]

The last recorded breeding spree was thought to have taken place during April–May 1987. Not a success. Water dried up before our eggs hatched, so that out of 30,000 potential toads, there were only 29.[449] Yes, 29! Our population crashed, big time. Only a few were reported in the following years (in 1988 the numbers had declined to ten or eleven). Such a sharp, deep decline – how could any creature come back from those minuscule numbers?

The date 15 May 1989 was the last recorded sighting of me, a solitary male, this precious amphibian. Was I the lone one that behavioural

Golden toad (*Incilius periglenes*) in its natural habitat,
Monteverde, Costa Rica, 1987.

ecologist Marty Crump had seen twelve months earlier? If I was, then
I had been keeping vigil for my other toads, faithful to the end, but the
wait was in vain.

Why? How did this happen? This was a region pretty much free from
direct human contact, so what threatened our small ecosystem? There
are several theories: erratic weather linked to global warming and the
El Niño–Southern Oscillation; our restricted range, which made deforestation an issue; chytridiomycosis and other diseases; and airborne pollution.
We were also thought to be vulnerable to ultraviolet light.

Which was it? Perhaps all of the above. The threats were interwoven,
and it was hard to separate one from the other. For example, researchers
have suggested that one of the culprits was ultraviolet light, which ham-
pered the development of toad embryos, and could have rendered us more
susceptible to a fatal chytrid-type fungal disease.[450] This, in turn, makes
those embryos more vulnerable to the disease, a disease which was killing
many amphibians around the world, not just us. Now, the toad embryos
were receiving more ultraviolet light because the pools of water in which
the eggs had been deposited were much shallower, because there had
been less rain. Rainfall had diminished significantly since 1976, owing to

El Niño-like weather conditions.[451] Changes in water levels may have been small at the beginning, but they were significant enough to change the course of our lives.

We lived in burrows but were active during daylight hours. Our forest cover was changing, our skin was drying out. Since 1976, during the dry season, the number of days without mist had increased. Moisture was vital for us and for many other creatures who shared the forest. Now the cloud line was above the forest, above the tree tops, whereas before it had been below the forest. If you find this difficult to imagine, think of a dress on a growing child . . . each year more leg is exposed . . . less cover – a rising hemline. By the time of the dry season of 1987, climate change had gone beyond the point of reversal, meaning that the whole of our habitat on the mountaintop was in trouble: the rising cloud line still meant shade, but now there was no mist.[452] These increasing numbers of days without mist were a trial for us golden toads; our skin was permeable and needed moisture. We wandered through our ecosystem during the day, but we were now vulnerable to desiccation. The drier conditions were dangerous. This erratic weather behaviour interfered with our reproductive efforts. Why didn't we stay in our burrows during the day? We weren't a noisy species – we were incapable of much vocalization because we had no vocal sacs or slits. It is thought that we had two calls: a release call and one given by the male during mating (we did become quite vocal during the mating season).[453] Our calls were quite soft and did not carry over a great distance. If you had bedded down on our mountain, you wouldn't have been kept awake by us. We tended to communicate via visual cues, by being physically present, in the flesh, so to speak, rather than relying on acoustics. That was probably the main reason we were the colours we were.

We were stunning, beautiful and precious, a necklace, but our chain's links were tarnished, corroded by climate change, disease and pollution. All you need is one or two loops to snap . . . then the gems come off, the jewels are lost. In our case, forever. I would have preferred to have continued to sparkle brightly, set off against the deep green of my cloud forest. Remember, males were orange, amber, the traffic-light colour for warning, the hue of vests worn by tradespeople so they can be easily seen. May we serve as a warning: keep watch over your remaining jewels, the gems of creation. Toads feature in many fairy tales, sometimes connected with precious gold, or with jewels such as diamonds.[454] Who knew that we, golden toads, were the embodiment of that valuable gold and needed protection? In many legends, toads are guardians of treasure. In this case, *we* were the treasure.

❊ ❊ ❊

The Pyrenean Ibex

(*Capra pyrenaica pyrenaica*) ('Celia', 2000): I was sort of the last – I will come to that, so be patient. All you need to know for now is that my name was Celia. I was the last *natural* Pyrenean ibex (do you detect a whiff of mystery?), also known by our Spanish name, *bucardo*, one of four subspecies of the Iberian ibex (Iberian wild goat, or Spanish ibex). A simpler name: wild goats. We had moved into mountainous regions 18,000 years ago, near the end of the Ice Age, accompanied by several closely related subspecies. One of the other subspecies, the Portuguese ibex, has also become extinct – the last known sighting of it was back in 1892.

We were hefty: the males weighed between 58 and 68 kilograms (128–50 lb). The markings of the male were grey and brown, with black on the mane, forelegs and forehead, but the females had brown fur and no black markings and were sometimes mistaken for deer. Our fur was short during the summer months, but for winter it grew long and thick, except on our necks; that fur remained short all year round. Young ibexes were brown, as the females were.

Our horns were impressive, especially those of the male. They were large, thick and curved outwards, between 78 and 100 centimetres (31–9 in.) in length. The females had shorter horns which were cylindrical in form. In a nineteenth-century book about hunting, lengths and girths of our horns were listed and compared.[455] The number of ridges that developed on the horns as we aged was thought to be an indicator of age, a bit like circles on a tree trunk. Our stunning horns made it easy to identify us among the animals painted on cave walls in southern France 30,000 years ago, and from the fifteenth century we have graced modern artwork, because we *were* breathtaking.[456]

We used to have a wide range, living in Spain, France, Portugal and Andorra. Large numbers of us roamed the Pyrenees (hence our name), near the French border, until our numbers started to decline in the nineteenth century and into the twentieth century, not helped by ongoing hunting. We lived in rocky regions and loved cliffs. We were quite the athletes: we could jump 1.8 metres (6 ft) without needing to take a running start and were able to climb near-vertical rock faces and leap across wide precipices. Our agility made it difficult for most predators to catch us, but having said that, when we perched on outlying rocks atop cliffs, this made us easy targets for skilled gunmen. We were highly sought after – something harder to obtain is often more highly prized.

In spring, we inhabited high regions, where we would mate. Females would migrate to more isolated areas, away from the males, to give birth in May (we usually gave birth to one kid), and then in winter we would descend to areas less covered in snow, because we could adapt to terrain that had short, hardy shrubs, or grasses. Our love of grass, herbs and lichens, combined with easy access to these food items, meant we were attracted to farmland. This led to competition with domestic animals, such as sheep, horses and domestic goats, and the land became overgrazed.

Some suggest that our inability to compete with other species for food, plus our high susceptibility to infections and diseases such as the bluetongue virus, which we contracted through contact with domestic

Celia, the last Pyrenean ibex (*Capra pyrenaica pyrenaica*).

animals, were reasons for our extinction. Of course, hunting and later, after we were protected, poaching (people wanted our enormous horns for their walls) were the main reasons, but the whole picture of why we went extinct is still shrouded in mystery. As I have already mentioned, during the past two centuries, our numbers declined. This observation was noted in a document as early as 1767, stating that we were becoming rare.[457] During the 1950s and '60s, our population decline continued to be a concern. Conservation measures were put in place to try to increase our dwindling numbers. In 1973 we were, finally, declared a protected species (or subspecies) but even so, our numbers continued to plummet until there were only thirty of us remaining, our last habitat being the Ordesa y Monte Perdido National Park, in the Spanish Central Pyrenees, near the French border. In 1982 authorities enlarged the park, but it was too late. Once – oh, in our heyday – there would have been 50,000 of us gracing high cliffs and the mountains, but by 1989 there were only six to fourteen of us.[458] In 1996 the IUCN declared us to be critically endangered. Though low in number, we were still regarded as the most important species (or subspecies) in the national park. Low numbers decreased our gene pool, which was already genetically weakened by low genetic diversity and inbreeding, partly a consequence of being restricted by the park's borders. We had a low rate of fertility, too, so this small population was not viable . . . it was only a matter of time until we became extinct.

We had fans among conservationists and other scientists, people try-ing to keep us going, against all odds. Even the Spanish authorities were becoming concerned about our small numbers. In 1989 a vet by the name of Alberto Fernández-Arias became involved in developing methods for artificial or assisted insemination of us. Matters worsened, though, because the last male Pyrenean ibex was sighted in 1991.[459] This really signalled the end of the dream of capturing wild ibexes and starting a breeding programme. The team didn't give up, carrying out experiments between close relatives of ours from southern Spain and ordinary nanny goats. This marked the beginning of a number of years of unsuccessful experiments, resulting in numerous miscarriages and stillborn young. Perhaps this was partly due to stress: captured wild Spanish ibexes were highly stressed, so eggs remained unfertilized. Some suggested that the domestic goat uterus was incompatible with the Spanish ibex embryo.[460] Did this mean that there was a cross-species barrier? Sadly, by the time scientists had managed to succeed, with goat surrogates giving birth to healthy ibexes, there was only one Pyrenean ibex left: me, Celia. Yes, I was the last. Scientists tried to mate me, but these attempts were unsuccessful; I was old, sterile and had congenital heart problems. I was probably a product of inbreeding too – so I came with some baggage![461]

Now, at the beginning of my ramble, I mentioned that I was the last *natural* Pyrenean ibex to go extinct. We were the first taxon to become 'de-extinct', but this was not a quick process. Now, have you wondered why I have a name? The reason is because I became part of a conservation programme. On 20 April 1999 I was caught in a trap, captured by a team of scientists (oh, I was scared! Handled by humans!), fitted with a radio transmitter, and blood and tissue samples were taken.[462] The tissue came from skin cells scraped from my ear, the cells preserved in liquid nitrogen. These cells were collected to use in the new science of cloning. This was a fortuitous move by the scientists because nine months later, on 6 January, my tracking device gave off a long, steady beep, which alerted park rangers that I was in trouble.[463] When they found me near the French border, I was dead, having been crushed by a falling tree. My end was so quick, I do not remember it. It was better than starving, or being attacked by a predator, or shot. Pyrenean ibexes had lifespans of between twelve and seventeen years; I had been fortunate, living to thirteen.

Eventually we, the Pyrenean ibex, had the fortune (or should I say *mis*fortune) to be the first creature to become 'de-extinct', the first species 'resurrected', thanks, in part, to me. Scientists used a cloning technique known as nuclear transfer, a method similar to the one used to clone Dolly the sheep seven years earlier. Genetic material was removed from the eggs of domestic goats and replaced with DNA from my tissue sample. Over four hundred embryos were formed, but only seven of the potential surrogate hosts, who were domestic goats, ibexes or hybrids of wild and domestic goats, became pregnant, and only one (a hybrid of a Spanish ibex and a goat) made it through pregnancy without miscarrying.[464] On 30 July 2003, extinction was reversed, the clock turned back, because a cloned female ibex, weighing 2 kilograms (4½ lb), was born via caesarean section. The kid had short, thick, grey-brown fur, a dark muzzle, a short tail and long, kicking legs. She had a normal heartbeat and wide-open eyes. Sadly, her life ended within minutes, her death caused by a lung defect, which meant she suffocated shortly after birth. (Some argue whether it was several minutes or ten minutes. Does it matter? She did not survive.) She had been born with an extra lobe in her left lung. This lobe was hard, lacking the sponginess of a normal lung, and it took up too much space in her chest cavity.[465] This meant that her left lung couldn't inflate properly; her lungs struggled to fill with air . . . she couldn't breathe, poor love. All her other organs appeared to be normal. Perhaps there were flaws in my DNA. Even though my cells had been preserved in ice, DNA degrades over time, so there may have been gaps in vital genetic information that is required to produce a healthy animal. There were also gaps in knowledge about my taxonomy: there was much scientists did not know about the Pyrenean ibex, much they will now never learn. I wouldn't really know about this . . . just repeating what I have heard . . . I am, or was, just a wild goat. An old wild goat. Maybe that too was part of the reason: the age of my tissue sample; it came from a fairly old Celia – I was not young when humans trapped me. If I had been in my prime, I may have been able to escape their clutches . . . and there would have been no cloning, no 'resurrection', no 'de-extinction'.

Old DNA, gaps, genetic mutations . . . do the causes really matter? She died. My kid. Her death meant that we, the Pyrenean ibex, were the first species or subspecies to have been declared extinct twice. I would have preferred to have won a competition for having 'the longest horns', or 'the feistiest temper'. I can't help wondering, though; I really can't stop wondering – after all, she *was* part of me – if she had survived, what then? There wasn't a Pyrenean male ibex anywhere, so she wouldn't have been able to produce a pure-blood Pyrenean ibex. Even if there had been a successful pregnancy with a subspecies of ibex, it still wouldn't have resulted in a Pyrenean ibex. Dreams, musings, wonderings. I wonder about all those stillbirths and miscarriages. There is a price to pay for attempting to resurrect a species, a species that will not be 'pure' anyway. Reviving extinct species needs to be balanced against saving endangered species. It's a bit of a balancing act, like the way we would scramble up rocks and skip away from danger . . . for a time.

I had my moment of glory, of fame. I was the 'hope' of 'de-extinction', the reason for the quickened heartbeats of several scientists. There are photos of me – I was a bit of a celebrity, with a pretty name to boot. Have I gone the way of today's celebrities, remembered for a brief time and then quickly forgotten, replaced by another? My profile should be as high as that of Dolly the sheep.

But . . . one ibex remains in the Ordesa y Monte Perdido National in Aragon. Me. I am preserved behind glass in the visitor's centre. I hope that my taxidermy form will inspire humans to care for the creatures that still exist on this Earth. My body may not rest deep in the ground, covered by dirt and rock, closed off from prying eyes, but I may serve a higher purpose, as a warning that magnificent animals are disappearing before your eyes. Conservationists are studying our extinction, gleaning ways to save endangered wild tigers who face similar problems, such as isolation, contracting diseases from domestic animals, inbreeding and fertility problems.[466] Conservation measures came too late for us; may time favour the tiger.

'Celia' means 'heavenly', an accidental reference to the place where the Pyrenean ibex now resides. 'Celia' can also be a contraction of 'Cecilia', meaning 'blind', but my glass eyes 'see': they watch all who enter through that door; its lintel frames my former home of rock and wildness. Keep your eyes open to the beauty and wonder of this earthly plain.

❀ ❀ ❀

The Baiji (Yangtze River) Dolphin

'If we can't save an appealing and charismatic dolphin – one that has lived on earth for more than twenty million years – what can we save?'[467]

(*Lipotes vexillifer*) (last authenticated sighting of a wild one was in 2002; declared functionally extinct 2006): *bai ji* means 'white dolphin' in Chinese: white is the colour of innocence, of sacredness. Our undersides, our bellies, were white, but our backs were a beautiful bluish-grey. Regardless of our colour, we were intertwined with divinity, viewed as symbols of purity, peace and innocence in our native China. These are recurring themes in many of the stories and legends about us.

In one story, a cruel stepfather beats his stepdaughter. He sets out to sell her, but as he crosses the Yangtze River (in China), a storm descends, wetting them. He sees her wet, young body and is consumed with lust. She breaks away and throws herself into the swirling water, transformed into a beautiful white dolphin, a baiji.[468] Another tale concerns an unfortunate general, who had been away from home for many years and mistakenly ends up sleeping with his daughter. When he realizes this, he throws himself into the Yangtze River and is changed into a porpoise. His daughter chases him into the waves and becomes a baiji.[499] There are many such folk tales, some more than 2,000 years old, the narrative changing slightly depending on the region that is edged next to the mighty Yangtze. For many fishermen and boatmen, we were revered as the incarnation of a protective river goddess. Some say that we were the reincarnation of a princess. This princess, now a goddess, had refused to marry a man chosen by her family, causing great shame and loss of face, so her father drowned her.[470] We were believed to be predictors of the weather, early weather forecasters: we were known as 'the worshipper of the wind' – if we were observed diving in and out of the waves, that meant strong winds or waves were on their way.[471]

We were prominent in legends and poetry, but we were also mentioned in academic texts. The oldest known reference to us is found in a work known as the *Er Ya* (*Erya, Erh-ya*), an early Chinese dictionary or lexicon. Researchers suggest that it dates from the third century BCE. Whoever wrote it got us wrong: in the *Er Ya*, we are described as being a type of shark.[472] One thing that is a little strange is that despite our high profile, we weren't subject-matter for classical Chinese art, such as sculpture, ceramics or painting.[473] I say 'strange' because other animals, such as the tiger, crane and even shrimp and fish, were drawn or modelled.

We were river dolphins, the only member of the mammal family called Lipotidae, and were not closely related to any living species of dolphin. Parts of our skeletons and our stomachs were unique: our stomachs were divided into three compartments.[474] So the extinction of the baiji meant the extinction of the entire ancient Lipotidae family. We, the Lipotidae, had separated from other river dolphins 16–20 million years ago, during the Miocene epoch. Our ancestors were marine dolphins who had managed to swim upriver and had evolved to living in fresh water. We were not the only species of river dolphin, but we were probably the first fresh-water species that became extinct due to humans. We were about 2.5 metres (8 ft) long and a hefty 167–220 kilograms (368–485 lb) in weight and had small heads; long, thin beaks – which were slightly upturned; many small, sharp teeth; and long mouth lines, so we looked as if we were smiling. If fortunate, we could live for 24 years. Females bred every two years. After a gestation period of ten-to-eleven months, a female birthed a single calf. This precious calf was nursed for many months. We had broad flippers and low, triangular dorsal fins. These white fins resembled light-coloured flags when spotted just below the surface of the murky waters of the Yangtze. This was another name gifted to us: 'white flag'. Our species name *vexillifer* means 'flag bearer'.[475] A white flag means 'surrender', doesn't it? If we had been carrying a red flag, maybe our circumstances would have changed for the better. An early warning: danger.

Most species of river dolphin have poor eyesight or are blind.[476] We, the baiji, had very small eyes and poor vision, but we managed by the skill of echolocation, or sonar.[477] We built up our own sound picture, with clicks and their echoes.[478] Echolocation was a vital tool. It helped us navigate for food and avoid predators. It also kept us in our groups. We lived in small groups of two to six, were quiet and shy, and were difficult to approach, and, unlike some dolphin species, we avoided boats. We were unique to China, confined solely to the great Yangtze and several of the lakes that were attached to that massive body of water, found in the middle and lower reaches, from the Three Gorges to the mouth of the Yangtze. This meant that we lived in a 1,700-kilometre (1,000 mi.) stretch of the great Yangtze. According to the writings of Guo Pu, a scholar of the Jin dynasty, the Yangtze was 'teeming' with baiji.[479] The great and mighty Yangtze was our mother, our whole world.

We were known in our homeland, revered for most of our time on this Earth, in our great mother water, but for those in the West, we were not 'discovered' until 1914, and then it was via a youth, a seventeen-year-old American named Charles Hoy, who had managed to shoot one of us near Chenglingji.[480] He took a photograph of the dead baiji and carted its skull and a couple of its vertebrae back to his country. Their final destination was the Smithsonian, and within that hallowed institution, far from our mighty river, scientists announced that we were a new species. In 1918 we were formally, or scientifically, named.

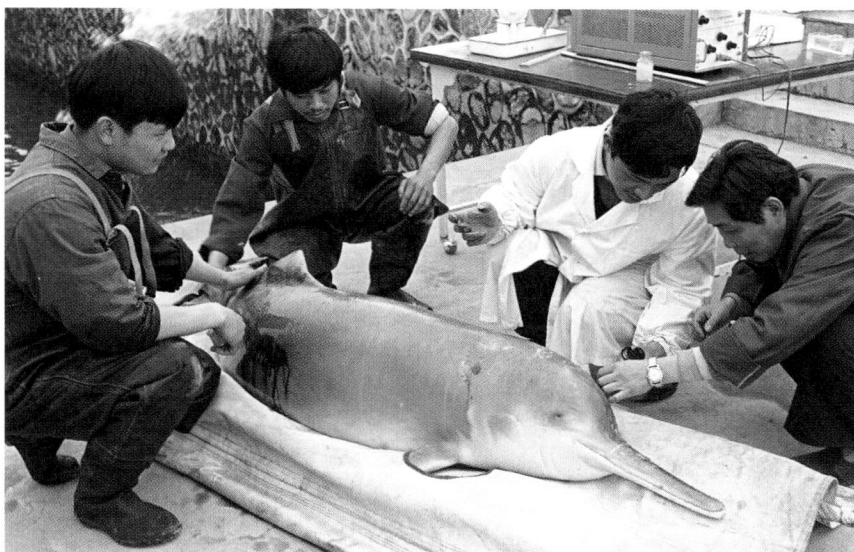

Qi Qi, the world's only captive Yangtze River dolphin (*Lipotes vexillifer*), being examined by researchers in the 1980s. Qi Qi passed away in July 2002 after living for more than 22 years at the CAS Institute of Hydrobiology in Wuhan.

Being held in reverence kept us safe; one does not usually kill that which is sacred. This changed, however, during the time of Mao Zedong, when religion and superstition were stamped out, and industrialization ruled the waves, as they say. Being stripped of our sacredness meant we could be hunted and stripped of our flesh and skin – our skins were fashioned into handbags and gloves.[481] What did that mean, wearing part of a goddess on one's hands? Power? Status? Or was it more a snubbing of beliefs, of peasant folklore? Industrialization meant huge environmental destruction as well, leading to starvation for many Chinese people. They needed a food source, so, to fill empty, gnawing bellies, they consumed what had once been sacred: the baiji. In 1994 work began to turn the magnificent Three Gorges into the largest hydroelectric dam ever built. This, of course, altered water levels and the existing sand banks. We used to congregate near sandbars, because the eddies in the water were rich in nutrients, which attracted many fish.

Other enormous (and smaller) dams were built across the Yangtze River, which served to alter the ecosystem: fish populations decreased and groups of dolphins became separated from each other. Our migratory routes were blocked, our breeding and feeding areas inaccessible. They were not the only reasons for our decline; opening up the country meant that more vessels were using the Yangtze. What used to be hundreds of boats became thousands. What noise! The density of these ships and the clamour of activity produced what is known as 'white noise', a sound that interfered with our echolocation skills, blocking out our ability to 'read' the world around us. Noise pollution served to confuse us; we became disorientated and greatly distressed. Many crashed into ships, becoming trapped, caught within the hard, rotating propellers, or became so confused that they were stranded, unable to swim.

Other factors were added to the mix that threatened us, including massive pollution, which sullied our water, our home. So many pollutants! Petroleum by-products, cyanides, heavy metals such as mercury and chromium, and synthetic chemicals. Stretches of our river became covered with oil. Fish, our food source, died of poisoning, and several massive spills of chemicals killed some of us immediately.[482] Other pollutants damaged our vital organs, triggered cancers, suppressed hormones, destroyed embryos and foetuses, and even altered the outer hair cells of our ears, causing deafness, which meant echolocation became impossible.[483] Our home, our waterway, had become home to a tenth of the world's human population: what hope did we have? Think of the amount of pollution, the run-off, the volume of water traffic, untreated sewerage. Overfishing robbed us of food, and many of us became entangled in longlines and nets and drowned. The worst of the fishing lines were the rolling hook longlines; these were about 100 metres (328 ft) long, set with about a thousand closely set, unbaited hooks. These were tied to the backs of boats, or anchored to river beds.[484] If that wasn't enough of a threat, new, extreme forms of fishing were put into place in order to catch larger numbers of fish. These methods included blasting the waters, or electrifying them.[485] How could we possibly survive?

Our numbers plummeted. In 1950 there were estimated to be between 5,000 and 6,000 of us; by 1980 that number had dropped to 400; by 1988 fewer than 200, and in 1998 it was estimated that there were only thirteen of us left in the Yangtze's waters.[486] In the 1980s attempts were made to set up a semi-natural reserve for us near the town of Tongling in Anhui province. We became popular, our name placed on beer labels,[487] cola, fertilizer . . .

we were even the name of a hotel. Tourist wishes, tourist dollars, tourist dreams . . . but there was a major problem: there were no captive baiji.

There were other efforts to save us, but bickering and incompetence halted any major progress towards securing our survival. One proposal would probably have been a success: it suggested capturing the last of us and transporting us to Tian'ezhou, an oxbow lake in Hubei province. This lake, which was alongside the Yangtze River, had a healthy fish population, as well as finless porpoises.[488] It had no ship traffic, little fishing and decreased amounts of pollution. It was hoped that we would be able to repopulate the Yangtze. In 1995 one baiji was captured and placed in the lake, but it died seven months later, having become entangled in netting.[489]

But . . . lack of money, poor planning, ignorance, incompetence and, the saddest of all, apathy, drove our decline. Many wasted years. We should have been an international conservation concern. We could have been saved. Let's just say that money – from fishing, transport and industry – became more important and that power struggles within bureaucracy, where things never move quickly, did not help matters.

One of us, though, did survive. He was captured in 1980 and became a national celebrity. He was known as Qi Qi (pronounced 'chee chee'). Several other baiji were captured, but they didn't survive for long, so attempts at breeding were unsuccessful. In 2002 Qi Qi died of old age and diabetes and was given a funeral. It was such an important occasion that it was broadcast on television. Songs were sung and flowers were placed on Qi Qi's coffin.[490]

One writer thought we had become the 'aquatic equivalent of the giant panda'.[491] There is a major problem with that analogy, being compared to the furry panda: they are still alive, whereas . . . well, the last one of us to be seen in the wild was photographed in 2002. There were expeditions to find us. In 2006 conservationists from a number of countries, including the United States, the United Kingdom and Switzerland, conducted an intensive six-week search for us, covering more than 3,500 kilometres (2,000 mi.) of the Yangtze without finding a single baiji.[492] High-powered binoculars, whistles to tune in to our echolocation . . . all to no avail . . . they were too late; by then, we were extinct.

We, the river goddess, the baiji, revered for centuries; we swift of fin, who loved our Mother Yangtze; of water, from water, we, we were put in the record books, placed on the ıucn extinct list, and became the first documented global extinction of a cetacean in recent history. We, the baiji, who swam in the Yangtze for 20 million years, became extinct within fifty years, due to human activity. An entire family of river dolphin, the only species in the genus *Lipotes* – which, interestingly, means 'left behind' – is no more. None have been 'left behind'; instead, the baiji have swum ahead, to join other divinities. Glimpses of the river goddess have disappeared, her stories preserved within the Yangtze's polluted depths and confined within pages and memories.

❄ ❄ ❄

The Pinta Island Tortoise

(*Chelonoidis abingdonii*) ('Lonesome George', 24 June 2012): hello, there. George here. Well . . . Lonesome George.

I was a species of Galápagos tortoise, found on Ecuador's volcanic Pinta Island, the northernmost of the larger islands of the Galápagos. This 60-square-kilometre (23 sq. mi.) island does not consist of fantastic island habitat, though, because Pinta houses an active shield volcano. We giant tortoises became well known: by the 1570s, the Spanish 'Insulae de los Galopegos' ('The Islands of the Tortoises') was even written on maps.[493] Other maps and oral reports enabled whalers and fur traders in the 1800s to find us on their way through these island-strewn waters. We, a supposedly delicious meal, were hunted and eaten – and there was plenty of flesh! And oil! Introduced species ate our eggs and our young hatchlings. At one stage, the Galápagos were home to fifteen species of tortoise. Sadly, four of these species are extinct, including my species, *Chelonoidis abingdonii*. We were the world's largest land-living, cold-blooded animal; our numbers decreased until there was just me. I became an 'endling', the last Pinta Island tortoise.

I had been left alone for most of my life, free from the awful encounters with humans that my forebears had to deal with, when tortoises were an easy and plentiful food supply. I was not 'discovered' or 'found' by humans until I was about seventy years old. I was never meant to be found! It was thought that my species had become extinct in the early part of the twentieth century. Pinta Island was quiet, uninhabited by humans, but I was not alone. There were gulls and hawks, fur seals and iguanas aplenty. In 1959 our habitat changed because several goats were released there by fishermen. These goats were to provide them with a ready source of meat, a job my ancestors had fulfilled. Now, creatures have a habit of multiplying – procreation is one of our urges (more about mine later). By 1970 those couple of goats had become a sizeable 20,000, which, of course, destroyed much of the island's vegetation.[494]

Well, around this time, on 1 December 1971, American snail biologist Joseph Vagvolgyi and his wife Maria spotted me, a giant tortoise, on their expedition to Pinta Island. Quite a change in size, eh? Joseph recorded our meeting: 'The tortoise was walking slowly when we first encountered him, but withdrew into his shell with a loud hiss as we moved closer to take his picture . . . he soon relaxed, and resumed his walk.'[495] What was surprising was that they just accepted that I was there and didn't regard this sighting as monumental, whereas for many, this would have been so incredible, because the last one of us was thought to have been collected back in 1906. The return of the dead! Interesting that the Spanish word *pinta* means 'spotted' and was the name given to my island. *Pinta* had been the name of one of Columbus's ships. Well, this snail man had spotted me – a bit hard to miss, I suppose . . . but why had I not been 'spotted' or 'found'

Lonesome George, the last known Pinta Island tortoise
(*Chelonoidis abingdonii*), who died in 2012.

earlier? Vagvolgyi's report led to several Galápagos National Park rangers capturing (or 'rescuing') me the following year, in order to bring me to a safer environment and with the intention of having me breed. My new and last home was the Tortoise Centre, part of the Charles Darwin Research Station, on Santa Cruz. I became famous, billed as 'the rarest creature on Earth' (what tosh!), an icon for the conservation movement and an entry in the Guinness World Records as 'the world's rarest living creature'.

My name – how did I acquire such a mournful name? Apparently, I was named after an American comedian, George Gobel, who was known as 'Lonesome George'; I didn't mind the connection to fame, or being named (meaningless to me; 'naming' is a human construct), but in my case, there was nothing funny about it.

Now, I know I was special, and that there was quite some excitement around the 'find', but no female Pinta tortoises could be found, either on Pinta Island or in any of the many zoos around the world. They tried to mate me with other giant tortoises, including two Española Island tortoises (*C. hoodensis*), which are closely related to my species, the Pinta, but the eggs did not produce any viable offspring, and if they had, they would have been hybrids, never pure giant Pinta tortoises.

Why were the eggs produced during this thirteen-year period infertile? Was it because of the mix of species, or were other factors at play? Biologists have pondered this, putting forward several reasons. One hypothesis is that I had been living in isolation for many years and therefore was deficient in terms of lessons in sexual behaviour.[496] I am not sure about this; I think my instincts would have helped me along in that department. Another suggestion is that sometimes mating comes about as a result of male competitiveness. I might have needed a dose of dominance, or sparring, to get, well, into the 'mood'. A ritual, such as raising one's head as high as possible and delivering a bite to the opponent, might also attract a mate.[497] How one reacts to and with others – our social life, I suppose – could be the difference between success and well . . . no young. All fine theories, but that is what they remain – theories. There was only me, and yes, I wasn't interested in the females. Perhaps if there had been another Pinta, a female Pinta Island tortoise, things would have been different. There was even a $10,000 reward offered for a female Pinta, but that money was never claimed.[498] An upside of this unsuccessful mating business is that researchers have been studying the genetics of giant tortoises in the Galápagos and have found several hybrids on Wolf Volcano on Isabela Island, with half or less Pinta ancestry. As I said earlier, they will remain hybrids only, but biologists hope these giant tortoises will populate Pinta Island again.[499] In 2010 some hybrid giant tortoises were introduced to Pinta, to help re-establish the ecosystem, assist with biodiversity and allow island foliage to recover from the damage caused by the goats (now eradicated from Pinta). We giant tortoises open up paths through forests and grasses, and our digestive tracts promote the germination and dispersal of seeds. I know there will never be a pure Pinta tortoise again, but, if these ones breed, there will be tortoises again on Pinta Island.

It is a bit embarrassing, but it needs to be said that at one time, after analysing DNA from three specimens of tortoise that had been collected on Pinta in 1906, it was thought that I might *not* be from Pinta, but had either been introduced from another island, or had found my way across from an island. What would this have done for my reputation, and for that of the Galápagos Research Centre? And for the booming tourist industry? Thankfully, another group of researchers managed to recover about three-quarters of the genetic sequence needed from the specimens to be able to say that I was from Pinta.[500] Imagine the fuss if they had come back with a different result!

One of the dangers of living in captivity is weight gain. I know I was never what one would call 'fast moving', but in confinement there was less incentive to be active. In 1980 I had a fall, and word got out that I had died. No, I was just badly hurt. Those in charge of my care thought that maybe my weight had been a contributing factor to my fall. They also discovered that I had a hormonal imbalance, so I was given medication and put on a diet![501]

Yes, I was applauded as an icon for conservation, acknowledged as a 'flagship' species, but such prominence, such fame, comes with risk: I became the target of several death threats. Yes! People chanting '*Muerte al Solitario Jorge!*' ('Death to Lonesome George!').[502] This danger came about due to disagreements between sea cucumber fishermen and conservationists. Back in 1986, the Ecuadorian government had taken measures to stop foreign fishermen entering the Galápagos, but illegal fishing had continued. On 3 January 1995, the offices of the Charles Darwin Research

Station (where I was based) and the GNPS (Galápagos National Park Service) were taken over by about thirty fishermen, and they threatened to kill the animals that were housed there (which included me!). This blockade persisted for three days. Now, this wasn't the first time I had been at risk. Back in 1992 several fishermen came to Santa Cruz and were planning to hold me hostage. Fortunately for me, and for the other animals, one of the key people at the Charles Darwin Research Station heard some rumours and had taken several precautionary measures, including swapping me for another large tortoise. Of course, I wouldn't have wanted any harm done to my tortoise 'double' (who, by the way, was female) but ... anyway, things settled down, as did the blockade in January 1995 – and another in September 1995.[503] Too much excitement for me!

I lived for nearly twenty more years, departing this Earth on Sunday, 24 June 2012. My death was thought to be caused by a cardiac arrest, at the tender age of what some scientists estimated to be about one hundred (though some put it lower, at eighty years old). I say 'tender age' because 80–100 years was still quite young, for we, the Pinta giant tortoise, could live to 150–200 years. No human has lived long enough to record our lifespan! We may have been the longest living animal on Earth. You can count the rings on tortoises' shell plates (as you would with a tree trunk), but that only works when we are young, until about the age of ten.[504] Actually, our distinctive saddleback shells were quite something; their front edges were rimmed, which allowed our long necks more room to stretch, meaning that we could grasp plants at a higher level and raise our heads high when vying for dominance.[505]

After my death, my magnificent 75-kilogram (165 lb) body was put on ice, and then it was subjected to the knife and brush, preserved as taxidermy until I looked 'like new'. This took more than a year of detailed work by George Dante, one of the best in the field. This work was not cheap: the bill exceeded $30,000, and my magnificent 75 kilograms had been reduced to about a third of that weight.[506] I was put on display at the American Museum of Natural History, in New York, but, after some controversy, I was moved back to the Galápagos. Even here there was heated discussion, the Ecuadorian government stating that its capital city, Quito, was the correct place for me, whereas others argued that the breeding station on Santa Cruz, where I spent my final forty years, was a more fitting final resting place.[507] I am now on display in the Symbol of Hope Exhibition Hall on Santa Cruz Island, in the Galápagos National Park, near my former enclosure.[508]

Back home, this is where I belong. You know, the Galápagos became well known due to a visit by Charles Darwin. I understand he used the thoughts and notes from his trip to construct what became a controversial scientific theory. Darwin had wondered whether there were different species of tortoise on different islands and had written up these ponderings and theories in his journal.[509]

Survival of the fittest? Perhaps not. Survival of the biggest? Not to be. You know, Darwin's descriptions of meeting giant tortoises were similar to those of Joseph Vagvolgyi, the snail guy. Unlike Vagvolgyi, Darwin used us for his amusement: 'I frequently got on their backs, and then, upon giving a few raps on the hinder part of the shell, they would rise up and walk away; but I found it very difficult to keep my balance.'[510] I suppose we could forgive Darwin, assuming he was so overcome by our magnificent saddleback with its frontal rim that he became confused, thinking the tortoise was a horse.

Ah, memories of my former life on the island are fading. Outside the enclosure where I lived was an information board which included these words: 'Whatever happens to this single animal, let him always remind us that the fate of all living things on Earth is in human hands.' One of your poets wrote: 'No man is an island, entire of itself.'[511] Perhaps no tortoise is an island, entire of itself . . . there is more to me, to other species of tortoises, than this giant endling.

❀ ❀ ❀

The Bramble Cay Melomys

(*Melomys rubicola*) (the IUCN declared the Bramble Cay melomys extinct in 2015. The Australian Government officially declared it extinct in 2019): Bramble Cay, Bramble Cay, Bramble Cay. Keep repeating those words. Perhaps they conjure up illustrations of an English countryside, replete with a hedgehog or two among a prickly thicket of brambles. But this is not the case. Bramble Cay is far from England, though its name came from European surveyors on HMS *Bramble*, who came across this little piece of island in 1845. A 'cay' is a small, low-lying island, formed from coral rubble, sand and sporting some vegetation. Bramble Cay is tiny, an island of just 5 hectares (12 ac), situated in the Torres Strait, off the coast of Papua New Guinea.

Water, coral, sun.
Clumps of lush vegetation.
Our Bramble Cay.

It was an idyllic setting for a small creature like us, the Bramble Cay melomys (*Melomys rubicola*), a native Australian rodent from the Muridae family. That is our scientific name; we were also known as the Bramble Cay mosaic-tailed rat, because our tails were made up of tiny, interlinking scales that resembled a mosaic (as is the case for all melomys), rather than the concentric, overlapping scales found on the tails of most mice and rats.[512] Yes, we were small but cute rodents. The negative connotations of 'rat' don't do us justice. We had large eyes and reddish-brown fur, which was lighter, almost grey-brown, on our bellies, and we were tiny enough to be cradled in your palm. It is said that we had a 'Roman nose'. The Indigenous people called us *maizub kaur mukeis*, from the Meriam Mir language.

No one is certain how we came to inhabit this little isle. Perhaps we arrived during a storm? This cay is at the northern tip of the Great Barrier Reef, so that is a possibility. Perhaps thousands of years ago there was a land bridge which we crossed? Our mode of transport remains a mystery.

We arrived, and we lived. Cut off from most of the world, among the most isolated of mammals. We had all we needed; being small, we didn't eat much. Only part of the cay had vegetation, so we stayed in the densely vegetated region, which provided us with food and shelter, and we avoided areas with high numbers of seabirds and turtles. It was warm. Life was pleasant . . . until . . . until humans interfered. No, no, *not* that they came here to destroy us. For generations Indigenous people from Erub Island sailed here to hunt turtles, birds and fish, and small numbers of Europeans arrived in the early days . . . *But* humans did destroy us . . . usually not face to face but, rather, through greed, or ignorance, or indifference . . . or apathy.

Bramble Cay melomys (*Melomys rubicola*), photographed in 2001.

We disappeared sometime between 2007 and 2011, the first mammalian species made extinct due to the effects of human-induced climate change.[513]

We loved the water
but it loved us too much.
An eternal hug.

Rising seas, with high tides, some associated with cyclonic storms, engulfed the vegetation on Bramble Cay, causing habitat loss. It is estimated that between 2004 and 2014, 97 per cent of the leafy plants that made up this cay, our home, were gone, owing to rising sea levels.[514] Once the food was gone, and we had nowhere to live, to shelter, to breed (our breeding season was quite lengthy), well, in such a remote area, it didn't take long for us to disappear forever. We *had* nowhere else to go, *could go* nowhere else. Our demise was fairly quick. In a 1979 scientific report, we were reported as numbering several hundred; in 1998 we were listed as being fewer than one hundred.[515] The last known sighting of one of us was in 2009. In 2015 our absence became official, and, based on this data, in 2015 the IUCN declared us to be extinct. The Australian government did not declare us extinct until 18 February 2019.

Hmm, the Australian government. For years several scientists had been trying to raise money for conservation; they knew our situation was precarious, but funding was not forthcoming. We were not charismatic enough; we were a rodent, not a whale or a panda. Finally, in 2011, and again in 2014, when funding and approval became available to allow us to be trapped and bred in captivity, it was too late – none of us were left. Not only had we disappeared, but tissue samples of us that had been collected earlier, to record and analyse genetic information, had vanished too.[516]

Like our tails, our tale is also a mosaic, our existence dependent on a low-lying island, with a particular habitat, but then the mosaic is flipped over, showing its underside of escalating tides of water which washed away our environment. Many of us were washed out to sea, exploring further realms, the journey ending in the depths of the ocean, our final resting place. The dark, destroying shadow side of the mosaic included scales of starvation and exposure for those who remained clinging to the cay's coral rubble, a place once associated with sweet thoughts of tropical bliss, now transformed into a nightmarish sinking grave.

The Indigenous people, who had custodial ties with this small clump of land, mourned our loss. As part of their grief, several Torres Strait islander artists, from the island of Erub (Maizub Kaur, which is the Meriam Mir name for Bramble Cay, lies 50 kilometres (31 mi.) north of Erub) created a family, or group, of Bramble Cay melomys out of waste, using ghost nets and other rubbish discarded by the fishing industry and found on shorelines. Their tribute to us has been on display at the Darwin Museum and Art Gallery, and can be viewed via a virtual gallery.[517] They hope that their work will highlight the fragility of island ecosystems and that our story serves as a cautionary tale, a call for humans to clean up their act for the health of all Earth's inhabitants.

Indigenous hands
mould our likeness from debris
a scarred warning.

A short portrait of a small creature. A mosaic of tragedy which continues, played out with further extinctions. Next time you see a mosaic, think of us, extinction scaled down, a mnemonic device.

Oh, I forgot to say that there is a tale about a group of Indigenous people, travelling from Erub to Maizub Kaur, who were turned into stone.

Some say that their ghostly canoe and its passengers, which include a mother and child, can be seen at times.[518] Who or what will be our ghosts?

❊ ❊ ❊

The Oʻahu Tree Snail

(*Achatinella apexfulva*) ('George', 1 January 2019): unlike others of my species, I had a name: I was George, an *Achatinella apexfulva*. I was also christened with another name: 'endling'.

Achatinella apexfulva: we were one of hundreds of species of snail that evolved in Hawaii. Once there were more than 750 species of land snail in Hawaii, including 200 species in the tree snail family.[519] It is thought that all species of tree snail in Hawaii are descendants of ancient molluscs. No one is sure how the snails arrived on the remote island of Oʻahu, in the Pacific – 3,800 kilometres (2,360 mi.) is a quite a distance, across the vast waters of the ocean. Perhaps as a passenger on a bird?[520] On a piece of timber washed up on shore?

Although we will never know how the first arrival occurred, what I can say is, what a family tree! The first of the 750-or-so species of land snail on Hawaii was described by European science back in 1787, when Captain George Dixon, after landing on the island, was given a lei which contained one of our shells.[521] Our species was endemic to the wet, tropical forests of the island of Oʻahu. Some species lived their entire lives on the one tree. We were not herbivores, though; instead, we fed off the fungus and algae that grew on the trees. Feeding on this fungus helped protect the trees from disease.

There were 41 *kāhuli* (the Hawaiian name for tree snail) species in the genus *Achatinella*, all either listed as endangered, or extinct. We were a colourful species, for *apexfulva* means 'yellow-tipped'. The tops of our shells tapered to a pale-mustard point. I was the size of a thumb and conical in shape and resembled a chocolate whirl, my smooth, glossy shell having brown-and-cream markings.

My species, and similar ones, have been likened to Christmas trinkets: ornate, delicately curved shells of different shades and patterns strung across trees. Not ordinary Christmas ornaments (if there *is* such a thing) but singing baubles! I understand that at Christmas time, carols are sung. We, too, would sing – or so it was thought. Our songs are enshrined in islanders' myths and legends. The singing snail has quite a ring to it. We were known as the *pūpū kani oe*, 'the shell that sounds long' or, more simply, 'the singing shell'.[522] Even the summer palace of King Kamehameha III, one of the Hawaiian kings, was called *Kaniakapupu*, 'the singing of the land shells', because it was an area rich in Oʻahu tree snails.[523] Our 'singing' was incorporated into traditional Hawaiian chants. One of them, 'Kāhuli Aku', now a popular children's song, is about snails calling to the golden plover to bring them water. Another of our 'songs' was to welcome a bridal couple: '*O ka leo o ke kahuli/ Aia i ke kuahiwi/ O ka pupu kani oe.*' (The voice of the snail/ There in the uplands/ It's the singing shell.)[524] In this love chant, the snails sing, signalling that the couple should be together.[525] We were active at night, so it was thought that this was the time when we sang, but our 'singing' was probably noise produced by chirping crickets.

Our low numbers were due to factors common in extinction stories: loss of habitat, predation and, in our case, over-collection. We were crafted into lei by the Hawaiians (some Oʻahu snail lei are still prized family heirlooms) and, like pretty and precious Christmas ornaments, collected by locals but, more particularly, by foreigners. We could be picked off a tree, placed in one's pocket as a memento of a holiday, or of a day's outing. This practice was rampant during the age of the great collectors, the Victorians. Visiting Europeans and descendants of missionaries would collect us in the thousands. Records from the nineteenth century claim that 10,000 or more shells could be gathered in a single day.[526] One individual, J. T. Gulick, an American missionary and naturalist, managed to collect an astonishing 44,500 snail shells in just three years.[527] In one report, Gulick told of riding into a forest with a group and returning late afternoon with more than 1,400 snails.[528] Foreigners would pay locals to fill up containers with us and then carry us out of the forests on horseback. Even though some collectors kept records of their finds, many of the snails were from different sites. Unfortunately, no accurate records have been found that have assisted scientific research.

We suffered a loss of habitat, because forests were felled when the land was settled by Polynesians. Hawaii had no native land mammals, but species such as pigs, goats, dogs and domestic livestock were brought in, and they altered the land. Intensive grazing damaged soil, native plants were eaten, and non-native vegetation invaded our home. Over-collecting and deforestation were also responsible for our decline, as was the fact that we were slow breeders. Another factor was that we had a number of introduced predators, the primary one being another snail. This snail, the rosy wolf snail (*Euglandina rosea*, or cannibal snail), was introduced to Hawaii in 1955 in order to control agricultural pests, particularly the introduced invasive African land snail, *Lissachatina fulica*. The introduction of the rosy wolf snail did not reduce the population of African land snails; instead, it reduced the population of the native snails! A voracious eater! It would follow snail slime trails and then consume the gastropod, often in one go (helped by its serrated tongue). Sadly, at least seven other snail extinctions in Hawaii have been hastened by this creature. You would think that snails would respect one another, wouldn't you? The rosy wolf

George the Oʻahu tree snail (*Achatinella apexfulva*),
the last of his species, who died in 2019.

snail has been placed on an IUCN list – not the list of endangered creatures, or even of extinct creatures; it has the misfortune to be included on the list of the top one hundred most invasive species. My story is a story about other snails too, isn't it?

We had other predators to contend with, including the rat and another introduced creature, Jackson's chameleon. What was a chameleon, native to East Africa, doing in Hawaii? People like exotic pets; some people even purchase illegal animals. In 1972 a pet shop owner on our island of O'ahu received a delivery of a dozen Jackson's chameleons. They seemed a bit stressed after their trip, so he let them out in his backyard, to recover. They escaped and colonized, surviving on what they could find in the wild, which included us.[529]

In 1981 O'ahu tree snails were federally listed (by the U.S. Fish and Wildlife Service) as endangered. In 1997 researchers from the University of Hawaii collected ten snails, which they believed to be the remaining specimens of *Achatinella apexfulva*.[530] This led to my unusual life: my parents were members of that last known wild population of *A. apexfulva*, found on several trees near O'ahu's Poamoho Trail. This meant that I was not born in a natural setting, the wild habitat of the tree snail; my life began and ended in an unnatural, artificially created habitat, a sort of laboratory. I was not alone there. There were offspring (kin, relatives) but by April 2011, I was on my own. I don't know what happened to the other snails, my companions – I think a disease, a pathogen, wiped them out. All gone, except for me . . . not sure why I survived . . . but I did.

Which is how, why, when and where I acquired my name: George. George. Named after the last member of the Pinta Island tortoise family. A name for a male, which didn't take into account my hermaphroditic nature, but . . . I was sexually mature from about 2012. No pressure, but researchers searched the area where they had collected the remaining *A. apexfulva*, searching for a mate for me (I may have possessed both male and female reproductive organs, but I still needed a partner), but none was found. I became the lone member of my species, living my fourteen years with scientists. Near the end of my life, I spent my days and nights with researcher David Sischo, a wildlife biologist who was in charge of the Snail Extinction Prevention Programme, a programme that cared for native endangered snails. Sischo and his team were trying to prevent further extinctions. My last two years were spent inside a specially equipped trailer, housed in a terrarium. Our living conditions (I shared lodgings with other endangered snails) were carefully monitored, with controlled lighting, temperature and humidity, trying to protect us snails from extinction. At times, there was excitement: in 2018, during the wake of Hurricane Lane, we were taken to Honolulu, in order to keep us safe, to keep us alive.

The Christmas tree. The ornaments are few, the precious Oʻahu one now permanently removed from its tree. It is not tucked away awaiting the next Christmas season, as if it were a Christmas decoration; it is simply . . . no longer there to sparkle on its tree. At fourteen years of age, it was my turn to search for the other snail baubles, who were probably twinkling rainbows, bright lights strung high on the Tree of Life. Oʻahu is nicknamed 'the gathering place'; now it was time for me to be back with other snails, no longer on my own. I understand that my bodily remains are preserved in ethanol and that my shell joins the 2 million other Hawaiian snail specimens in the Bernice Pauahi Bishop Museum's malacological collection, though a portion of my foot was removed in 2017, sent to San Diego Zoo's Institute for Conservation Research's 'Frozen Zoo' to provide DNA if they ever decide to clone me.[531] So, packed away . . . boxed or stored in several different places, my two-toned whirl a reminder of the permanency of extinction. Did you know that we, the often-overlooked, or ignored, snails, have disproportionately suffered from extinction of our members? Land snails and slugs account for approximately 40 per cent of all known animal extinctions since 1500.[532] Most people don't know that, and I would suggest that most people don't care.

Now it is your turn to sing, because my song ceased on 1 January 2019, New Year's Day. As you were singing 'Auld Lang Syne' – a phrase that means 'olden times or 'as time goes by' – as you were welcoming in the new year, there was an ending of our 'olden times', the extinction of a species, the end of the 'endling', of me, George, the last of my species. The 'endling' of a year, of a species, of a life.

Sing, sing a song of mourning for the *Achatinella apexfulva*, for George.

References

1. Extinction

1 J. M. Sinclair, ed., *Collins English Dictionary*, 3rd edn (Sydney, 2001), p. 549.

2 Perhaps it helps to think about the Holocaust and the 6 million people who perished. It is hard to imagine 6 million people, but as an individual, with his or her unique story, we then obtain entry or glimpse into something of the numbers.

3 Michael Blencowe, *Gone: A Search for What Remains of the World's Extinct Creatures* (London, 2021), p. 13.

4 American Museum of Natural History, 'Shelf Life 12: Six Extinctions in Six Minutes,' www.amnh.org, December 2015; 'Major Mass Extinctions', www.britannica.com, accessed 7 July 2024; Gabe Allen, 'The End-Ordovician Mass Extinction Wiped Out 85 Percent of Life', www.discovermagazine.com, 13 September 2022; Sam Noble Museum, 'End-Ordovician Extinction', https://samnoblemuseum.ou.edu, accessed 9 July 2024.

5 Ibid.; Advancing Earth and Space Sciences (AGU), 'Scientists Reconstruct Ancient Impact that Dwarfs Dinosaur-Extinction Blast', https://news.agu.org, 9 April 2014.

6 E. O. Wilson, *Half-Earth: Our Planet's Fight for Life* (New York, 2016), p. 9.

7 Tim Flannery and Peter Schouten, *A Gap in Nature: Exploring the World's Extinct Animals* (Melbourne, 2001), p. xvi; 'Birds are among the best-studied animal groups, but their prehistoric diversity is poorly known due to low fossilization potential. Hence, while many human-driven bird extinctions (i.e., extinctions caused directly by human activities such as hunting, as well as indirectly through human-associated impacts such as land use change, fire, and the introduction of invasive species) have been recorded, the true number is likely much larger': R. Cooke et al., 'Undiscovered Bird Extinctions Obscure the True Magnitude of Human-Driven Extinction Waves', *Nature Communication*, XIV/8116 (2023).

8 Laura Clark, 'One-Tenth of Native Mammals in Australia Are Extinct: Blame Cats And Foxes', Smithsonian Magazine, www.smithsonianmag.com, 11 February 2015.

9 Tim Green, 'The Thing about Extinction', www.bbc.co.uk/lastchancetosee, accessed 30 May 2023.

10 Ibid.

11 Catherine Finn, Florencia Grattarola and Daniel Pincheira-Donoso, 'More Losers than Winners: Investigating Anthropocene Defaunation through the Diversity of Population Trends', *Biological Reviews*, XCVIII/5 (October 2023), pp. 1732–48.

12 The IUCN Red List of Threatened Species, www.iucnredlist.org, accessed 19 March 2022.

13 Elizabeth Kolbert, *The Sixth Extinction: An Unnatural History* (London, 2014), p. 17.

14 For more information, see 'The IUCN Green Status of Species' and 'Effective Protected Areas', www.iucnredlist.org, accessed 31 May 2024.

15 M. R. O'Connor, *Resurrection Science: Conservation, De-Extinction and the Precarious Future of Wild Things* (New York, 2015), p. 121.

16 Beth Shapiro, *How to Clone a Mammoth: The Science of De-Extinction* (Princeton, NJ, 2015), p. ix; Piers Anthony, *The Source of Magic* (New York, 1979), quoted in Shapiro.

17 For more information on this particular project, and on the wider field of de-extinction, see 'How De-Extinction Works: Methods, Examples and Step-By-Step Process', Colossal Laboratories and Biosciences, https://colossal.com, accessed 31 May 2024, and Revive & Restore, https://reviverestore.org, accessed 31 May 2024.

18 Torill Kornfeldt, *The Re-Origin of Species: A Second Chance for Extinct Animals*, trans. Fiona Graham (Brunswick, VIC, 2018), p. 25.

19 Ibid., p. 26.
20 Ibid., p. 27.
21 Ibid.
22 Shapiro, *How to Clone a Mammoth*, p. 164.
23 Ibid., p. 165.
24 Kornfeldt, *The Re-Origin of Species*, p. 31.
25 Shapiro, *How to Clone a Mammoth*, p. ix.
26 Ibid., p. 180.
27 Ibid.
28 Kornfeldt, *The Re-Origin of Species*, p. 75.
    Kornfeldt notes that 154 embryos were
    implanted into 44 goats, whereas Shapiro
    states that it was 208 embryos (*How to
    Clone a Mammoth*, p. 8). In a sense, it
    doesn't matter; a large number of embryos
    were involved. It is worth remembering
    that Dolly the sheep was the success story
    from 277 embryos.
29 Shapiro, *How to Clone a Mammoth*, p. 26.
30 To read more about the coelacanth,
    see Samantha Weinberg, *A Fish Caught
    in Time: The Search for the Coelacanth*
    (London, 1999).
31 'Pookila (New Holland Mouse)', Zoos
    Victoria, www.zoo.org.au, accessed
    8 August 2021.
32 The scientific community is yet to reach
    a consensus in terms of its classification.
    Some classify it as still being in the genus
    Solenodon, so its binomial name is *Solenodon
    cubana*, whereas others claim that there
    is enough biological evidence for it to
    have its own genus, *Atopogale*, being of
    the family Solenodontidae and having
    a binomial name of *Atopogale cubana*.
    Whichever classification or name is used,
    the Cuban solenodon remains one of
    only two living solenodon species.
33 Jeremy Madeiros, 'A Record Year for
    Bermuda's National Bird – 2022 Cahow
    Recovery Program Update', www.
    nonsuchisland.com, 30 December 2022.
34 University of Sydney news, 'Wallace's
    Biggest Bee Found', www.sydney.edu.au,
    22 February 2019; Patrick Barkham,
    'World's Largest Bee, Missing for 38 years,
    Found Alive in Indonesia', *The Guardian*,
    www.theguardian.com, 22 February 2019.
35 John Whitfield, *Lost Animals: The Story of
    Extinct, Endangered and Rediscovered Species*
    (London, 2020), p. 210.
36 'Rare, Egg-Laying Mammal, Named After
    Sir David Attenborough, Seen for the First
    Time in 60 Years in Indonesia's Cyclops
    Mountains', BBC *Wildlife Magazine*,
    www.discoverwildlife.com, 11 November
    2023.
37 'Bizarre Mammal Believed to Be Extinct
    Is Rediscovered by "Euphoric" Scientists',
    Sky News, https://news.sky.com,
    10 November 2023.
38 Brian Swimme and Thomas Berry, *The
    Universe Story: From the Primordial Flaring
    Forth to the Ecozoic Era: A Celebration of the
    Unfolding of the Cosmos* (New York, 1992),
    p. 243.
39 Center for Ecozoic Studies, 'Naming a
    New Geological Era: The Ecozoic Era,
    Its Meaning and Historical Antecedents',
    https://ecozoicstudies.org, accessed 7 July
    2024.
40 Caspar Henderson, *The Book of Barely
    Imagined Beings: A 21st Century Bestiary*
    (London, 2012), p. 373.
41 Swimme and Berry, *The Universe Story*,
    p. 249.
42 Henderson, *Book of Barely Imagined Beings*,
    p. 373.
43 Swimme and Berry, *The Universe Story*,
    p. 260.

2. *Memorializing Grief*
1 Aldo Leopold, *A Sand Almanac and Other
   Writings on Ecology and Conservation* [1949]
   (New York, 2013), p. 98.
2 Todd McGrain, *The Lost Bird Project*
   (Hanover, NH, and London, 2014), p. 6.
3 Ibid., p. 2.
4 Christopher Cokinos, *Hope Is the Thing
   with Feathers: A Personal Chronicle of
   Vanished Birds* (New York, 2000), p. 12.
5 Ibid. Cokinos noted that the Carolina
   parakeet was forgotten before its
   extinction.
6 Scott Weidensaul, *Living on the Wind:
   Across the Hemisphere with Migratory Birds*
   (New York, 1999), p. 195.
7 *Stand Up Guys* (dir. Fisher Stevens, 2013).
   Other sources for this quote include
   Banksy and Ernest Hemingway.
8 Tim Dee, cited in Robert MacFarlane,
   Landmarks (London, 2015), p. 24.
9 Adam Nicolson, *The Seabird's Cry:
   The Lives and Loves of Puffins, Gannets
   and Other Ocean Voyagers* (London, 2017),
   p. 19.

10 Katrina Merkies and Olivia Franzin, 'Enhanced Understanding of Horse–Human Interactions to Optimize Welfare', *Animals*, XI/5 (May 2021), p. 2.

11 Gary Kowalski, *The Souls of Animals*, 2nd edn (Walpole, NH, 1999), p. 139. In Kowalski's footnote, he gives credit for this contrast between 'biology' and 'biography' to Professor Tom Regan.

12 Nicolson, *The Seabird's Cry*, p. 20.

13 Brett L. Walker, *The Lost Wolves of Japan* (Seattle, WA, and London, 2005), p. 13.

14 Jeffrey Masson and Susan McCarthy, *When Elephants Weep: The Emotional Lives of Animals* (London, 1996), p. 21; Masson and McCarthy use this definition when writing about emotions.

15 These terms were coined by Australian philosopher Glenn Albrecht; see Panu Pihkala, 'Climate Grief: How We Mourn a Changing Planet', BBC Future, www.bbc.com, 3 April 2020.

16 Leopold, *A Sand Almanac*, p. 45.

17 McGrain, *The Lost Bird Project*, p. 13.

18 Ibid., p. 82.

19 Ibid., p. 85.

20 Ibid., p. 13.

21 There are many, such as Christopher Cokinos and Julian Hume, but the work of Errol Fuller is particularly poignant and encompasses the fields of vintage photography, painting and writing. The past gifts us some (more to do with illustrations of new species found, rather than the as-yet-unknown concept of extinction), including John James Audubon.

22 Joel Sartore, *Rare: Portraits of America's Endangered Species* (Washington, DC, 2010), n.p.

THE PORTRAITS

1 Scott Weidensaul, *The Ghost with Trembling Wings* (New York, 2002), p. 191.

2 Ibid.

3 Edward Brooke-Hitching, *The Sky Atlas* (London, 2019), p. 20.

4 Ibid., p. 21.

5 Ibid.: 'This Lascaux artwork allows us to view the cosmos through Ice Age eyes.'

6 Weidensaul, *The Ghost with Trembling Wings*, p. 192.

7 Richard Ellis, *No Turning Back, The Life and Death of Animal Species* (New York, 2004), p. 148.

8 Lutz Heck, *Animals: My Adventure* (London, 1954), p. 141.

9 Ellis, *No Turning Back*, p. 148.

10 Weidensaul, *The Ghost with Trembling Wings*, p. 196.

11 See the profile of 'The Tarpan' for more information about the Heck brothers.

12 Heck, *Animals: My Adventure*, p. 142.

13 Ellis, *No Turning Back*, p. 149; Weidensaul, *The Ghost with Trembling Wings*, p. 199.

14 Heck, *Animals: My Adventure*, p. 154.

15 David Day, *The Doomsday Book of Animals: A Unique Natural History of Vanished Species* (London, 1981), p. 189.

16 The Tauros Programme, www.taurosproject.com, accessed 30 November 2021; Rewilding Europe, https://rewildingeurope.com, accessed 30 November 2021.

17 Day, *The Doomsday Book of Animals*, p. 27.

18 Anton Gill and Alex West, *Extinct* (London, 2001), p. 137.

19 Ibid., p. 138.

20 Errol Fuller, *Dodo: From Extinction to Icon* (London, 2002), p. 17. Writer Jan den Hengst states that *doudo* is not a Portuguese word but offers the term *passaro doido*, which means 'crazy bird': Jan den Hengst, *The Dodo: The Bird that Drew the Short Straw* (Marum, 2003), p. 20.

21 Ellis, *No Turning Back*, p. 162. In Fuller, *dodaersen* is translated as 'fat behinds': *Dodo: From Extinction to Icon*, p. 17.

22 Gill and West, *Extinct*, p. 155.

23 Michael Blencowe, *Gone: A Search for What Remains of the World's Extinct Creatures* (London, 2021), p. 154.

24 For the story of the monkeys in the garden, see den Hengst, *The Dodo*, p. 26; Day, *The Doomsday Book of Animals*, p. 28.

25 den Hengst, *The Dodo*, p. 20.

26 'A True Report, 1599', cited in Julian P. Hume, *Extinct Birds*, 2nd edn (London, 2017), p. 156.

27 Ibid.

28 Gill and West, *Extinct*, p. 147.

29 Ibid., p. 145.

30 Ibid., p. 147.

31 English traveller Peter Mundy described two dodos in his writings about his

travels in Surat. Although he had visited
Mauritius, he did not see them there. It
seems that when sailing past Mauritius,
he recollected seeing two dodos in India.
Fuller, *Dodo: From Extinction to Icon*, p. 66;
Hume, *Extinct Birds*, p. 156.

32 Errol Fuller, *Extinct Birds*, revd edn
(Ithaca, NY, 2001), p. 194.

33 Gill and West, *Extinct*, p. 155.

34 Fuller, *Dodo: From Extinction to Icon*,
pp. 102–5. The painting is dated 1626.

35 Gill and West, *Extinct*, p. 155.

36 Hume, *Extinct Birds*, p. 157.

37 Fuller, *Dodo: From Extinction to Icon*, p. 30.

38 Blencowe, *Gone*, p. 151. For more
information, see J. P. Hume, A. S. Cheke
and A. McOran-Campbell. 'How Owen
"Stole" the Dodo: Academic Rivalry and
Disputed Rights to a Newly-Discovered
Subfossil Deposit in Nineteenth Century
Mauritius', *Historical Biology*, XXI/1–2
(October 2009), pp. 33–49.

39 Gill and West, *Extinct*, p. 161.

40 Ibid.

41 Ibid., pp. 161–3.

42 Hume, *Extinct Birds*, p. 158.

43 Day, *The Doomsday Book of Animals*, p. 30.

44 Geoffroy Atkinson, 'A French Desert
Island Novel of 1708', *PMLA*, XXXVI/4
(December 1921), pp. 509–28.

45 Fuller, *Extinct Birds*, p. 204.

46 Ibid., p. 203.

47 Ibid.

48 Hume, *Extinct Birds*, p. 160.

49 Julian Hume and Lorna Steel, 'Fight
Club: A Unique Weapon in the Wing
of the Solitaire, *Pezophas solitaria* (Aves:
Columbidae), an Extinct Flightless Bird
from Rodrigues, Mascarene Islands',
Biological Journal of the Linnean Society,
CX/1 (September 2013), pp. 32–44 (p. 32).

50 It was Julien Tafforet. Tafforet's account
was undiscovered until the latter part of
the nineteenth century. Hume, *Extinct
Birds*, p. 159.

51 Day, *The Doomsday Book of Animals*, p. 30.

52 Gizzard stones came to be known as
'bezoar stones'. Some believed these
contained astonishing medicinal
properties, including the power to heal
dysentery, leprosy and epilepsy. The stones
were also thought to be an antidote to
poison.

53 Hume, *Extinct Birds*, p. 159.

54 'Turdus Solitarius: The Solitaire', Ian
Ridpath's Star Tales, www.ianridpath.com/
startales/solitaire.html, accessed 27 June
2024.

55 Ibid.

56 Ibid. For a history of the evolution
of constellation studies, see Lisa
Bohnwagher, 'Constellation Noctua:
A Galactic Transformation',
https://medium.com, 11 May 2018.

57 Fuller, *Extinct Birds*, p. 205.

58 Georg Steller, *De Bestiis Marinis*
(The Beasts of the Sea) (1751), p. 13,
https://digitalcommons.unl.edu,
accessed 7 November 2021.

59 Ibid., p. 25.

60 Ibid.

61 Ibid.

62 Ibid., p. 15.

63 Ibid., pp. 26, 45.

64 Day, *The Doomsday Book of Animals*, p. 218.

65 Steller, *De Bestiis Marinis*, p. 46.

66 Day, *The Doomsday Book of Animals*, p. 218.

67 Rudyard Kipling, *The Jungle Book* [1894]
(New York, 1968), p. 126.

68 Ibid., p. 127.

69 Ibid.

70 Day, *The Doomsday Book of Animals*, p. 218.

71 Christopher Cokinos, *Hope Is the Thing
with Feathers: A Personal Chronicle of
Vanished Birds* (New York, 2000), p. 311.

72 Sources differ, some stating the hunt took
place in June, others that it happened in
July.

73 Molly Oldfield, *The Secret Museum*
(London, 2013), p. 132.

74 Gill and West, *Extinct*, p. 176.

75 Day, *The Doomsday Book of Animals*, p. 44.

76 Ibid.

77 Cokinos, *Hope Is the Thing with Feathers*,
p. 314.

78 Errol Fuller, *The Great Auk* (New York,
1999), p. 400.

79 Oldfield, *The Secret Museum*, p. 132.

80 Gill and West, *Extinct*, p. 187; Oldfield,
The Secret Museum, p. 132; Fuller, *The Great
Auk*, p. 401.

81 Fuller, *The Great Auk*, p. 396.

82 Ibid., p. 401.

83 Ellis, *No Turning Back*, p. 159.

84 Gill and West, *Extinct*, p. 181.

85 Ibid.

86 Ibid.

87 Cokinos, *Hope Is the Thing with Feathers*, p. 314.

88 Gill and West, *Extinct*, p. 180.

89 Charles Kingsley, *The Water Babies* (Ware, 1994), p. 201.

90 Ibid., p. 203.

91 Gill and West, *Extinct*, p. 194.

92 Cokinos, *Hope Is the Thing with Feathers*, p. 330.

93 Ibid.

94 Tim Flannery and Peter Schouten, *A Gap in Nature: Exploring the World's Extinct Animals* (Melbourne, 2001), p. 34.

95 Gill and West, *Extinct*, p. 195.

96 Hume, *Extinct Birds*, p. 154.

97 Gill and West, *Extinct*, p. 201.

98 Ibid. In 1898 a great auk skin and egg fetched £630 (equivalent to £50,000 today) at auction.

99 Sources differ on whether it took place in June or July. Jeremy Gaskell also questions the year, looking at evidence that points to another expedition which netted a similar outcome. Jeremy Gaskell, *Who Killed the Great Auk?* (Oxford, 2000), p. 129. In Todd McGrain, *The Lost Bird Project* (Hanover, NH, and London, 2014), p. 35, there is discussion about a bird which may have been a great auk, captured and killed on Fogo Island in 1888.

100 For more information about the ceremony, see *Apology to the Great Auk*, Marcus Coates, www.marcuscoates.co.uk, accessed 20 May 2024.

101 Modern ideas question the notion of their extinction. The Mi'kmaq say the Beothuk left the coast because they were driven out of the area by the new settlers, but they went on to intermarry with other Indigenous nations on the mainland. This theory seems to have been confirmed by recent DNA testing: James A. Tuck, with update by David Joseph Gallant and Michelle Filice, 'Beothuk', *Canadian Encyclopedia*, www.thecanadianencyclopedia.ca, 6 February 2006, updated 22 July 2022; and 'Thought to Be Extinct, Beothuk DNA Is Present in Living Families, Genetics Researcher Finds', CBC News, www.cbc.ca, 8 May 2020.

102 Steller, cited in Blencowe, *Gone*, p. 34.

103 Steller, in Georg Steller, *Journal of the Sea Voyage from Kamchatka to America and Return on the Second Expedition, 1741–1742*, trans. and ann. Leonhard Stejneger, American Geographical Society Research Series No. 2, in American Geographical Society, *Bering's Voyages*, vol. II (New York, 1925), p. 237, https://content.wisconsinhistory.org, accessed 11 July 2021.

104 Fuller, *Extinct Birds*, p. 71.

105 Steller, cited in Blencowe, *Gone*, p. 34.

106 Fuller, *Extinct Birds*, p. 69.

107 Steller, cited ibid., p. 70.

108 Day, *The Doomsday Book of Animals*, p. 46.

109 This is according to Steller's description of the abundance of spectacled cormorants, cited ibid.

110 Hume, *Extinct Birds*, p. 86; Blencowe, *Gone*, p. 38.

111 Hume, *Extinct Birds*, p. 85.

112 Ibid., p. 87.

113 Blencowe, *Gone*, p. 42.

114 Ibid., p. 41.

115 Ibid., p. 42.

116 Rosamond Purcell, *Swift as a Shadow: Extinct and Endangered Animals* (Boston, MA, and New York, 1999), no. 50.

117 Charles Darwin, 'March 16–17, 1834', *Narrative of the Surveying Voyages of His Majesty's Ships Adventure and Beagle between the Years 1826 and 1836, Describing their Examination of the Southern Shores of South America, and the Beagle's Circumnavigation of the Globe*, vol. III (London, 1839), p. 251, scanned from a copy from the Balfour and Newton Libraries, Cambridge, http://darwin-online.org.uk, accessed 2 March 2022.

118 J. J. Austin et al., 'The Origins of the Enigmatic Falkland Islands Wolf', *Nature Communications*, IV/1552 (March 2013), www.nature.com. The LGM was approximately 20,000 years ago, during the last phase of the Pleistocene epoch.

119 Carlo Meloro, 'Falklands "Wolf" that Baffled Darwin Was Actually More Like a Jackal', *The Conversation*, https://theconversation.com, 10 January 2017.

120 These were discovered by thirteen-year-old Dale Evans, a budding naturalist. They have become known as the Evans warrah. The other remarkable fact about

this discovery is that they are the only remains that have been found in their own habitat, a natural fatality, rather than specimens collected by naturalists during the 1800s: https://falklands-museum.com/the-warrah, accessed 9 July 2024.

121 Dan Whipple, 'Alas, poor warrah . . .', *New Scientist*, CLXXX/2426–8 (2003), pp. 80–81.

122 Flannery and Schouten, *A Gap in Nature*, p. 66.

123 Darwin, *Narrative of the Surveying Voyages of His Majesty's Ships Adventure and Beagle*, p. 251.

124 Cited online at Falkland Islands Museum and National Trust, www.falklands-museum.com, accessed 2 March 2022.

125 H. A. Bryden, *Kloof and Karroo: Sport, Legend and Natural History in Cape Colony, with a Notice of the Game Birds, and of the Present Distribution of Antelopes and Larger Game* (London and New York, 1889), p. 394.

126 Errol Fuller, *Lost Animals: Extinction and the Photographic Record* (London, 2013), p. 196.

127 Day, *The Doomsday Book of Animals*, p. 208.

128 Ibid.

129 Ibid.

130 Bryden, *Kloof and Karroo*, p. 401.

131 Ibid.

132 Fuller, *Lost Animals*, p. 199.

133 'Losing the Quagga', Elizabeth Hawksley Blog, http://elizabethhawksley.com, 5 January 2020.

134 Ibid.

135 Day, *The Doomsday Book of Animals*, p. 208.

136 Bryden, *Kloof and Karroo*, p. 398.

137 Ibid.

138 F. Martin Duncan, *Cassell's Natural History* (London and New York, 1913), p. 350, https://archive.org.

139 Fuller, *Lost Animals*, p. 199.

140 Bryden, *Kloof and Karroo*, p. 393.

141 Ibid., p. 402.

142 Jim Endersby, 'Equus quagga and Lord Morton's Mare', *The Guardian*, www.theguardian.com, 14 September 2007.

143 For more information about the Heck brothers and back-breeding, see the portraits for 'The Aurochs' and 'The Tarpan'.

144 Weidensaul, *The Ghost with Trembling Wings*, p. 209.

145 For more information about the history and the current research projects, visit The Quagga Project, www.quaggaproject.org, accessed 22 February 2024, and Weidensaul, *The Ghost with Trembling Wings*, pp. 209–12.

146 Weidensaul, *The Ghost with Trembling Wings*, p. 211.

147 Ibid., p. 212.

148 *Khumba* (dir. Anthony Silverston, 2013, Triggerfish Animation Studios, Cape Town).

149 Thomas Pringle, from 'Afar in the Desert', cited in Bryden, *Kloof and Karroo*, p. 402. Pringle, a Scottish writer, is sometimes referred to as the father of South African poetry.

150 Susanna Forrest, *The Age of the Horse: An Equine Journey through Human History* (London, 2016), p. 26.

151 Ibid., p. 31.

152 Ibid.

153 There are differences of opinion regarding the year of her death. Some say it was in 1876, others, December 1879. David Day writes that the tarpan died on Christmas Day, 1879: Day, *The Doomsday Book of Animals*, p. 212.

154 Weidensaul, *The Ghost with Trembling Wings*, p. 204.

155 Ibid., p. 205.

156 Heck, *Animals: My Adventure*, p. 158.

157 Forrest, *The Age of the Horse*, p. 49.

158 Ibid., p. 51.

159 For more information about the tarpan in the United States, see Dixie Meadows Tarpan Horses, https://dixiemeadowstarpans.com, accessed 6 November 2021, and Tarpan Horse Conservation Project, www.thcponline.org, accessed 6 November 2021.

160 'Tarpans', Hope's Legacy Equine Rescue, www.hopeslegacy.com, accessed 9 July 2021.

161 David Day mentions a Mongolian legend that tells of the Torguls, a centaur-like tribe descended from a tarpan and a princess. Day, *The Doomsday Book of Animals*, p. 213.

162 Jeffrey A. Lockwood, *Locust: The Devastating Rise and Mysterious Disappearance of the Insect that Shaped*

the *American Frontier* (New York, 2004), p. 26.

163 Ibid., p. 157.
164 Ibid., p. 21.
165 Ibid.
166 Ibid., p. 3.
167 Chuck Lyons, '1874: The Year of the Locust', www.historynet.com, 5 February 2012.
168 Lockwood, *Locust*, p. 20.
169 Matt Reimann, 'In One Year, 12 Trillion Locusts Devastated the Great Plains – and then They Went Extinct. They Ate "Everything but the Mortgage"', https://medium.com, 16 February 2017.
170 Blencowe, *Gone*, p. 120.
171 Jeffrey Lockwood, 'The Death of the Super Hopper: How Early Settlers Unwittingly Drove Their Nemesis Extinct, and What It Means for Us Today', *High Country News*, www.hcn.org, 3 February 2003.
172 Lockwood, *Locust*, p. 13.
173 Laura Ingalls Wilder, *On the Banks of Plum Creek* [1937] (London, 2014), p. 56.
174 Lockwood, *Locust*, p. 13. I thank Lockwood for pointing out how locusts and their behaviour became parts of speech.
175 Ibid.
176 Ibid., p. 14.
177 Ingalls Wilder, *On the Banks*, p. 165.
178 Lyons, '1874: The Year of the Locust'.
179 Ibid.
180 Ingalls Wilder, *On the Banks*, p. 167.
181 In 1877 Nebraska passed a Grasshopper Act, which required every able-bodied man between the ages of sixteen and sixty to work for at least two days eliminating locusts at hatching time, or face a $10 fine: Lyons, '1874: The Year of the Locust'.
182 Reimann, 'In One Year, 12 Trillion Locusts Devastated the Great Plains'.
183 Lyons, '1874: The Year of the Locust'.
184 Ibid.
185 Observing the seventh year as a Sabbath rest for the land was a commandment: Lev. 25:4; Lockwood, *Locust*, p. 44.
186 Lockwood, *Locust*, p. 45.
187 'The Great Minnesota Grasshopper Miracle', Kinship Radio, https://kinshipradio.org, 7 August 2014.
188 Jack El-Hai, 'A Plague of Locusts', www.wondersandmarvels.com, accessed 29 September 2021.

189 Lockwood, *Locust*, p. 128. In 1901 Criddle, assisted by Harry Vane, invented what became known as Criddle mixture, a bait that assisted in controlling grasshoppers for the next thirty years. The ingredients were copper acetoarsenite, salt and horse manure (or bran or sawdust). N. J. Holliday, 'Norman Criddle: Pioneer Entomologist of the Prairies', *Manitoba History*, 51 (February 2006).
190 Jeffrey Lockwood, 'Entomological Storytelling: Why We Wrote an Opera about Locusts (Really!)', *Entomology Today*, https://entomologytoday.org, 16 October 2018. Three professors at the University of Wyoming, including Lockwood, wrote the opera. Lockwood was the librettist.
191 A comparison proposed by Lockwood, *Locust*, p. 229, and in Lockwood, 'The Death of the Super Hopper'.
192 R. Das et al., 'The Biomechanics of the Locust Ovipositor Valves: A Unique Digging Apparatus', *Journal of the Royal Society Interface*, XIX/188 (March 2022).
193 Lockwood, *Locust*, p. 55.
194 Ibid., p. 158.
195 Ibid., p. 45. Interestingly, Lockwood points out that apart from angels, the only other creatures with the full use of their limbs are mythical creatures: Pegasus and the griffin.
196 Day, *The Doomsday Book of Animals*, p. 160. A different source suggests that the wolf was slightly larger: 50–60 centimetres (20–24 in.) tall, its body 80–110 centimetres (31–43 in.) long: Ryoko Takeishi, 'DNA Study Offers Third Theory on Origin of Extinct Japanese Wolf', *Asahi Shimbun*, www.asahi.com, 13 June 2022.
197 Brett L. Walker, *The Lost Wolves of Japan* (Seattle, WA, and London, 2005), pp. 20, 27, 45.
198 Pleistocene wolves were thought to have populated the Japanese archipelago at different times between 57,000 and 35,000 years ago. Alex K. T. Martin, 'Researchers Trace the Evolutionary Origins of the Japanese Wolf', *Japan Times*, www.japantimes.co.jp, 11 May 2022.
199 Martin, 'Researchers Trace the Evolutionary Origins of the Japanese Wolf' and Takeishi, 'DNA Study Offers Third Theory on Origin of Extinct Japanese Wolf'.

200 Walker, *The Lost Wolves of Japan*, p. 9.
201 Ibid., p. 132.
202 Ibid., p. 77.
203 Ibid., p. 70.
204 Ibid., p. 71.
205 Ibid., p. 70.
206 Ibid., p. 217.
207 'Japanese Wolf', Extinct Animals, www.extinctanimals.org, 28 March 2022.
208 For a modern take on the problems of industrialization in Japan, and wolf lore, watch the Studio Ghibli animated film *Princess Mononoke* (dir. Hayao Miyazaki, 1997).
209 Fuller, *Extinct Birds*, p. 194. Also mentioned in Flannery and Schouten, *A Gap in Nature*, p. 124.
210 Aldo Leopold, *A Sand Almanac and Other Writings on Ecology and Conservation* [1949] (New York, 2013), p. 97.
211 Cokinos, *Hope Is the Thing with Feathers*, p. 208.
212 Joel Greenberg, *A Feathered River across the Sky: The Passenger Pigeon's Flight to Extinction* (New York, 2014), p. 47.
213 Cokinos, *Hope Is the Thing with Feathers*, pp. 207–8.
214 Ibid., p. 200.
215 Hume, *Extinct Birds*, p. 167.
216 McGrain, *The Lost Bird Project*, p. 53.
217 Scott Russell Sanders, ed., *Audubon Reader: The Best Writings of John James Audubon* (Bloomington, IN, 1986), p. 117.
218 Errol Fuller, *The Passenger Pigeon* (Princeton, NJ, and Oxford, 2015), p. 30.
219 Fuller, *Extinct Birds*, p. 189.
220 Flannery and Schouten, *A Gap in Nature*. p. 124.
221 Day, *The Doomsday Book of Animals*, p. 32.
222 Sanders, *Audubon Reader*, p. 120.
223 Fuller, *Extinct Birds*, p. 192.
224 Day, *The Doomsday Book of Animals*, p. 34.
225 Hume, *Extinct Birds*, p. 169.
226 Cokinos, *Hope Is the Thing with Feathers*, p. 201.
227 Day, *The Doomsday Book of Animals*, p. 32.
228 Cokinos, *Hope Is the Thing with Feathers*, p. 209.
229 Day, *The Doomsday Book of Animals*, p. 36.
230 McGrain, *The Lost Bird Project*, p. 55.
231 Barbara Allen, *Pigeon* (London, 2009), p. 177.
232 Day, *The Doomsday Book of Animals*, p. 36.
233 Purcell, *Swift as a Shadow*, no. 2.
234 Day, *The Doomsday Book of Animals*, p. 36.
235 Ellis, *No Turning Back*, p. 174.
236 Hume, *Extinct Birds*, p. 168.
237 '[I]n terms of absolute extinction, an extra factor comes into play: the peculiar evolution of the birds that meant they could survive – psychologically, emotionally, and physically – only in vast numbers': Fuller, *The Passenger Pigeon*, pp. 86–7.
238 'I Vacuumed a Passenger Pigeon Today', Ohio History Connection Natural History Blog, www.ohiohistory.org, 19 August 2013.
239 Cokinos, *Hope Is the Thing with Feathers*, p. 243.
240 Ibid., p. 264.
241 Ibid., p. 267.
242 Greenberg, *A Feathered River across the Sky*, p. 189.
243 Michelle Johnson, 'What Does the Passenger Pigeon Have to Do with Lyme Disease?', https://wiscontext.org, 27 July 2018.
244 Cokinos, *Hope Is the Thing with Feathers*, p. 208.
245 Ibid., p. 1.
246 'The Last Carolina Parakeet', John James Audubon Center at Mill Grove, https://johnjames.audubon.org, accessed 2 April 2023.
247 Cokinos, *Hope Is the Thing with Feathers*, p. 15.
248 The other parrot, the only surviving parrot species of the two native to the United States, is the thick-billed parrot, now only found in Mexico.
249 Fuller, *Extinct Birds*, p. 243.
250 Cokinos, *Hope Is the Thing with Feathers*, p. 17, and Kevin R. Burgio, 'The Tragic Story of America's Only Native Parrot, Now Extinct for Over 100 Years', *The Conversation*, https://theconversation.com, 28 March 2018.
251 Cokinos, *Hope Is the Thing with Feathers*, p. 17.
252 Fuller, *Extinct Birds*, p. 240.
253 Fuller, *Lost Animals*, p. 75.
254 Cokinos, *Hope Is the Thing with Feathers*, p. 49.
255 Cited ibid., p. 47. Nuttall made this observation in 1840.
256 Purcell, *Swift as a Shadow*, no. 1.

257 Cokinos, *Hope Is the Thing with Feathers*, p. 36.
258 In some literature, there are references to the Carolina parakeet being susceptible to a type of apoplexy, or stroke: ibid., p. 36.
259 Fuller, *Lost Animals*, p. 75.
260 Cited in Brett Westwood and Stephen Moss, *Natural Histories: 25 Extraordinary Species that Have Changed Our World* (London, 2015), p. 290.
261 Cokinos, *Hope Is the Thing with Feathers*, p. 35.
262 Kevin R. Burgio et al., 'The Two Extinctions of the Carolina Parakeet', *Bird Conservation International*, XXXII/3 (July 2021), pp. 1–8; Tammana Begum, 'Reviving the Cold Case of the Carolina Parakeet Extinction', Natural History Museum, www.nhm.ac.uk, 27 July 2021. It should be noted that David Day mentioned this back in 1981: Day, *The Doomsday Book of Animals*, p. 68, and Fuller, *Extinct Birds*, p. 243. More recent research focuses on what being two subspecies meant for parrot extinction and how this knowledge can help bird conservation today.
263 Begum, 'Reviving the Cold Case of the Carolina Parakeet Extinction'.
264 Ibid.
265 Burgio et al., 'The Two Extinctions of the Carolina Parakeet', p. 6, and Begum, 'Reviving the Cold Case of the Carolina Parakeet Extinction'.
266 Fuller, *Extinct Birds*, p. 239.
267 Fuller, *Lost Animals*, p. 72.
268 Fuller, *Extinct Birds*, p. 240.
269 Fuller, *Lost Animals*, p. 77.
270 Ibid.
271 There is a memorial sculptured by Todd McGrain at Kissimmee Prairie Preserve, Okeechobee, Florida.
272 Day, *The Doomsday Book of Animals*, p. 210.
273 Ibid.
274 Ibid., p. 212. The body of water Day refers to as 'Lake Azrak' is more commonly known as the 'Azraq Oasis' or the 'Azraq Basin'.
275 Ibid., pp. 210, 212.
276 Hume, *Extinct Birds*, p. 43.
277 Day, *The Doomsday Book of Animals*, p. 128.
278 Hume, *Extinct Birds*, p. 43.
279 Ibid.
280 Ibid.
281 Errol Fuller, *Lost Animals*, p. 44.
282 Cokinos, *Hope is the Thing with Feathers*, p. 144. The 1916 fire resulted in 'nearly 13,000 acres burned – about 20 per cent of the island'; ibid., p. 143.
283 Fuller, *Lost Animals*, p. 44.
284 Ellis, *No Turning Back*, p. 177.
285 Hume, *Extinct Birds*, p. 43.
286 Day, *The Doomsday Book of Animals*, p. 128.
287 Cokinos, *Hope Is the Thing with Feathers*, p. 178.
288 Ibid., p. 126.
289 Ellis, *No Turning Back*, p. 178; in Cokinos, *Hope Is the Thing with Feathers*, p. 181, Cokinos names the year: 1930.
290 Cokinos, *Hope Is the Thing with Feathers*, p. 182.
291 Or after his mother-in-law. Both were named Martha. Perhaps it is meant to be Martha's Vineyard, a collective, minus the apostrophe?
292 The notion (and I would add that it is a far-fetched one) that Shakespeare may have written these words about Martha's Vineyard was suggested by McGrain in *The Lost Bird Project*, p. 79.
293 Day, *The Doomsday Book of Animals*, p. 224.
294 Gill and West, *Extinct*, p. 226; Robert Paddle, *The Last Tasmanian Tiger: The History and Extinction of the Thylacine* (Cambridge, 2000), p. 7.
295 Eric Guiler and Philippe Godard, *Tasmanian Tiger: A Lesson to Be Learnt . . .* (Perth, 1998), p. 45.
296 Some sources state 90 degrees, others that the gape could be up to 150 degrees.
297 Gill and West, *Extinct*, p. 238.
298 Ibid., p. 241; and Paddle, *The Last Tasmanian Tiger*, pp. 205–7, 212. Paddle challenges this view, calling it 'placental chauvinism'.
299 Benjamin Gray, *Extinct: Artistic Impressions of Our Lost Wildlife* (Melbourne, 2021), p. 86.
300 'The Tasmanian Wolf in London', *Braidwood Dispatch and Mining Journal*, 26 May 1909, cited in David Maynard and Tammy Gordon, *Tasmanian Tiger: Precious Little Remains* (Launceston, TAS, 2014), p. 31.
301 Gill and West, *Extinct*, p. 238.
302 Ibid., p. 239.
303 Ibid., p. 225.

304 Cited in Guiler and Godard, *Tasmanian Tiger*, p. 78. Oxley was incorrect because three sightings had been recorded in the south in 1805, but he was correct in stressing that the thylacine was not common.

305 Penny Olsen, *Upside Down World: Early European Impressions of Australia's Curious Animals* (Canberra, 2010), p. 30.

306 Cited in Gill and West, *Extinct*, p. 227.

307 John Oxley, 'Account of the Settlement at Port Dalrymple' (1810), cited in Guiler and Godard, *Tasmanian Tiger*, p. 78.

308 Gill and West, *Extinct*, p. 228.

309 Ibid., p. 231.

310 Fuller, *Lost Animals*, p. 171.

311 According to Diana Chase and Valerie Krantz, *The Stories Behind the Legends: Legendary Animals* (Melbourne, 1995), p. 9. Tanneries were paid £3/18 for each of the 3,482 skins sent to England to be made into waistcoats, but Kathryn Medlock, from the Tasmanian Museum and Art Gallery, is uncertain whether this is true, because no such waistcoat is known to exist: David Owen, *Thylacine*, revd edn (Sydney, 2011), p. 42.

312 For many years, it was thought that Benjamin was actually female (no film or photographs revealed the presence of testicles). New research, via a single frame of photo footage, suggests that Benjamin was, in fact, male. Fuller states that thylacine expert Stephen Sleightholme is adamant that Benjamin was definitely male: Fuller, *Lost Animals*, p. 239.

313 Gill and West, *Extinct*, p. 243.

314 Carol Freeman, *Paper Tiger: How Pictures Shaped the Thylacine* (Hobart, 2014), p. 177.

315 Rodney Dillon, Tasmanian Aboriginal and Torres Strait Islander Commissioner, *The Mercury*, 31 January 2002, cited in Owen, *Thylacine*, p. 167.

316 Leigh Maynard's *How the Tasmanian Tiger Got Its Stripes* (Lindfield, 2004) comes from the Nuenonne people of Bruny Island, off the southeast coast of Tasmania. Maynard heard the story from his grandmother, Gussie Maynard. This legend appears to be the same as the one told to Quaker Joseph Cotton in the 1830s by Timler, an Indigenous Elder. It was attributed to Mannalargenna, chief and wise man of the North-East Coast Federation of Tribes: Owen, *Thylacine* p. 59. Cotton's great-grandson adapted these tales, and they were published as Jackson Cotton, *Touch the Morning: Tasmanian Native Legends* (Hobart, 1979), pp. 17–18. See Notes no. 1, in Owen, *Thylacine*, p. 207. Although there were no records of thylacine presence on Bruny Island, they knew of them (they had two names for them) and may have seen them when visiting the Tasmanian mainland. Another myth comes from the Kunwinjku people, from mainland Australia. They tell of two ancestral thylacines hunting a kangaroo. They fall off a cliff into a river and turn into archerfish (these fish have stripes on their bodies).

317 Owen, *Thylacine*, p. 70. Owen adds yet another layer of suggestion, mentioning that no thylacine remains have been uncovered in middens or rock shelters.

318 Wildlife biologist Nick Mooney thinks this would have been the case: Nick Mooney, 'So Near and Yet So Far', in *The Tasmanian Tiger: Extinct or Extant?*, ed. Rebecca Lang (Sydney, 2014), pp. 37–49 (p. 48).

319 Gray, *Extinct*, p. 86.

320 Blencowe, *Gone*, p. 111.

321 Ibid., p. 113.

322 Liam O'Brien, 'In the Shadow of the Xerces Blue', *Bay Nature*, https://baynature.org, 14 March 2019. This behaviour is known as 'tending'.

323 Blencowe, *Gone*, p. 117.

324 Ibid., p. 118. Although O'Brien, 'In the Shadow of the Xerces Blue', writes that Lange netted several, rather than a single, Xerces blue butterfly, Blencowe writes about Lange's solitary butterfly and how it became part of Lange's entomological collection.

325 In 2022 research was carried out on mitochondrial DNA from a Xerces blue butterfly. Scientists compared it to its closest living relative, the silvery blue butterfly (*Glaucopsyche lygdamus*). Results showed that they were distinct species, not different populations of butterfly. Research also revealed that low genetic diversity, combined with several other factors, had made the Xerces blue butterfly a vulnerable species. Major populations

had been on the decline for thousands of years, perhaps due to climate change: Spanish National Research Council, 'An Icon of Anthropogenic Extinction: Xerces Blue Butterfly Genome Sequenced', https://phys.org, 13 July 2023. For more information, see Tony de-Dios et al., 'Whole-Genomes from the Extinct Xerces Blue Butterfly Can Help Identify Declining Insect Species', *eLife*, https://elifesciences.org, 4 September 2023.

326 Hume, *Extinct Birds*, p. 19.

327 Ibid.; Day, *The Doomsday Book of Animals*, p. 25.

328 On the same date, T. E. Lawrence wrote these words in his private field notebook: 'All day deputations, fusillades, coffee, ostrich eggs'. T. E. Lawrence's notebook, 5 June 1917, British Library, MS 45915, T. E. Lawrence Society Blog, https://telsociety.org.uk, accessed 20 June 2022.

329 Hume, *Extinct Birds*, p. 20.

330 Peter Goodfellow, *Birds of the Bible* (Oxford, 2013), p. 75.

331 Michael Bright, *Beasts of the Field* (London, 2006), p. 245.

332 Ibid., p. 247.

333 Hume, *Extinct Birds*, p. 19.

334 Douglas Russell, 'The Mysterious Story of the Syrian Ostrich Egg', BBC Radio 4, www.bbc.co.uk, 27 August 2015.

335 Foreword by John H. Baker, in James T. Tanner, *The Ivory-Billed Woodpecker* [1942] (Mineola, NY, 2003), p. v.

336 Audubon wrote: '[the Ivory-billed Woodpeckers] . . . never failed to remind me of some of the boldest and noblest productions of that inimitable artist's pencil'; www.audubon.org/birds-of-america/ivory-billed-woodpecker, accessed 9 July 2024. Also Day, *The Doomsday Book of Animals*, p. 140.

337 Tanner, *The Ivory-Billed Woodpecker*, p. 61.

338 Ibid. Tanner also said our call resembled a 'head in a bucket' sound: Cokinos, *Hope Is the Thing with Feathers*, p. 114.

339 Cokinos, *Hope Is the Thing with Feathers*, p. 114.

340 Day, *The Doomsday Book of Animals*, p. 142.

341 Phillip Hoose, *The Race to Save the Lord God Bird* [2004] (New York, 2014), p. 9.

342 Ibid., p. 27

343 Tanner, *The Ivory-Billed Woodpecker*, p. 55. Ivory-billed woodpeckers have also been found in burial sites in Illinois and Nebraska; Benjamin E. Leese, 'Scarlet Scalps and Ivory Bills: Native American Uses of the Ivory-Billed Woodpecker', *Passenger Pigeon*, LXVIII/3 (Fall 2006), pp. 212–25 (p. 218). According to Leese, the ivory-billed woodpecker served as an important religious symbol to a number of Nations of the Midwest and Upper Plains, particularly the Siouan Nations. In his article, Leese makes reference to the Pawnee, the Omaha, the Potawatomi, the Sac and the Fox Nations. Ibid.

344 Tanner, *The Ivory-Billed Woodpecker*, p. 58.

345 Cokinos, *Hope Is the Thing with Feathers*, p. 94.

346 Hume, *Extinct Birds*, p. 248.

347 Ibid.

348 Purcell, *Swift as a Shadow*, no. 25. Another writer records 800 hectares (2,000 ac) as the minimum area required for a breeding pair: Day, *The Doomsday Book of Animals*, p. 142.

349 Hume, *Extinct Birds*, p. 248.

350 Tanner, *The Ivory-Billed Woodpecker*, p. 44.

351 Hume, *Extinct Birds*, p. 247.

352 Cokinos, *Hope Is the Thing with Feathers*, p. 65.

353 Hume, *Extinct Birds*, p. 247.

354 For example, the state of Florida brought in a non-game protection act in 1901, but this did little for the low numbers of the ivory-billed woodpecker: Cokinos, *Hope Is the Thing with Feathers*, p. 97. In recent years, there has been some debate in ornithological circles concerning Tanner's findings about the ivory-billed woodpeckers' need for old growth forests: Mark A. Michaels, 'The Legacy of James T. Tanner's Ivory-Billed Woodpecker Research', National Aviary, www.aviary.org, accessed 14 September 2022.

355 Fuller, *Lost Animals*, p. 108. According to Phillip Hoose, this quote comes from p. 5 of Tanner's 1939 report for the Audubon Society, 'Report of the Ivory-Billed Woodpecker Fellowship before the National Association of Audubon Societies, October, 1939', which was found in Box 1 of Tanner's Cornell file: Hoose, *The Race to Save the Lord God Bird*, p. 194.

356 Cokinos, *Hope Is the Thing with Feathers*, p. 89.

357 Fuller, *Lost Animals*, p. 102.

358 Tanner, *The Ivory-Billed Woodpecker*, p. 100.

359 James T. Tanner, 'Present Status of the Ivory-Billed Woodpecker', *Wilson Bulletin*, LIV/1 (March 1942), pp. 57–8.

360 Tanner was called up for military service. It is interesting to note that as the ivory-billed woodpecker disappeared, a soon-to-become-famous cartoon character, Woody Woodpecker, appeared in 1940. He was not based on the ivory-billed woodpecker; rather, the cartoon character was a western acorn woodpecker, a bird that had annoyed cartoonist Walter Lantz. In the episode 'Dumb Like a Fox' of *The Woody Woodpecker Show* (aired 7 January 1964), a museum offers a monetary reward for the capture of a *Campephilus principalis*, an ivory-billed woodpecker. Some people assumed this was the species to which Woody belonged. Due to this incorrect identification, Woody made it into the headlines when the ivory-billed woodpecker was declared extinct by the United States: D. D. Degg, 'U.S. Declares Woody Woodpecker Extinct', *Daily Cartoonist*, www.dailycartoonist.com, 30 September 2021.

361 Fuller, *Lost Animals*, p. 108.

362 Ibid., p. 98.

363 Tanner, *The Ivory-Billed Woodpecker*, p. 55.

364 Hoose, *The Race to Save the Lord God Bird*, p. 44.

365 Hume, *Extinct Birds*, p. 248.

366 For more details about unconfirmed sightings, see Hoose, *The Race to Save the Lord God Bird*, Chapters Fourteen and Fifteen.

367 May R. Berenbaum, *The Earwig's Tail: A Modern Bestiary of Multi-Legged Legends* (Cambridge, MA, 2009), p. 11.

368 Ibid., pp. 10–11.

369 Ibid., p. 12.

370 Ibid., p. 13.

371 In 2023 the government of St Helena and the St Helena National Trust negotiated the repatriation of a St Helena Earwig specimen from the AfricaMuseum to the Museum of St Helena, where it is now on display. See 'Extinct Giant Earwig Returns to St Helena after 56 Years', www.africamuseum.be, May 2023.

372 Jeremy Hance, 'Gone for Good: World's Largest Earwig Declared Extinct', *Mongabay*, https://news.mongabay.com, 19 November 2014.

373 The St Helena Earwig is sometimes known by this name; Fabian Haas, 'The Giant Earwig of St Helena: The Dodo of the Dermaptera', www.earwigs-online.de, accessed 10 May 2021.

374 Jeremy Hance, 'Gone for Good: World's Largest Earwig Declared Extinct', *Mongabay*, https://news.mongabay.com, 19 November 2014; see also https://iucn.org/content/global-appetite-resources-pushing-new-species-brink-iucn-red-list, accessed 17 October 2024.

375 Ibid.

376 Marie Woolf, 'The Great Earwig that Could Bring a Country to a Standstill', *The Independent*, 27 November 2005, cited in 'St Helena Island: New Airport Threatens Scores of Animals', Dear Kitty. Some blog, https://dearkitty1.wordpress.com, 27 November 2005.

377 Day, *The Doomsday Book of Animals*, p. 49.

378 Hume, *Extinct Birds*, p. 149.

379 Day, *The Doomsday Book of Animals*, p. 48.

380 Ibid.

381 Hume, *Extinct Birds*, p. 150. With the exception of these two confirmed sites, other breeding grounds for the Eskimo curlew remain a mystery. This is remarkable, when one considers their (once) enormous numbers.

382 Day, *The Doomsday Book of Animals*, p. 48.

383 Fuller, *Extinct Birds*, p. 163.

384 Day, *The Doomsday Book of Animals*, p. 48.

385 Ibid., p. 49.

386 Ibid.

387 Fuller, *Lost Animals*, p. 59.

388 Day, *The Doomsday Book of Animals*, p. 49.

389 Fuller, *Lost Animals*, p. 56.

390 Cited in Ellis, *No Turning Back*, p. 179, from Scott Weidensaul, *Living on the Wind: Across the Hemisphere with Migratory Birds* (New York, 1999).

391 See 'Eskimo Curlew', EDGE of Existence programme, ZSL, www.edgeofexistence.org, accessed 31 May 2024.

392 Jon McCracken of Bird Studies Canada, cited in Amy Lewis, 'The Eskimo Curlew

Hasn't Been Seen in 55 Years. Is It Time to Declare It Extinct?', National Audubon Society News, www.audubon.org, 20 April 2018.

393 'The Legend of St Beuno', Call of the Curlew, www.curlewcall.org, 7 November 2019.

394 James H. Brown and C. Robert Feldmeth, 'Evolution in Constant and Fluctuating Environments: Thermal Tolerances of Desert Pupfish (*Cyprinodon*)', *Evolution*, xxv/2 (1 June 1971), pp. 390–98 (p. 391).

395 'Chief Tecopa', Mojave Desert, http://mojavedesert.net, 10 June 2022.

396 Katherine Rivard, 'The Extraordinary Lives of Death Valley's Endangered Devils Hole Pupfish', www.nationalparks. org, accessed 6 July 2024. See also Wainwright Lab, University of California, 'Explosive Evolution in Pupfish', https://fishlab.ucdavis.edu, 5 May 2011.

397 Day, *The Doomsday Book of Animals*, p. 269.

398 'This is the last known collection of the Tecopa pupfish': Robert R. Miller, James D. Williams and Jack E. Williams, 'Extinctions of North American Fishes during the Past Century', *Fisheries*, xiv/6 (November 1989), pp. 22–38 (p. 30).

399 Department of the Interior, 'Proposed De-Regulation of the Tecopa Pupfish', *Federal Register*, xliii/128 (3 July 1978), pp. 28, 805–28, 963 (pp. 28, 842).

400 Alan Levitt, 'Extinction to Remove Fish from Endangered Species List', Department of the Interior, Fish and Wildlife Service News release, 3 July 1978.

401 'Death Valley Fish Declared Extinct', *New York Times*, www.nytimes.com, 19 November 1981.

402 Arcadio Valdés González et al., 'The Extinction of the Catarina Pupfish *Megupsilon aporus* and the Implications for the Conservation of Freshwater Fish in Mexico', *Oryx Journal*, liv/2 (March 2020), pp. 154–60.

403 '*Rheobatrachus silus* – Southern Gastric-Brooding Frog', Australian Government Department of Climate Change, Energy, the Environment and Water, Species Profile and Threats Database, www.environment. gov.au, 21 October 2009.

404 Ibid.

405 M. J. Tyler and M. Davies, 'Larval

Development', in *The Gastric Brooding Frog*, ed. M. J. Tyler (London, 1983), pp. 44–57.

406 Ibid.

407 Queensland Environmental Protection Agency, *National Recovery Plan for the Stream-Dwelling Rainforest Frogs of the Fungella Region of Mid-Eastern Queensland 2000–2004* (2001), p. 18, www.dcceew.gov.au; J. Winter and K. McDonald, 'Fungella. The Land of Cloud', *Australian Natural History*, xxii/1 (Winter 1986), pp. 39–43, https:// museum-publications.australian.museum.

408 Queensland Environmental Protection Agency, *National Recovery Plan*, p. 18.

409 Gray, *Extinct*, p. 42.

410 Tim Flannery, *Life: Selected Writings* (Melbourne, 2019), p. 294.

411 Ibid.

412 Gray, *Extinct*, p. 42; Christopher Rojas, 'The Southern Gastric-Brooding Frog', Embryo Project Encyclopedia, https://embryo.asu.edu, 26 January 2015.

413 M. J. Tyler, and M. Davies, 'Superficial Features', in *The Gastric Brooding Frog*, ed. Tyler, pp. 5–15.

414 Flannery, *Life*, p. 294.

415 Ibid., p. 295.

416 Tim Flannery, *A Warning from the Golden Toad* [2005], book 7 of Penguin Books's Green Ideas series (2021), p. 65.

417 'Lost Frog DNA Back from the Dead: Lazarus Project', University of Newcastle Australia News, www.newcastle.edu.au, 18 March 2013.

418 Gray, *Extinct*, p. 80.

419 Heather Saul, 'Extinct Frog Brought Back to Life: Lazarus Project Named One of 2013 Best Inventions', *The Independent*, www.independent.co.uk, 22 November 2023.

420 Ibid.

421 For a fuller discussion concerning the controversy, see 'Inventing Indigenous Solutions to the Environmental Problem', www.ecopsychology.org, accessed 11 July 2024; Adrianus Nooij, 'The Chief Seattle Speech: An Authentic Indigenous American History or a Symbolized Fabulation?', BA thesis, 2007, Luleå University of Technology, and Ann Medlock, 'Chief Seattle Speaks – Or Does He?', www.annmedlock.com, accessed 11 July 2024.

422 Hume, *Extinct Birds*, p.362.

423 Parker Bauer, 'Of a Fire on the Marsh', *American Scholar*, https://theamericanscholar.org, 5 March 2018.

424 James D. Rising, 'Ecological and Genetic Diversity in the Seaside Sparrow', *Birding* (September/October 2005), p. 493, www.aba.org.

425 Bauer, 'Of a Fire on the Marsh.'

426 Paul W. Sykes Jr, 'Decline and Disappearance of the Dusky Seaside Sparrow from Merritt Island, Florida', *American Birds*, XXXIV/5 (September 1980), pp. 728–37 (p. 732), https://sora.unm.edu.

427 Bauer, 'Of a Fire on the Marsh'.

428 Hume, *Extinct Birds*, p. 362.

429 Ibid.

430 Bauer, 'Of a Fire on the Marsh'.

431 Rising, 'Ecological and Genetic Diversity in the Seaside Sparrow', p. 494.

432 Bauer, 'Of a Fire on the Marsh'.

433 Rising, 'Ecological and Genetic Diversity in the Seaside Sparrow', p. 494.

434 Ibid.

435 Hume, *Extinct Birds*, p. 362: 'The disastrous attempt to hybridise the last male Dusky Seaside Sparrows with females of the subspecies *A. m. peninsulae* is another example of human apathy, bad politics and arrogant taxonomic philosophy, all of which conspired to doom this bird to extinction.'

436 Rising, 'Ecological and Genetic Diversity in the Seaside Sparrow', p. 494.

437 'Dusky Seaside Sparrow', www.extinctanimals.org, accessed 15 January 2022.

438 Mark Jerome Walters, *A Shadow and a Song* (White River Junction, VT, 1992), p. 181.

439 Bauer, 'Of a Fire on the Marsh'.

440 Cited in Walters, *A Shadow and a Song*, p. 182.

441 Bauer, 'Of a Fire on the Marsh'.

442 Marty Crump, *In Search of the Golden Frog* (Chicago, IL, and London, 2000), p. 150.

443 Jay M. Savage, 'An Extraordinary New Toad (*Bufo*) from Costa Rica', *Revista de Biología Tropical*, XIV/2 (1966), pp. 153–67 (p. 153). Savage is the first to point out that the true discoverer of the golden toad was Mr Jerry James of Monteverde, back in 1963, though credit is often given to Savage

(p. 161). James said that he had only seen the toads near the beginning of the rainy season, during April and May (p. 157).

444 Flannery, *Life*, p. 293.

445 In 1972 this region became known as the Monteverde Cloud Forest Biological Reserve. At the time, the Reserve covered approximately 328 hectares (810 ac). It has since expanded to include 14,200 hectares (35,089 ac).

446 Martha L. Crump, Frank R. Hensley and Kenneth L. Clark; 'Apparent Decline of the Golden Toad: Underground or Extinct?', *Copeia*, 2 (May 1992), pp. 413–20 (p. 413).

447 On Monteverde, see https://selvatura.com/monteverde, accessed 10 July 2024; Lauren Carter and Andrea Vella, 'Field Expedition to Costa Rica: Costa Rica: The Monteverde Cloud Forest', http://publish.illinois.edu, accessed 10 July 2024.

448 Crump's diary entry for 20 April 1987, cited in Flannery, *Life*, p. 291.

449 Jason DeGroot, '*Incilius periglenes*', Animal Diversity Web (ADW), http://animaldiversity.org, accessed 8 November 2023.

450 Flannery, *Life*, p. 295.

451 Ibid.

452 Ibid., p. 292.

453 Susan K. Jacobson and John J. Vandenberg, 'Reproductive Ecology of the Endangered Golden Toad (*Bufo periglenes*)', *Journal of Herpetology*, XXV/3 (September 1991), pp. 321–6, cited in DeGroot, '*Incilius periglenes*'.

454 In the French fairy tale 'The Fairies' (also known as 'Diamonds and Toads') by Charles Perrault, the good, hard-working daughter spits out diamonds and flowers, while the lazy one coughs up vipers and toads. In the German tale 'Frau Holle', the good child spits out gold pieces, rather than diamonds and flowers.

455 In *Big Game Shooting* (1894), cited in 'The Return of the Pyrenean Ibex: Hunters as Key Stakeholders', Pyrenean Way – GRIO, www.pyreneanway.com, 24 May 2020.

456 Torill Kornfeldt, *The Re-Origin of Species: A Second Chance for Extinct Animals*, trans. Fiona Graham (Brunswick, VIC, 2018), p. 67.

457 'What Can We Learn from Vanishing Wildlife Species: The Case of the

Pyrenean Ibex', *ScienceDaily*, www.sciencedaily.com, 6 April 2021.

458 Kornfeldt, *The Re-Origin of Species*, p. 68.

459 Ibid., p. 69.

460 Beth Shapiro, *How to Clone a Mammoth: The Science of De-Extinction* (Princeton, NJ, 2015), p. 147.

461 In *Big Game Shooting* (1894), 'The Return of the Pyrenean Ibex'.

462 Kornfeldt, *The Re-Origin of Species*, p. 72.

463 Some sources cite the date as 5 January 2000.

464 Kornfeldt, *The Re-Origin of Species*, p. 75; Shapiro, *How to Clone a Mammoth*, p. 143.

465 Kornfeldt, *The Re-Origin of Species*, p. 76.

466 Candice Gaukel Andrews, 'Studies of Extinct Ibex Could Save Today's Tigers', Natural Habitat Adventures, www.nathab.com, 2 August 2022.

467 Mark Carwardine, *Last Chance to See: In the Footsteps of Douglas Adams* (London, 2009), p. 310.

468 Samuel Turvey, *Witness to Extinction: How We Failed to Save the Yangtze River Dolphin* (Oxford, 2008), p. 3.

469 Ibid., p. 4.

470 Carwardine, *Last Chance to See*, p. 306.

471 Turvey, *Witness to Extinction*, p. 4.

472 Ibid., p. 5.

473 Ibid., p. 6.

474 'Baiji', https://au.whales.org, accessed 7 November 2023.

475 This name is due to an error. The word *qi* means 'flag/banner', and sounds similar to *ji*, which means 'dolphin'. This means that the scientific binomial for the species, *Lipotes vexillifer*, coined by Gerrit S. Miller Jr in 1918, is based on a misunderstanding: Turvey, *Witness to Execution*, p. 9.

476 Fuller, *Lost Animals*, p. 189.

477 Carwardine, *Last Chance to See*, p. 306.

478 Similar to bats.

479 Carwardine, *Last Chance to See*, p. 306.

480 Fuller, *Lost Animals*, p. 188.

481 There was a factory built for this purpose: Carwardine, *Last Chance to See*, p. 308. According to Turvey, this factory may have been fictitious, or short lived: Turvey, *Witness to Extinction*, p. 27.

482 Turvey, *Witness to Extinction*, p. 36.

483 Ibid.

484 Ibid., p. 38. '[B]etween 50 and 60 per cent of all dead baiji found by Chinese researchers

in the 1970s and 1980s were riddled with dozens or even hundreds of hook marks, their skins torn and ulcerating – clear signs of having been killed by long-lines': Turvey, *Witness to Extinction*, p. 39.

485 Fuller, *Lost Animals*, p. 191.

486 Carwardine, *Witness to Extinction*, p. 308, and John Whitfield, *Lost Animals: The Story of Extinct, Endangered and Rediscovered Species* (London, 2020), p. 208.

487 The local brewery made its own Baiji Beer, which included the baiji's scientific name, *Lipotes vexillifer*, on the bottle cap, 'probably the only beer in the world to carry a scientific name': Turvey, *Witness to Extinction*, p. 51.

488 Carwardine, *Last Chance to See*, p. 308.

489 There may have been other causes associated with the dolphin's death. She was underweight, even starving, at the time of her death. Had she, the solitary baiji, been bullied by the porpoises in the lake? Had she been ill, or injured during her capture?: Turvey, *Witness to Extinction*, p. 76.

490 Fuller, *Lost Animals*, p. 193; Turvey, *Witness to Extinction*, p. 78.

491 Carwardine, *Last Chance to See*, p. 306.

492 Whitfield, *Lost Animals*, p. 208.

493 Blencowe, *Gone*, p. 126.

494 Henry Nicholls, *Lonesome George: The Life and Loves of a Conservation Icon* (New York, 2006), p. 150. The goats continued to breed. By the end of the 1970s, an estimated 41,390 had been eradicated.

495 Cited ibid., p. 1.

496 Ibid., p. 22.

497 Ibid.

498 Ibid., p. 130.

499 'Lonesome George', Galápagos Conservancy, www.galapagos.org, accessed 30 November 2023.

500 Nicholls, *Lonesome George*, p. 71, and Peter Young, *Tortoise* (London, 2003), p. 129.

501 Nicholls, *Lonesome George*, p. 16.

502 Ibid., p. 92.

503 Ibid., pp. 97–8.

504 Ibid., p. 14.

505 Blencowe, *Gone*, p. 128.

506 Natasha Geiling, 'Lonesome George, the Last Tortoise of His Kind, Is on Posthumous Display in NYC', *Smithsonian Magazine*, www.smithsonianmag.com, 26 September 2014.

507 Geiling, 'Lonesome George',

508 Blencowe, *Gone*, p. 137.

509 From Darwin's *Journal of Researches*, about his 1839 trip on the *Beagle*, 'There is every reason for believing that several of the islands possess their own peculiar varieties or species of tortoise.' Cited in Nicholls, *Lonesome George*, p. 51.

510 From Charles Darwin, entry for 26–27 September 1835, *Journal of Researches into the Geology and Natural History of the Various Countries Visited by HMS 'Beagle'* (London, 1939), cited in Young, *Tortoise*, p. 13; Blencowe, *Gone*, p. 127.

511 John Donne, from *Devotions upon Emergent Occasions*, 'Meditation XVII', (1623). This line is from a paragraph in the essay. Through the years the text has been adapted, often presented as a poem.

512 Sandy Ingleby and Abram Powell, 'Bramble Cay Melomys, *Melomys rubicola*', https://australian.museum, 28 June 2021.

513 Gray, *Extinct*, p. 18.

514 Hannah Seo, 'Extinction Obituary: How the Bramble Cay Melomys Became the First Mammal Lost to the Climate Crisis', *The Guardian*, www.theguardian.com, 1 June 2022.

515 Ibid.; Gray, *Extinct*, p. 18.

516 Seo, 'Extinction Obituary'.

517 Brendan Mounter, 'Torres Strait Artists Give Extinct Native Rodent New Life while Flagging First Climate Change Loss', ABC Far North, www.abc.net.au, 19 August 2021. Although the exhibition has finished, it can be seen via a virtual gallery, accessed 28 August 2022.

518 Ibid.

519 Christie Wilcox, 'Lonely George the Tree Snail Dies, and a Species Goes Extinct', *National Geographic*, www.nationalgeographic.com, 8 January 2019.

520 Ed Yong, 'The Last of Its Kind', *The Atlantic*, www.theatlantic.com, July 2019.

521 'RIP George: The Last Known Land Snail of His Kind Dies', Department of Land and Natural Resources (Hawai'i), https://dlnr.hawaii.gov, 4 January 2019.

522 Janice Crowl, 'Kahuli Homecoming', *Hana Hou!*, XIV/2 (April–May 2011).

523 Ibid.

524 Ibid.

525 Ibid.

526 Wilcox, 'Lonely George the Tree Snail Dies'.

527 John Thomas Gulick (1832–1923) studied Hawaiian snails, particularly those of the genus *Acatinella*. Gulick was one of the pioneers of evolutionary thinking, and his ideas were based on his studies of snails. He came up with the term 'divergent evolution' and corresponded with Darwin about his theories. Sadly, Gulick's enormous snail collection would have contributed enormously to their demise: Purcell, *Swift as a Shadow*, no. 59.

528 Ibid.

529 Brenden S. Holland, Steven L. Montgomery and Vincent Costello, 'A Reptilian Smoking Gun: First Record of Invasive Jackson's Chameleon (*Chamaeleo jacksonii*) Predation on Native Hawaiian Species', *Biodiversity and Conservation*, XIX/5 (May 2009), pp. 1437–41 (p. 1438).

530 Tabitha Whiting, 'Why Does It Matter that a Snail Died in Hawaii?', https://medium.com, 16 January 2019.

531 Ibid.

532 Wilcox, 'Lonely George the Tree Snail Dies'.

Bibliography

Avery, Mark, *A Message from Martha: The Extinction of the Passenger Pigeon and Its Relevance Today* (London, 2014)

Bailey, Col, *Shadow of the Thylacine: One Man's Epic Search for the Tasmanian Tiger* (Melbourne, 2013)

—, *Lure of the Thylacine: True Stories and Legendary Tales of the Tasmanian Tiger* (Melbourne, 2016)

Blencowe, Michael, *Gone: A Search for What Remains of the World's Extinct Creatures* (London, 2021)

Bodsworth, Fred, *Last of the Curlews* [1954] (London, 1966)

Carwardine, Mark, *Last Chance to See: In the Footsteps of Douglas Adams* (London, 2009)

Cokinos, Christopher, *Hope Is the Thing with Feathers: A Personal Chronicle of Vanished Birds* (New York, 2000)

Corwin, Jeff, *100 Heartbeats: The Race to Save Earth's Most Endangered Species* (New York, 2009)

Day, David, *The Doomsday Book of Animals: A Unique Natural History of Vanished Species* (London, 1981)

den Hengst, Jan, *The Dodo: The Bird that Drew the Short Straw* (Marum, 2003)

Ellis, Richard, *No Turning Back: The Life and Death of Animal Species* (New York, 2004)

Flannery, Tim, *Life: Selected Writings* (Melbourne, 2019)

—, *A Warning from the Golden Toad* [2005] (Dublin, 2021)

—, and Schouten, Peter, *A Gap in Nature: Discovering the World's Extinct Animals* (Melbourne, 2001)

Ford, Fred, *John Gould's Extinct and Endangered Mammals of Australia* (Canberra, 2014)

Forrest, Susanna, *The Age of the Horse: An Equine Journey through Human History* (London, 2016)

Freeman, Carol, *Paper Tiger: How Pictures Shaped the Thylacine* (Hobart, 2014)

Fuller, Errol, *The Great Auk* (New York, 1999)

—, *Extinct Birds*, revd edn (Ithaca, NY, 2001)

—, *Dodo: From Extinction to Icon* (London, 2002)

—, *Lost Animals: Extinction and the Photographic Record* (London, 2013)

—, *The Passenger Pigeon* (Princeton, NJ, 2015)

Gaskell, Jeremy, *Who Killed the Great Auk?* (Oxford, 2000)

Gill, Anton, and West, Alex, *Extinct* (London, 2001)

Gray, Benjamin, *Extinct: Artistic Impressions of Our Lost Wildlife* (Melbourne, 2021)

Greenberg, Joel, *A Feathered River across the Sky: The Passenger Pigeons' Flight to Extinction* (New York, 2014)

Grihault, Alan, *Dodo: The Bird Behind the Legend* (Cassis, 2005)

Guiler, Eric R., *Thylacine: The Tragedy of the Tasmanian Tiger* (Oxford, 1985)

—, and Godard, Philippe, *Tasmanian Tiger: A Lesson to Be Learnt . . .* (Perth, 1998)

Heise, Ursula K., *Imagining Extinction: The Cultural Meanings of Endangered Species* (London, 2016)

Hoose, Phillip, *The Race to Save the Lord God Bird* [2004] (New York, 2014)

Hume, Julian P., *Extinct Birds*, 2nd edn (London, 2017)

Jones, Ryan Tucker, *Empire of Extinction: Russians and the North Pacific's Strange Beasts of the Sea, 1741–1867* (Oxford, 2014)

Kingsley, Charles, *The Water Babies* (Ware, 1994)

Kolbert, Elizabeth, *The Sixth Extinction: An Unnatural History* (London, 2014)

Kornfeldt, Torill, *The Re-Origin of Species: A Second Chance for Extinct Animals*, trans. Fiona Graham (Brunswick, VIC, 2018)

Lang, Rebecca, ed., *The Tasmanian Tiger: Extinct or Extant?* (Sydney, 2014)

Lockwood, Jeffrey A., *Locust: The Devastating Rise and Mysterious Disappearance of the Insect that Shaped the American Frontier* (New York, 2004)

McGrain, Todd, *The Lost Bird Project* (Hanover, NH, and London, 2014)

MacPhee, Ross D. E., *End of the Megafauna: The Fate of the World's Hugest, Fiercest, and Strangest Animals*, illus. Peter Schouten (New York, 2019)

Maynard, David, and Gordon, Tammy,
    Tasmanian Tiger: Precious Little Remains
    (Launceston, TAS, 2014)
O'Connor, M. R., *Resurrection Science:*
    Conservation, De-Extinction and the Precarious
    Future of Wild Things (New York, 2015)
Oldfield, Molly, *The Secret Museum* (London, 2013)
Owen, David, *Thylacine: The Tragic Tale*
    of the Tasmanian Tiger (Sydney, 2011)
Paddle, Robert, *The Last Tasmanian Tiger:*
    The History and Extinction of the Thylacine
    (Cambridge, 2000)
Parish, Jolyon C., *The Dodo and the Solitaire:*
    A Natural History (Bloomington, IN, 2013)
Piper, Ross, *Extinct Animals: An Encyclopedia*
    of Species that Have Disappeared during
    Human History (Westport, CT, 2009)
Purcell, Rosamond, *Swift as a Shadow: Extinct*
    and Endangered Animals (Boston, MA,
    and New York, 1999)
Sanders, Scott Russell, ed., *Audubon Reader:*
    The Best Writings of John James Audubon
    (Bloomington, IN, 1986)

Shapiro, Beth, *How to Clone a Mammoth:*
    The Science of De-Extinction (Princeton, NJ,
    and Oxford, 2015)
Tanner, James T., *The Ivory-Billed Woodpecker*
    [1942] (Mineola, NY, 2003)
Walker, Brett L., *The Lost Wolves of Japan*
    (Seattle, WA, and London, 2005)
Walters, Mark Jerome, *A Shadow and a Song*
    (White River Junction, VT, 1992)
Weidensaul, Scott, *The Ghost with Trembling*
    Wings: Science, Wishful Thinking, and the
    Search for Lost Species (New York, 2002)
Westwood, Brett and Moss, Stephen, *Natural*
    Histories: 25 Extraordinary Species that Have
    Changed Our World (London, 2015)
Whitfield, John, *Lost Animals: The Story of*
    Extinct, Endangered and Rediscovered Species
    (London, 2020)
Wilson, Edward O., *Every Species Is a Masterpiece*
    (Dublin, 2021)

Acknowledgements

My deepest thanks to Rhys, Bernadette, Di (who read every word – again!), Leah, Leanne, Kate, Kim and Christine. I thank Harry for faithful companionship and Leaf for keeping my lap warm.

For the Xerces blue photos, I thank the Collaborative Invertebrate Laboratories at the Field Museum and Dr Bruno de Medeiros for use of the imaging equipment (funded by the Science Innovation Grant, Grainger Bioinformatics Center and the Field Museum). I also thank Stephanie Ware at Morphology Labs and Dr Elizabeth Postema, Post-Doctoral Researcher for training and use of the equipment, and Jessica Wadleigh, Collections Assistant in Insects for taking the photos.

This book could not have been written without the ability to draw on previous research undertaken by ornithologists, zoologists, writers, scholars, poets and dreamers. I have tried to acknowledge all sources, but if I have overlooked anyone, my heartfelt apologies.

To Michael Leaman and the staff at Reaktion, you are wonderful, as always. Thank you for your patience; this has been a difficult book to write, particularly during several rough years. This book has been written through a mist of continual tears: for the animals, and for my late husband.

A special 'thank you' to Errol Fuller, whose work has inspired me for a long time, and to David Day, whose book *The Doomsday Book of Animals* I purchased many years ago. This book could not have been written without their work residing in my bookcase, and in my heart.

May we remember the animals, those gone, and those still present. They are kin.

Photo Acknowledgements

The author and publishers wish to express their thanks to the sources listed below for illustrative material and/or permission to reproduce it. Some locations of artworks are also given below, in the interest of brevity:

Alamy Stock Photo: pp. 34 (*bottom*; Michel Denis-Huot/hemis.fr), 132 (Dave Watts); from Otto Antonius, 'Beobachtungen an Einhufern in Schönbrunn. I. Der syrische Halbesel (*Equus hemionus hemippus* J. Geoffr.)', *Der Zoologische Garten*, I (July 1928): p. 123; from David L. Belding, *Fifty-First Annual Report of the Commissioners on Fisheries and Game for the Year 1916* (Boston, MA, 1917), photo MBLWHOI Library, Woods Hole, MA: p. 128; Ian Bell/EHP/Queensland (CC BY 4.0): p. 212; British Library, London (MS Or 2784, fol. 233v): p. 149; photo Marty Crump: p. 192; from Samuel Daniell, *African Scenery and Animals* (London, 1804), photo Smithsonian Libraries, Washington, DC: p. 77; from Charles Darwin, *The Zoology of the Voyage of HMS Beagle*, part II: *Mammalia* (London, 1838), photo Library of Congress, Rare Book and Special Collections Division, Washington, DC: p. 73; from Daniel Giraud Elliot, *The New and Heretofore Unfigured Species of the Birds of North America* (New York, 1869), vol. II, photo Smithsonian Libraries, Washington, DC: p. 68; from *Endangered Wildlife of California* (Sacramento, CA, n.d.): p. 175; Field Museum, Chicago, IL, photos Jessica Wadleigh: pp. 141, 144; from Leopold Josef Fitzinger, *Bilder-Atlas zur wissenschaftlich-populären Naturgeschichte der Säugethiere in ihren sämmtlichen Hauptformen* (Vienna, 1860): p. 55; Hawai'i Department of Land and Natural Resources: p. 216; from François Leguat, *Voyage et avantures . . . en deux isles desertes des Indes orientales* (London, 1708), vol. I, photo Zentralbibliothek Zürich: p. 50; Library of Congress, Washington, DC: p. 146; Manchester Museum, the University of Manchester, Entomology Collection, photo © Manchester Museum: p. 160; from Franz Xaver Mettenleiter (and his sons), *Naturhistorisches Bilderbuch: Vorlegeblätter beim Unterricht in der Naturgeschichte und zum Nachzeichnen* (Munich, 1875), photo Universitätsbibliothek der Technischen Universität Braunschweig: p. 34 (*top*); © Museums Victoria (CC BY 4.0): p. 180; National Museum of Natural History, Smithsonian Institution, Washington, DC: pp. 113, 129 (photo David Price); The Natural History Museum, London: pp. 47, 92; Nature Picture Library/naturepl.com: pp. 85 (© Wild Wonders of Europe/Widstrand), 152 (© John Cancalosi); The New York Public Library: p. 24; from John Ray, ed., *The Ornithology of Francis Willughby* (London, 1678), photo Wellcome Library, London: p. 42; from Philipp Franz von Siebold, *Fauna japonica*, vol. V: *Mammalia* (Leiden, 1842), photo Ernst Mayr Library of the Museum of Comparative Zoology, Harvard University, Cambridge, MA: p. 102; University of Pittsburgh, Archives and Special Collections: pp. 62, 107, 116; USFWS: pp. 167 (Christina

Index

Page numbers in *italics* refer to illustrations

Allee effect 16
Arabian ostrich 144–50, *146, 149*
　eggs 147–8
　feathers 144–5, *147*
　names 145
　range of Arabian Ostrich *144*
　and Richard Meinertzhagen 148, *150*
　roar of Arabian Ostrich 148
　and T. E. Lawrence 147
Audubon, John James 108, 118–19, 169
　Carolina Parakeet 116
　Great Auk 62
　Passenger Pigeon 107
aurochs 35–40, *34*
　Jaktorów forest, last one 38
　Lascaux 35
　Polish nobility hunts 37
　'rewilding' 40
　see also Heck brothers

baiji dolphin 199–205
　description of 201
　echolocation 201, 203
　Er-Ya 200
　expeditions to find 204
　Hoy, Charles 201
　hydroelectric dams 202
　legends and sacredness 199–200,
　　202, 204–5
　Lipotidae family 200, 205
　Qi Qi 204
Bering expedition 67
Bodsworth, Fred, *The Last of the Curlews*
　(novel) 172

Bramble Cay melomys 210–14
　artwork by Torres Strait Islanders
　　213
　description and name 211
　extinct because of human-induced
　　climate change 212–13

Carolina parakeet 115–21, *116*
　Bartsch and 'Doodles' 118–19
　care for rest of the flock 119
　causing fear 117
　'Incas' 115, 120–21
　names 115
　sport 118
　two subspecies of Carolina
　　parakeet 120
　see also Audubon, John James
Carroll, Lewis, *Alice's Adventures
　in Wonderland* 41, 45, 48
Church, George 14, *15*
Cincinatti Zoo 112, *114,* 121
cloning 16
coelacanth 18–19
Cuvier, Georges 9–10

Daniell, Samuel, 'The Quagga' 77
Darwin, Charles 73, 76, 210
　lithograph of the Falkland Islands
　　wolf or fox 73
de-extinction/resurrection science 14
dodo 40–49, *42, 47*
　Clark, George 46–8
　in Japan, India and London 44–5
　names 40–41, 43

Owen, Richard 47–8
    Savery Roelandt, paintings 46, 48
    sub-fossil remains 46–7
    Van Neck's and Verken's
        descriptions 43–4
    see also Carroll, Lewis
dusky seaside sparrow 183–9
    description 183
    fires 187
    habitat 183, 186–7
    Merritt Island 184
    mosquito control and DDT/flooding
        184–5
    last four living (Walt Disney
        World) 187–8
    poem by Brian Sharp 188–9

Ecozoic era 22
Eskimo curlew 166–73
    call 167–9
    hunting/market hunting 170–71
    migratory routes 168–9
    names 166
    Rocky Mountain locust, link to 171
    sculpture of 173
    World Curlew Day (21 April) 173
    see also Audubon, John James;
        Bodsworth, Fred
extinction
    causes 12
    dates of mass extinction 10–11
    island extinctions 12

Falklands wolf 72–6, 73
    fur trade 75–6
    London Zoo 76
    names 72
    see also Darwin, Charles 73, 76
Fitzinger, Leopold Josef, 'Steller's sea
    cow' 55

golden toad 189–94
    causes of extinction 192
    changes in rain/mist levels 193
    colours and description 190
    'discovery' by Jay Savage 189
    mating and breeding 191
    Monteverde Cloud Forest
        reserve 190
    names 189–80
    as poster amphibian 190
great auk 59–66, 62
    calls for protection 64
    description 60
    eggs 59
    Fogo Island, 'sorry' ceremony 66
    Funk Island 63–4
    Geirfuglasker 65
    last Great Auk hunt 65–6
    name 61–2
    Vikings 60–61
    see also Kingsley, Charles
grief 25–32
    ecological 29

heath hen 125–30
    'boom' of 127
    'Booming Ben' 125, 127, 129–30
    conservation movement's
        beginnings 126
    courtship display 127
    Gross, Alfred, 129–30
    hunting 125
    Martha's Vineyard 125–6, 129–30
Heck brothers and backbreeding 38–9,
    83, 87–9

IUCN 13
ivory-billed woodpecker 150–59
    and Alexander Wilson 151, 153
    call of the ivory-billed woodpecker
        151

courtship of the ivory-billed
woodpecker 153–4
Cuban ivory-billed woodpecker 158
description 150–51
and J. J. Kuhn 155–6
and James T. Tanner 151, 155–7
logging of old growth forests 155,
157–8
and Stephen Lyn Bales 156
see also Audubon, John James

Japanese wolf 100–105, *102*
names 100–101
Okawa Shrine 103
rabies 103–4
sacredness of 101, 103–5
Shinto wolf shrines 101–2

Khumba 84
Kingsley, Charles, *The Water Babies* 63
Kipling, Rudyard
The Jungle Book 57–8
The White Seal 58

Lazarus species 18–22
Leguat, François, 'The Rodrigues
solitaire' 50
Linnaeus, Carl 127

McGrain, Todd 26, 30–31, 66, 173
mammoths 8, 14–15, 16
Mettenleiter, Franz Xaver, 'Aurochs'
34

O'ahu tree snail 214–18
and David Sischo 217
'George' 214, 217–18
introduced species 215–17
land snail and slug extinctions
218
name 214

singing of the snails/chants/songs
215
Victorian shell collectors 215
Ormerod, Georgiana Elizabeth, *Rocky
Mountain Locust* 92

passenger pigeon 105–15, *107*
calls 109
excommunication of passenger
pigeon 110
last wild passenger pigeon 112
Martha 105–6, 112–14
names 106
pigeon hunting and trapshooting
110–12
Shufeldt, R.W. 114
star 115
superstitions 106
see also Audubon, John James
Pearson, G., *Ostrich Hunt in Palestine*
146
Pinta Island tortoise 205–10
controversy of location of body
for permanent display 209–10
and Joseph Vagvolgyi 206–7
'Lonesome George' 205–7, 209
mating attempts 207
target of death threats 208–9
see also Darwin, Charles
Pyrenean ibex 194–9
breeding programme 196
Celia 194, 197–9
cloned female ibex 17, 197–8
de-extinction 197–8
description 194

Quagga 77–84
breeding program 82
debate about species and
subspecies 78
DNA analysis on quagga 78

and H. A. Bryden 82
Khoekhoe 77, 79
names 77–8
and Reinhold Rau 83
in royal zoo 81
zebras 77–8, 79
see also Khumba

Rocky Mountain locust 89–100, 92
and Albert Child 93–4
Eskimo curlew link 89
'Grasshopper Day' 96–7
invasion 92–3
keystone species 99
Locust: An Opera 89, 98
Mormons 96
name 90
and Norman Criddle 97
swarming 91
see also Wilder, Laura Ingalls
Rodrigues solitaire 49–54, 50
bony knob (musket ball) 52
and François Leguat 49, 50, 51, 53–4
and Julien Tafforet 53
'marriages' 52–3
Turdus Solitarius and
constellations 54

St Helena Earwig 159–65
names 159, 160–61, 163
nurturing qualities 161–2
postage stamp 164
Project Hercules 164
removal of habitat 163–5
repatriation to St Helena Museum
165
Savery, Roelandt (attrib.), *The Dodo
and other Birds 47*
Shapiro, Beth 14
Siebold, Philipp Franz von, 'Japanese
Wolf' *102*

southern gastric-brooding frog and the
northern gastric-brooding frog/
Eungella gastric-brooding frog
178–83
call 179
chytridiomycosis 181–2
climate change 181
decline 178–9
description 179–80
gastric-brooding method 180–81
habitat 179
Lazarus Project 182
spectacled cormorant 66–72, 68
bones on Bering Island 71
description 67
and John Milton 71
and Leonhard Stejneger 70–71
name 67
specimens 70
Steller, Georg 55–7, 67–8, 70
Steller's sea cow 54–9, 55
cow 54–5
description 56
mermaid ivory 58
and Vitus Bering 57–8
see also Kipling, Rudyard
Syrian wild ass 122–4
death of last in captivity 124
description 122
and T. Aharoni 124

Tarpan 84–9
back-breeding 87 89
Lascaux 86
names 84–5
and Tadeusz Vetulani 87
see also Heck brothers 87–9
Tecopa pupfish 174–8
bathhouse 176
description 174
name 176

and Robert Miller 177
    Tecopa Hot Springs 176–7
Tenniel, John 24, 45
    illustration for *Alice's Adventures in
        Wonderland* 24
thylacine 131–40
    'Benjamin' 131, 137, 139
    bounty 136
    (depicted in) Indigenous rock art 133
    legal protection 137
    names 131
    parallel evolution 133–4
    skins sent to England 136
    tourist trade 137–8
    Wurrawana Corinna constellation
        139

trilobite fossils 7
Umwelt 27, 28

Wolf, Joseph, 'Spectacled cormorant' 68
Weidensaul, Scott 83–4
Wilder, Laura Ingalls 94–5

Xerces butterfly 140–44
    description 140
    habitat 140–43
    and Jean Baptiste Boisduval 141
    Lobo Creek 143
    mutation (in Xerces Blue Butterfly)
        143
    and Pierre Lorquin 141
    and William Lange 143